P9-DHO-782

# 11 CORE TRUTHS TO BUILD YOUR LIFE ON

# foundations

## A PURPOSE-DRIVEN® DISCIPLESHIP RESOURCE

**Teacher's Guide**
VOLUME TWO

# tom HoLLaDay & kay waRRen

ZONDERVAN™

GRAND RAPIDS, MICHIGAN 49530 USA

We want to hear from you. Please send your comments about this
book to us in care of zreview@zondervan.com. Thank you.

**ZONDERVAN**™

*Foundations Teacher's Guide, Volume 2*
Copyright © 2003 by Tom Holladay and Kay Warren

Requests for information should be addressed to:
Zondervan, *Grand Rapids, Michigan 49530*

ISBN 0-310-24075-1

All Scripture quotations, unless otherwise indicated, are taken from the *Holy Bible: New International Version*®. NIV®. Copyright © 1973, 1978, 1984 by International Bible Society. Used by permission of Zondervan. All rights reserved.

Scripture quotations marked GNT (also known as the TEV) are taken from *Today's English Version*. Copyright © American Bible Society 1966, 1971, 1976, 1992. Used by permission.

Scripture quotations marked LB are taken from *The Living Bible* © 1971. Used by permission of Tyndale House Publishers, Inc., Wheaton, IL 60189. All rights reserved.

Scripture quotations marked MESSAGE are taken from THE MESSAGE. Copyright © by Eugene H. Peterson 1993, 1994, 1995. Used by permission of NavPress Publishing Group.

Scripture quotations marked NASB are taken from the NEW AMERICAN STANDARD BIBLE®, Copyright © The Lockman Foundation 1960, 1962, 1963, 1968, 1971, 1972, 1973, 1975, 1977, 1995. Used by permission.

Scripture quotations marked NCV are taken from *The Everyday Bible, New Century Version*, copyright © 1987 by Worthy Publishing, Fort Worth, TX 76137. Used by permission.

Scripture quotations marked NJB are taken from *The New Jerusalem Bible,* copyright © 1985 by Darton, Longman & Todd, Ltd. and Doubleday, a division of Bantam Doubleday Dell Publishing Group, Inc. Reprinted by permission.

Scripture quotations marked NKJV are taken from the *New King James Version*. Copyright © 1979, 1980, 1982 by Thomas Nelson, Inc. Used by permission. All rights reserved.

Scripture quotations marked NLT are taken from the *Holy Bible, New Living Translation,* copyright © 1996. Used by permission of Tyndale House Publishers, Inc., Wheaton, IL 60189. All rights reserved.

Scripture quotations marked RSV are taken from the Revised Standard Version of the Bible, copyright 1946, 1952, 1971 by the Division of Christian Education of the National Council of the Churches of Christ in the USA. Used by permission.

The website addresses recommended throughout this book are offered as a resource to you. These websites are not intended in any way to be or imply an endorsement on the part of Zondervan, nor do we vouch for their content for the life of this book.

All rights reserved. No part of this publication may be reproduced, stored in a retrieval system, or transmitted in any form or by any means—electronic, mechanical, photocopy, recording, or any other—except for brief quotations in printed reviews, without the prior permission of the publisher.

*Interior design by Beth Shagene*

*Printed in the United States of America*

03 04 05 06 07 08 09 /❖ ML/ 10 9 8 7 6 5 4 3 2 1

# Contents

## Volume 2

# Salvation
## Part 1

**Life Change Objectives**

To give you an understanding of God's gift of salvation that enables you to:

• Love God more deeply for what he did for you.

• Tell others more confidently what God can do for them.

---

**Summary Teaching Outline**

The Problem: Man's Need for Salvation

    The nature of God

    The nature of man

The Provision: God's Solution to Sin

    Three central truths about how we are saved

    Seven descriptions of salvation

       1. Substitution: Jesus died in my place.

       2. Justification: Jesus made me right with God.

       3. Reconciliation: Jesus made peace with God possible.

       4. Adoption: Jesus made me a part of God's family.

       5. Redemption: Jesus purchased my salvation with his blood.

       6. Propitiation: Jesus satisfied God's justice.

       7. Forgiveness: Jesus sent my sins away from me.

    Three aspects of salvation: past, present, and future

### Teaching Tip

If you've taught for any length of time, you've discovered how easily we can fail to pray as we prepare to teach. It's not that we don't know that prayer is important; it's simply that we forget. Most of us must remind ourselves to pray. You might try writing "Pray" in big letters at the beginning of your teaching notes.

Depend on God in a new and fresh way as you begin to teach this study. Tell him in prayer, "Lord, I don't want the result of this study to be what I on my own strength and ability can accomplish. I pray that you would do through me what only you can do in people's lives: change hearts and transform minds."

In Los Angeles the rivers have been encased in concrete and turned into flood channels leading to the ocean. When heavy rains come, these channels quickly fill with swiftly flowing water. From time to time someone falls into a channel, and the result is often fatal. The slippery concrete gives a person nothing to grab on to in the rapidly moving waters and no way to get out. Unless rescued, certain death awaits at the tunnels that lead to the sea. Those who fall in the water cannot rescue themselves—they can't even call out for help as they struggle to breathe. The only hope is for someone to see their plight and to call the emergency rescue team to lower ropes to get them out of that water.

This flood channel is a picture of the spiritual need of all mankind. Without God, we are all headed for certain disaster. We cannot save ourselves, no matter how great our desire or effort. The good news is: God sees our need and he sent someone to rescue us!

If I had to sum up all that the Bible says in one sentence, it would be this:

**The major theme of the Bible is God's eternal plan to rescue us from our sin through Jesus' birth, his death on the cross, and his resurrection.**

**God knew from the beginning that his creation would need a Savior, so he set in motion all that would be necessary to accomplish the salvation of his children.**

**While the message of the cross is a familiar one to many, we must guard against attitudes of complacency, boredom, forgetfulness, and, most of all, "I've heard it before." There are so many layers of truth about Christ's work on the cross that we can never come to the point where there is nothing more to learn.**

It's easy when a subject like salvation is announced to lean back in our chair and think, "I have this one figured out." It seems much more easily understood than the Trinity of God or the divinity of Jesus. So we let our minds wander to the tasks we have in front of us tomorrow or maybe the situations we faced today, thinking, "This is one of the subjects I already understand."

When we do that, we're somewhat like the college student who, after one class in psychology, feels they can now understand every motivation of their parents and friends. A little knowledge becomes dangerous when it keeps us from looking deeper and knowing more. The more we understand about our salvation, the more we comprehend the greatness of God's love for us.

**In the study today we will be concentrating on:**

**The problem: the need for salvation**

**The provision: the solution of salvation**

**In the next session we will look at:**

**The promise: the security of salvation**

Discussion question 1 can be used here.

# The Problem: Man's Need for Salvation

**To understand man's need for salvation we must look at two things: the nature of God and the nature of man.**

## *The nature of God*

**We underestimate our need for a Savior because we underestimate who God is.**

The nature of God cannot and will not allow what is evil to continue.

**1. God is <u>HOLY</u>.**

Read with me Isaiah 57:15 and Psalm 99:9. Circle the word "holy" each time it is used.

**For this is what the high and lofty One says—he who lives forever, whose name is holy: "I live in a high and holy place, but also with him who is contrite and lowly in spirit, to revive the spirit of the lowly and to revive the heart of the contrite."**

**—Isaiah 57:15**

**Exalt the Lord our God and worship at his holy mountain, for the Lord our God is holy.**

**—Psalm 99:9**

Holy, you may remember from an earlier study, means to be separate, set apart, different. God is not like us. He is a God of perfection. And we are a people who struggle daily with our imperfections and sins.

Look at Habakkuk 1:13.

**Your eyes are too pure to look on evil; you cannot tolerate wrong.**
—Habakkuk 1:13

God is certainly aware of all of the evil in our world, and this verse reminds us that God cannot tolerate evil in his presence. It's amazing how we can fool ourselves into feeling a sense of moral superiority by our being tolerant of the sins of others. When we tolerate our sins and the sins of others, we are showing the worst kind of intolerance—we are being intolerant of the heart and the desires of God.

**God cannot tolerate anything that is evil.**

Look again at the word *cannot*. God cannot tolerate the presence of evil. God is repulsed by our sin. Sin is utterly offensive to all that he is.

The Bible often speaks of God as being offended by sin (Matt. 13:41–42; Deut. 4:25; Prov. 6:16–19). If we say that someone offends us, we usually mean they've been rude to us or hurt our feelings. When the Bible says God is offended by sin, it doesn't mean he's had his feelings hurt and is now in a corner having a pity party. It doesn't mean he'll get over his bad mood if you leave him alone for a while. It means God is justifiably angry because of our sin. Why? Because of his nature. Because of who he is.

2. **God is <u>RIGHTEOUS</u> <u>AND</u> <u>JUST</u>.**

**Holiness has more to do with God's character.**

**Righteousness and justice have to do with God's dealings with mankind in relation to his character.**

Because God is holy, he always deals with us with righteousness and justice.

Righteousness simply means that what God does is always right; he never makes a mistake. When God looks at my actions or behavior, he never judges me wrongly. He is always right on the money with his assessments. He sees me for who I really am every time!

God's justice is always fair and without vindictiveness. The so-called justice we see in many books, movies, and TV shows is motivated by anger and personal revenge. The angrier you are at the bad guys, the happier you are when they "get what they deserve." God's justice is not like that. God's justice grows out of the holiness of his character. It is a pure justice.

You and I can fudge on how we apply fairness. God cannot. The perfection of his character will not allow it. God said from the beginning that the penalty for sin would be separation from him and death. When we sin, it would be contrary to God's holy character for him to say, "We'll let this one go. I didn't really mean what I said about judgment."

**The LORD is gracious and righteous; our God is full of compassion.**
—Psalm 116:5

**The Lord is fair in everything he does, and full of kindness.**
—Psalm 145:17 (LB)

Notice in these verses that God's justice is linked to his compassion and to his kindness. Who would want a God who was not fair, who condemned one and blessed another simply based on chance or whim. It is comforting to know that God is just, but it is also sobering. Why? Because of the way we have treated God!

Look with me at the nature of man.

## The nature of man

Man's nature is the exact opposite of God's. While God is holy, righteous, and just, man is unholy, unrighteous, and unjust. When God created us, he made us to be holy, but we became unholy. At the moment of mankind's fall in the Garden of Eden, everything changed.

1. **Our nature: we are sinful.**

   **The Bible records Adam and Eve's sinful choice to disobey God's instructions not to eat from the tree of the knowledge of good and evil (Gen. 2:17; 3). Without knowing it, they unleashed the onslaught of evil and decay that permeates our world today. God cursed them and all of their offspring.**

   The Bible tells us God instructed Adam that he could eat from any tree in the Garden of Eden except from the "tree of the knowledge of good and evil." Adam and Eve chose to disobey God's instructions (Gen. 3). Just like small children told not to touch Grandma's prized vase, they made a beeline for the one thing in the whole garden that was off-limits to them. Because of their decision to disobey, all mankind now is born with a sin nature. But we can't just blame Adam and Eve for our troubles.

2. **Our choice: we sin.**

   **God says that all of us are considered guilty because of our relationship to Adam and because of our own choices (Rom. 5:18–19; 3:10–18).**

   Romans 3:10–18 tells us there is no one righteous, not one! On top of the sinful nature we inherited from Adam, we all choose on our own to disobey God. Anyone who has children or remembers what it was like to be a child knows that you don't have to teach a child to misbehave. They do it all by themselves. As parents, we spend hours repeatedly teaching and training our children how to overcome their natural inclination to misbehave and disobey. The sin nature is within all of us, and when given the opportunity, we choose to sin even more. There's no room for feeling superior to Adam and Eve or for condemning them. All of us would have done exactly the same thing they did!

**3. Our condition: we are lost (Luke 19:10).**

Go back with me to the person in the flood channel. Spiritually, we're *all* in the rushing waters of the channel, headed for an eternity without God. Because spiritually we're all in the same lost condition, it's easy to fool ourselves into thinking it really isn't all that bad. We compare ourselves with others and think, "I'm doing as good as everyone around me." We're staying afloat, but we're headed toward destruction. We all are in desperate need of being rescued!

One of the reasons we fail to see our need for the Savior is our inability to clearly see the desperation of our situation. The consequences of being lost are deeper and more terrible than we can imagine. Look with me at some of what it means to be lost—realizing that these are just the tip of the iceberg.

> Discussion question 2 can be used here.

---

 **A Closer Look**

*What Are the Consequences of Sin and Lostness?*

- **Sentenced to physical and spiritual death (Gen. 3:19; John 3:18; Rom. 6:23)**
- **Separated from God (Eph. 2:12)**
- **Dominated and controlled by sin (Eph. 2:1–3; Rom. 6:6)**
- **Spiritual blindness (2 Cor. 4:3–4)**
- **Without understanding (Rom. 3:11)**
- **Enemies of Christ (Matt. 12:30)**
- **Objects of God's wrath (Eph. 2:3)**
- **Considered children of the Devil (John 8:44)**

**The Bible portrays mankind's lostness as the most pitiful condition imaginable. Not only is our life on earth wasted as we live for self and selfish desires but the consequence is eternal separation from God (Rom. 6:23; Luke 13:3; Matt. 25:46).**

---

Those of us who have trusted Christ for salvation should get down on our knees and thank him *every day* for taking us out of our condition of sin. Some of you sitting here right now may very well still be in this condition of being lost. Most of the people you meet each day are lost, in need of salvation—the people you work with, your neighbors, maybe even your family members.

God is holy; we are sinful. God is just; we break God's commandments.

A holy and just God cannot say, "I feel benevolent today, so let's just pretend it never happened." He can't say, "I'll let you off just this one time."

Because he is holy. And he is just.

And this holy God loves us and wants to bring us back into a relationship with him. How can he do that? From our perspective it seems that his holiness would demand that he judge us for our sin, no matter how great his love for us. But God had a different plan, a plan more wonderful than we could ever imagine.

## The Provision: God's Solution to Sin

**God's solution is the last three words in this verse: faith in Jesus.**

**God presented him as a sacrifice of atonement, through faith in his blood. He did this to demonstrate his justice, because in his forbearance he had left the sins committed beforehand unpunished—he did it to demonstrate his justice at the present time, so as to be just and the one who justifies those who have faith in Jesus.**

**—Romans 3:25–26**

Circle "just" and "the one who justifies." That is how God solved this problem. He does not ignore or wink at our sin. Instead, he himself takes the just penalty for our sin through the willing sacrifice of Jesus. He justifies us by taking the penalty for us.

Do you ever find yourself taking your salvation for granted? It's all too common for us to think with greater joy about the occurrences of our daily lives than we do about our eternal salvation. Why do we do that? One reason is that we don't see—we can't see while we are on this earth—the depth of what happens when we are saved. We don't see how lost and in need of God we are. Before we become Christians we tend to think of ourselves as "almost there" when it comes to a relationship with God. The truth is, our sins have separated us from God by a distance that couldn't be measured in light years!

There are three central truths about salvation that every one of us needs to have cemented deep in our hearts. If you misunderstand any of these truths, you will misunderstand how you and I are saved. Understand these truths and you will not only understand your own salvation, but you can be a person who can be used by God to help many, many people find a saving faith in Jesus.

## Three central truths about how we are saved

1. **Salvation is not by works but by <u>GRACE</u>.**

Read with me Ephesians 2:8–9.

**For it is by grace you have been saved, through faith—and this not from yourselves, it is the gift of God—not by works, so that no one can boast.**
—**Ephesians 2:8–9**

Our salvation is only by God's grace. That last phrase, "so that no one can boast," is a reminder of what we are like as human beings. If we were able to get to heaven based on something we had done, we would spend all of eternity boasting about how well we had done it, how quickly we had done it, and how it had been accomplished with more humility than anyone we knew!

Mercy is when God doesn't give us what we do deserve.

Grace is God giving us what we do not deserve.

Salvation is a gift—and you cannot earn a gift.

> Imagine coming to a friend's house who has invited you over to enjoy a meal. You finish the delicious meal and then listen to some fine music and visit for a while. Finally, you stand up and get your coat as you prepare to leave. But before you leave you reach into your pocket and say, "Now, how much do I owe you?" What an insult! You don't do that with someone who has graciously given you a meal. Isn't it strange, though, how this world is running over with people who think there's something they must do to pay God back?[1]

Our salvation is a gift, graciously given by God.

2. **Salvation is not initiated by us, but by <u>GOD</u>.**

**It's not man reaching <u>UP</u> to God, but God reaching <u>DOWN</u> to man.**

**When we were unable to help ourselves, at the moment of our need, Christ died for us, although we were living against God. Very few people will die to save the life of someone else. Although perhaps for a good person someone might possibly die. But God shows his great love for us in this way: Christ died for us while we were still sinners.**
—**Romans 5:6–8** (NCV)

Salvation is not something we as humans initiated. You may think your salvation was your idea, but it was not. God initiated the contact and made forgiveness available to us—before we even asked. God reached down to us in the most dramatic and loving way possible, through Jesus' death on the cross. Jesus came to show us the way to salvation. He paid the ultimate price for the sins of each one of us.

We needed God to give us a way back to him, and he did that through Jesus Christ.

3. **Salvation is not an afterthought with God; it is his <u>ETERNAL PLAN</u>.**

**You were bought . . . with the precious blood of Christ, who was like a pure and perfect lamb. Christ was chosen before the world was made, but he was shown to the world in these last times for your sake.**
—1 Peter 1:18–20 (NCV)

**It is God who saved us and chose us to live a holy life. He did this not because we deserved it, but because that was his plan long before the world began—to show his love and kindness to us through Christ Jesus.**
—2 Timothy 1:9 (NLT)

Salvation is not an afterthought with God; he knew before he created the world that Adam and Eve would sin and would need a way back into a relationship with him. First Peter 1:18–20 tells us that Christ was chosen to die for our sins before the world began.

Salvation is not God's Plan B, put in place after the fall of man in the Garden of Eden. Look at 2 Timothy 1:9. It was always God's plan to show his love to the world through Jesus Christ. The Old Testament is not an example of a way of salvation that didn't work, forcing God to devise another plan as a result. The sacrificial system that you read about in the Old Testament was put in place to look forward to God's ultimate plan: salvation through his Son. God used the sacrificial system in the Old Testament to demonstrate deep spiritual truths that would become a reality with Christ's death and resurrection.

Think of it this way: the Old Testament is filled with neon signs that point the way to Jesus. The sacrificial system—a big sign pointing to Jesus. The tabernacle of worship—pointing to Jesus. The words of the prophets—flashing Jesus, Jesus, Jesus.

**Split Session Plan:** If you're teaching this study over two sessions, end the first session here.

I have in my hand an album of wedding photographs. Imagine a groom and bride having this delivered to them a month or so after their wedding. Can you imagine the bride saying to her new husband, "Let's not look at these, honey. After all, we were at the ceremony and saw everything that happened for ourselves. I know my father paid a lot for these pictures, but we're too busy right now to look at them." Not a chance! They would not be able to stop themselves from looking at the pictures of their commitment to each other.

I have a second album of pictures in my hand, filled with pictures of our salvation (hold up your Bible). The pictures in the Bible of our salvation are painted with incredibly vivid words. God did not want us to miss the picture of all that he does for us in salvation. The Bible is literally packed with these pictures. We're going to look at seven of the most often used pictures of salvation in the New Testament. Think of this as turning the pages in a photo album. Each turn of the page brings a gasp—a picture more beautiful than you could ever imagine.

> **Teaching Tip**
>
> Bring a photo album to show at this point. You could even turn the pages in this album as you talk about each of these pictures of our salvation. You'll come back to this again at the end of the study.

## Seven descriptions of salvation

### 1. <u>SUBSTITUTION</u>: Jesus died in my place.

Jesus died for *you*—he took your place.

Here's the picture. You and I deserve to die for our sins. It should have been us dying on that cross, but Jesus took our place. Jesus, who did not deserve to die, died for you and for me.

Anne Ortlund writes:

> If you have ever been the victim of an action that's blatantly unfair, consider Jesus. Acquitted by the highest court of the land ("I find no basis for a charge against him," John 19:4, 6), He is led away and roughly nailed to a cross to die anyway!
>
> Even in this crisis, the habit of His life continues; He prays. "Father, forgive them. . . ."
>
> Who is "them"?
>
> Not just the Italian soldiers carrying out the act.
>
> Not just the Jewish mob shouting, "Let His blood be on us and on our children!"
>
> Father, forgive all people from Adam on: "all have sinned." All are responsible for His death.
>
> Forgive me. . . .
>
> Forgive you. . . .[2]

Look at 1 Peter 3:18. Jesus, who was not guilty, suffered for your sin. He took your place.

**For Christ died for sins once for all, the righteous for the unrighteous, to bring you to God. He was put to death in the body but made alive by the Spirit.**

—1 Peter 3:18

What does it mean when we say that Jesus became our substitute?

- **He was made sin for me (2 Cor. 5:21).**
- **He bore my sin in his body on the cross (1 Peter 2:24).**
- **He suffered once to bear the sins of others (Heb. 9:28).**
- **He was tortured for others' sin (Isa. 53:4–6).**
- **He was made a curse for me (Gal. 3:13).**

Look at each of these phrases *personally*. The truth that he was made sin means *my* sin. He bore *my* sin on the cross. He suffered for *me*. What happened on the cross was personal!

Can you comprehend the magnitude of this truth? It's almost too huge to fathom. Jesus, the perfect, sinless Son of God had your sin put on him. All the garbage, all the ugliness that is in you and me—Jesus assumed it all.

This is why Paul could write in Galatians 2:20,

**I have been crucified with Christ and I no longer live, but Christ lives in me. The life I live in the body, I live by faith in the Son of God, who loved me and gave himself for me.**

—**Galatians 2:20**

Circle the words "himself for me." Jesus took your place. Jesus took my place.

## 2. <u>JUSTIFICATION</u>: Jesus made me right with God.

When we sin, we sin against the God who made us. It's a spiritual slap in his face—we break trust and break relationship with our Creator. How is that relationship put back together again? Jesus justifies us. He makes us right with God.

Look at Acts 13:39 and Romans 4:25.

**Through him everyone who believes is justified from everything you could not be justified from by the law of Moses.**

—**Acts 13:39**

**He was delivered over to death for our sins and was raised to life for our justification.**

—**Romans 4:25**

Justification is a picture from the courtroom: a legal term meaning "acquittal." Jesus, by giving himself for our sins, makes it possible for God to bring the gavel down and declare us eternally "Not guilty!" When God declares us not guilty, he not only chooses not to hold us accountable for our sins, he wipes out any record of our sins. And (don't miss this!) God applies the record of Jesus' righteousness to our accounts! God now looks at you and at me as justified—"just-as-if-I'd" never sinned.

Warren Wiersbe writes,

> My friend Dr. Roy Gustafson has the finest illustration of justification I have ever heard. It seems that there was a man in England who put his Rolls-Royce on a boat and went across to the continent to go on a holiday. While he was driving around Europe, something happened to the motor of his car. He cabled the Rolls-Royce people back in England and asked, "I'm having trouble with my car; what do you suggest I do?" Well, the Rolls-Royce people flew a mechanic over! The mechanic repaired the car and flew back to England and left the man to continue his holiday.
>
> As you can imagine, the fellow was wondering, "How much is this going to cost me?" So when he got back to England, he wrote the people a letter and asked how much he owed them. He received a letter from the office that read: "Dear Sir: There is no record anywhere in our files that anything ever went wrong with a Rolls-Royce." That is justification![3]

Suppose Satan came before God and said of you, "You can't let him (or her) into heaven, their life was filled with sin. Look in the books, God, you'll see pages and pages of their ugly sin." If this were to happen, God would open those books and say, "I have no record of even one sin that they committed during their entire life."

Discussion question 3 can be used here.

### 3. RECONCILIATION: Jesus made peace with God possible.

Reconciliation means bringing together two people who have suffered a breakdown in their relationship. Jesus, by his death on the cross, gave us the opportunity to have our relationship with God healed and renewed.

**God was in Christ, making peace between the world and himself. . . . God did not hold the world guilty of its sins. And he gave us this message of peace.**

—2 Corinthians 5:19 (NCV)

**For if, when we were God's enemies, we were reconciled to him through the death of his Son, how much more, having been reconciled, shall we be saved through his life!**

—Romans 5:10

### Jesus is the bridge between God and man.

Look at this simple picture that has helped millions of people to understand what it means to be reconciled with God. We stand on one side of a gulf between us and God—a Grand Canyon–sized separation from God created by our sin. The bridge that spans this gap between us and God is the cross of Christ.

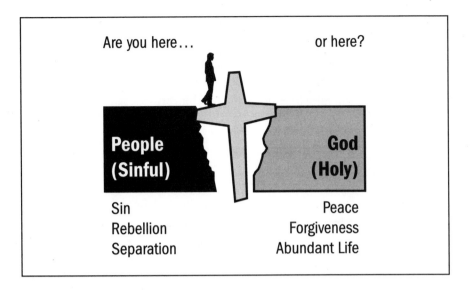

We can't cross this relational great divide through our own efforts. We need Jesus to reconcile us with God. From our perspective we see that some people live more moral lives than others. But from God's perspective, only a perfect person can bridge that gap. That's why we need Jesus. Listen to this description that James Kennedy gives us:

> Suppose that you were trying to cross from one cliff to another one which is a hundred feet away. It is five thousand feet down to the rocks below. You have, however, a one-inch-thick piece of rope which is capable of holding up several tons. There is a difficulty though, for you have only fifty feet of rope. I say, "Do not worry! I have fifty feet of thread. We can tie my thread to your rope and then tie that to trees on either cliff and then you can go across." You decline my offer and I respond, "What is the matter? Do you not trust the rope?" "Yes," you say, "I trust the rope but I do not trust the thread." Then let's change the story and make it ninety feet of rope and only ten feet of thread. You're still not comfortable. Then suppose we make it ninety-nine feet of rope and only one foot of thread. One inch of thread? You see, if you have one inch of thread, you will be just as dead on the rocks below as if you tried to cross on a hundred feet of thread. The rope obviously represents what Christ has done and the thread represents what we have done. We must trust in Christ alone. As Charles Spurgeon put it, "If we have to put one stitch into the garment of our salvation, we shall ruin the whole thing."[4]

Discussion question 4 can be used here.

## 4. <u>ADOPTION</u>: Jesus made me a part of God's family.

Adoption—the picture of a nursery and an orphan baby. Spiritually, we all were orphans. We were outside of God's family, but because of Jesus' death on the cross, believers are adopted and given the status of being children of God.

Adoption stresses the family relationship in salvation. Justification gives us the right legal standing before God, but adoption puts us into God's very own family. We often hear people make the statement that we are all God's children. This is not true. We are all God's creation, but the only way to be a child of God is to be adopted into his family through Jesus Christ.

**He predestined us to be adopted as his sons through Jesus Christ, in accordance with his pleasure and will.**

—Ephesians 1:5

**And since we are his children, we will share his treasures—for all God gives to his Son Jesus is now ours too.**

—Romans 8:17 (LB)

**For you did not receive a spirit that makes you a slave again to fear, but you received the Spirit of sonship. And by him we cry, "*Abba,* Father."**

—Romans 8:15

If you have ever had a friend or family member adopt a child, you know what a detailed and exhaustive procedure it is. Every legal document has to be just right, and the adoptive parents are put through extensive background, character, and financial checks. As painstaking as this process is, it is but a fraction of what God went through to adopt us. He faced the real pain of the cross. Our adoption papers were signed in blood—the blood that Jesus shed on the cross.

God has brought you into his family. On the cross he sealed the legal transaction and made the loving choice to make you his child. You are God's child by God's choice. Say that with me, would you? "I am God's child by God's choice."

5. <u>REDEMPTION</u>: **Jesus purchased my salvation with his blood.**

 **A Fresh Word**

*Redemption*

**The Greek word for redemption refers to slaves being purchased in the marketplace. In the spiritual sense, all of us were slaves to sin until Jesus purchased us out of the slave market and set us free from sin's bondage. Because he bought and paid for us with his blood, we now belong exclusively to him.**

The picture here is of a busy marketplace in a large city. The courtyard is packed with merchants selling vegetables, pottery, meat, and wine. At the center of this market there is a different kind of sale going on—people are being sold as slaves. To really understand this picture, you must visualize yourself up on that slave block. Prospective buyers are eyeing you—talking about you as a thing instead of as a person. They begin to bid on you. As each successive bid is shouted out, you look at the faces of those that would enslave you. Whether they seem kind or cruel, you know they are bidding to use you for their own purposes. Just as the auction is winding down to an end, a stranger stands. He puts in a bid a thousand times higher than the last—greater than anyone could match—and the crowd gasps. As the auctioneer hastily accepts his bid, you look into this stranger's eyes and realize, "He's the only one here who's not bidding to use me. He's bidding to set me free!"

Jesus paid the price for your redemption. Jesus paid the price to set you free. Look at these verses.

> **For he has rescued us from the dominion of darkness and brought us into the kingdom of the Son he loves, in whom we have redemption, the forgiveness of sins.**
>
> —Colossians 1:13–14

> **God paid a ransom to save you from the impossible road to heaven which your fathers tried to take, and the ransom he paid was not mere gold or silver, as you very well know. But he paid for you with the precious lifeblood of Christ, the sinless, spotless Lamb of God.**
>
> —1 Peter 1:18–19 (LB)

6. <u>PROPITIATION</u>: **Jesus satisfied God's justice.**

I dare you to say this word three times as fast as you can. This is the most unfamiliar word of these seven. When we say that Jesus was our propitiation, it means he completely satisfied all of God's righteous demands. Jesus' sacrifice was enough—it was sufficient for God. All of my best efforts cannot come close to being enough or sufficient to meet God's standards and demands for holiness and perfection. Jesus covered us with his blood and brought us into God's presence.

**A Fresh Word**

*Propitiation*

**To propitiate is to bring satisfaction or to fulfill a demand or requirement. In heathen circles it was a word that meant "to appease the gods." The biblical sense of the word speaks of that which satisfies the justice of God so that mercy is given.**

**The picture of propitiation in the Old Testament is the "mercy seat," the cover of the ark of the covenant in first the tabernacle and later the temple. This is the place where blood was sprinkled as an offering for the sins of the people.**

The picture in this word is a portrait that takes place at the temple, at the altar where the sacrifices are made.

Once a year, according to God's instructions in Leviticus 16, the high priest was to sprinkle the blood of a sacrifice on the cover of the ark of the covenant that was placed in the Holy of Holies in the tabernacle and, later, the temple of worship. This cover was called the "atonement cover" or the "mercy seat." There were three elements involved in this offering: the high priest, the blood of the sacrifice, and the mercy seat on which the offering was placed. Jesus became all three of these for us. He is the High Priest who makes an offering for our sin. He is the sacrifice who shed his blood for our sin. He is the place of mercy where we find forgiveness for our sin. Jesus fulfilled every picture in the Old Testament system of sacrifices, a system that God put into place to look forward to the sacrifice of his Son.

**He is the atoning sacrifice for our sins, and not only for ours but also for the sins of the whole world.**

—1 John 2:2

**This is love: not that we loved God, but that he loved us and sent his Son as an atoning sacrifice for our sins.**

—1 John 4:10

### 7. <u>FORGIVENESS</u>: Jesus sent my sins away from me.

The final picture is simple, but it may be the most moving of all. He forgives us of our sins. *Aphiemi* is the Greek word usually used for God's forgiveness of us in the New Testament. It literally means to "send away from." That is what God has done with our sins—sent them away from us. Would you read with me Ephesians 1:7 and Colossians 2:13.

**In him we have redemption through his blood, the forgiveness of sins, in accordance with the riches of God's grace.**

—Ephesians 1:7

**When you were dead in your sins and in the uncircumcision of your sinful nature, God made you alive with Christ. He forgave us all our sins.**

—Colossians 2:13

A graphic picture from the Old Testament sacrificial system showing the forgiveness of sin is the scapegoat. The placing of the blood on the mercy seat on the day of atonement was seen only by the high priest. Fellowship was restored with God through this act of faith, but the people of Israel couldn't see it happening. It was hidden from their view. God gave a visual object lesson to them to reassure them that their sin was covered.

A goat was selected to symbolically take the sins away from the people. Blood was sprinkled on it and it was led to the edge of the wilderness where it was set free to wander, never to be seen again. The scapegoat was a picture of Israel's "covered" sin.

Jesus was our scapegoat. God put all of our sins on him, even though he was innocent and pure. When our sins are put on him, we never see the guilt of them again.

Look at the picture God gives us in Psalm 103:12. "As far as the east is from the west." How far is that? You can't measure it. It's farther apart than we could ever reach. That's what forgiveness means.

**As far as the east is from the west, so far has he removed our transgressions from us.**

—Psalm 103:12

**You will throw away all our sins into the deepest part of the sea.**

—Micah 7:19 (NCV)

I've always liked what Corrie ten Boom says about Micah 7:19. God throws our sins into the deepest part of the sea, and then he puts up a "no fishing" sign.

But what if you don't feel forgiven? What if you have asked God for forgiveness but have a hard time believing that he has forgiven you? Martin Luther was once asked whether he felt his sins were forgiven. His answer, "No, I don't feel they are forgiven. I know they are because God says so in his Word."[5]

Look at me for just a moment. Your forgiveness is not based on your feelings, but on God's promise. And God promised that when we trust in Jesus for forgiveness he puts our sins as far as the east is from the west. He throws our sins into the deepest part of the sea. Some of you have been allowing Satan to continue to heap guilt on you for sins that God has already forgiven. Will you accept by faith the truth that God has forgiven you?

As we finish the look at our salvation, three statements can be made if you are already a Christian

## Three aspects of salvation: past, present, and future

1. In the <u>PAST</u>, I was saved from the <u>PENALTY</u> of sin (justification).

2. In the <u>PRESENT</u>, I am being saved from the <u>POWER</u> of sin (sanctification).

3. In the <u>FUTURE</u>, I will be saved from the <u>PRESENCE</u> of sin (glorification).

**This means that while Jesus' death accomplished all that God intended it to—Jesus said, "It is finished"—we have not experienced all there is to experience of salvation. There is more to look forward to!**

Discussion question 5 can be used here.

As we look through this biblical album of pictures of our salvation, here's the shocker. Right there in the middle of every picture is *you!* You are redeemed. You are adopted. You are justified. Jesus died in your place. Jesus gave himself as an offering for your sins. You are reconciled to God. You are forgiven!

Some of you may not yet have received God's gift of salvation. Let today be the day you step across the line and become a believer in Jesus Christ. You don't have to understand all of this information to become a Christian. In fact, few if any of us understood all of this when we became Christians. At the start, there are only a few basic truths to understand:

## Key Personal Perspective

**Does someone have to be able to understand all the truths we've discussed today to be saved? No.**

**To be saved you need to know only three truths:**

1. **I am a sinner.**
2. **Jesus died in my place.**
3. **If I ask God to forgive me for rebelling against him and I trust in Jesus as my Lord, he will save me.**

**No one can say these three truths are difficult to understand. The truth of our salvation is simple enough for a child to understand, yet deep enough to study the rest of your life and never fully comprehend.**

**The bottom line question: Have you accepted God's gift of forgiveness for your sin, paid for by Jesus' death on the cross?**

If you have not yet accepted God's gift of salvation, you can do that now. Pray those three truths in a simple prayer. "Father, I admit to you that I am a sinner. I thank you that Jesus died in my place. I ask you now to forgive me for rebelling against you and I trust in Jesus as the Lord, the manager of my life. Father, I trust you to give me the gift of salvation."

Let's pray and thank God one more time for all he did to make a relationship with him possible for us. Thank him for dying in your place, for justifying you, for reconciling you to him, for adopting you into his family, for redeeming you from slavery to sin, for covering your sins by his blood, and for forgiving all your sin completely and eternally.

**Begin working on memory card 6, "The Truth about Salvation."**

# Appendix

## *Supplemental Resource*

The doctrine of election and predestination is one of the most difficult doctrines that Christians try to understand. In simple terms, election means to choose certain people for a certain purpose, just as we elect government officials. Spiritual election addresses the question of how God chooses us for salvation.

There are two main streams of thought concerning election: Calvinism and Arminianism. Calvinism (named after John Calvin, a sixteenth-century theologian) emphasizes words like *elect, chosen,* or *predestine.* Calvinists typically believe that only certain people are chosen to be saved, and that God passes over the non-elect. They base their views on verses like 1 Peter 1:1–2.

> Peter, an apostle of Jesus Christ, To God's elect, strangers in the world, scattered throughout Pontus, Galatia, Cappadocia, Asia and Bithynia, who have been chosen according to the foreknowledge of God the Father, through the sanctifying work of the Spirit, for obedience to Jesus Christ and sprinkling by his blood: Grace and peace be yours in abundance.
>
> —1 Peter 1:1–2

Arminianism (named after James Arminius, another sixteenth-century theologian) emphasizes words like "whosoever" and "not willing that any should perish." It bases its views on verses like John 3:16 and 2 Peter 3:9. Arminians typically believe in free will and that God in his foreknowledge sees who will respond with faith in Christ and then elects them based on that foreknowledge.

> The Lord is not slow in keeping his promise, as some understand slowness. He is patient with you, not wanting anyone to perish, but everyone to come to repentance.
>
> —2 Peter 3:9

We believe that Scripture teaches both truths, and to exclude one set of verses or emphasize one over the other is unbalanced. God allows us the freedom to choose to love him or not. Our freedom to choose cannot supercede the sovereign election of God. These are ideas that are difficult to reconcile with our finite minds. In the end it must be a matter of trust.

The most frightening thought that haunts some is this: "What if I want God but he doesn't want me?" The truth is, that will never happen! If there is a desire for God in your heart, you're one of the elect!

## Discussion Questions

1. What simply amazes you about God's salvation?

2. Do you think any of us felt as lost as we truly were before we were saved? Have you seen any examples that show that the more lost someone knows they were the more appreciative they are of the gift of salvation?

3. The truth of justification is difficult for many to understand. What causes us to struggle to see ourselves as not guilty before God? What is it that has helped you to increase your faith in God's promise that we are justified?

4. In what ways do we take credit for or become prideful concerning the gift of salvation? What has encouraged you to keep before you daily the truth that salvation is completely by grace?

5. The seven pictures of salvation that we looked at in this study are among the greatest treasures in any of our lives.

    1. Substitution: Jesus died in my place.
    2. Justification: Jesus made me right with God.
    3. Reconciliation: Jesus made peace with God possible.
    4. Adoption: Jesus made me a part of God's family.
    5. Redemption: Jesus purchased my salvation with his blood.
    6. Propitiation: Jesus satisfied God's justice.
    7. Forgiveness: Jesus sent my sins away from me.

    Which of these has the most immediate emotional impact on you?

    Which of these would you like to understand better?

    Which could you use to help someone you know to better understand how to become a believer?

# Salvation
## Part 2

**Life Change Objective**

To give you an assurance of your salvation that results in a deepening security in God's love and an appreciation for God's grace.

**Summary Teaching Outline**

Why do so many people lack assurance of their salvation?

The Promised Security of Salvation

 The sovereign decision of the Father

 The high-priestly work of Jesus

 The sealing power of the Spirit

The Personal Assurance of My Salvation

 How do I handle doubts about my salvation?

 What if I can't remember when I became a Christian?

 What happens to my relationship to God when I sin?

 Are there any proofs that I am a Christian?

## Review

- The major theme of the Bible is God's eternal plan to rescue us from the penalty, power, and presence of sin through the death and resurrection of his Son, Jesus.

- God's nature is holy, righteous, and just. Man is sinful both by nature and by choice. God's solution? He has provided us a Savior!

- We looked at seven descriptions of what Jesus did for us on the cross:

1. Substitution: Jesus died in my place.
2. Justification: Jesus made me right with God.
3. Reconciliation: Jesus made peace with God possible.
4. Adoption: Jesus made me a part of God's family.
5. Redemption: Jesus purchased my salvation with his blood.
6. Propitiation: Jesus satisfied God's justice.
7. Forgiveness: Jesus sent my sins away from me.

**Even though God has provided us with all of these riches, many Christians remain unsure of their salvation. Last time we looked at the problem (our need for salvation) and the provision (the solution of salvation). In this session we'll look at how to be confident of your salvation.**

I want you to see how great a gift you've been given in your salvation. It's my prayer that you will sense in a deeper way than ever before the depth of security that you have in the love of God.

Max Lucado tells a parable of God's grace at the beginning of his book on Ephesians. Four brothers, because they disobey their father, become lost a long way from home. They each deal in different ways with the fact that they cannot get back home. One brother builds a hut and decides that where the brothers are now living is good enough. A second brother sits in judgment of the first brother for building the hut. The third brother begins the impossible task of building a path back to home on his own strength. When their elder brother comes to lead them back home, all three decide instead to stay where they are. They become stuck in their solutions to being separated from their father. Only the fourth brother, the youngest, decides to openly confess his disobedience and to depend upon his eldest brother's gracious offer to carry him back home. Lucado writes:

> All four brothers heard the same invitation. Each had an opportunity to be carried home by the elder brother. The first said no, choosing a grass hut over his father's house. The second said no, preferring to analyze the mistakes of his brother rather than admit his own. The third said no, thinking it wiser to make a good impression than an honest confession. And the fourth said yes, choosing gratitude over guilt.
>
> "I'll indulge myself," resolves one son.
> "I'll compare myself," opts another.
> "I'll save myself," determines the third.
> "I'll entrust myself to you," decides the fourth.[1]

Salvation is a matter of entrusting ourselves to God's grace. Do you have to understand everything about the doctrine of salvation in order for salvation to work? No. You don't have to understand the inner workings of a car to drive it or a watch to tell time.

There are, however, great benefits to understanding the doctrine of salvation. The more you understand your salvation the more you see how deeply the world around you needs Jesus Christ. He is God's only way to salvation!

The more you understand about your salvation, the more secure you become in that salvation. Once you entrust yourself to God, you can rest secure in his promise of salvation.

But many believers live lives of quiet doubt, wondering if they truly are saved. They know they have prayed a prayer of commitment to God and that they are trying to follow God in daily life. But there are moments when they wonder, Did it work? It almost seems too good to be true. These questions might come to mind infrequently or may be almost constant companions.

## Why Do So Many People Lack the Assurance of Salvation?

- **Because they cannot pinpoint a <u>SPECIFIC</u> <u>TIME</u> when they received Christ.[2]**

  The question, "When did you trust Jesus for your salvation?" is a question that troubles some, especially when others are so confident of the exact time. You hear them answer, "I became a believer on November 4, 1989, at 7:14 in the evening. The temperature that day was 45 degrees Fahrenheit and we had 1.2 inches of rainfall." They seem to know everything so exactly! And you do not. You can point to the period of time when you gave your life to Christ, but you don't know the exact day.

  Although there is certainly a moment in time when you cross the line and give your heart to Jesus, some of us remember the exact timing of that moment better than others. You may have come to Christ when you were older, or you may have had a Christian friend who helped you to remember the day, or you may have had a dramatic moment of personal crisis: for whatever reason the exact day and time stuck in your mind. But let me ask you, do you have to remember the exact time for Jesus to have saved you? Of course not. My salvation is not dependent on my remembering the day, but on my trusting in Jesus for forgiveness and life direction.

- Because they question the <u>CORRECTNESS</u> of the way they expressed faith in Christ.

  **"Did I pray the right prayer? Did I know everything I needed to know? Should I have felt differently?"**

  You've seen these little gospel tracts such as *Four Spiritual Laws* or *Steps to Peace with God*. These are great tools for sharing your faith in Christ with others. Sometimes we get the feeling that unless we had someone read one of those little booklets to us—and read every page—something might have gotten left out. Maybe we didn't do it right. I remind you that people have been becoming Christians for thousands of years without the wonderful tools we have today.

  Some think they should have felt differently. How did you feel emotionally when you became a believer in Jesus? Let's take a quick survey (you can say yes to more than one of these). How many of you felt goose bumps running up and down your arms? How many of you felt a sense of great relief? How many felt no great emotion at all? How many felt a warm sense of God's love for you?

  You see how differently we all feel? That's because we all feel differently! God has wired us differently. That, compared with the variety of circumstances that we are in as we come to Christ, causes us to have a wide range of emotions when we become believers.

- Because of <u>SINS</u> they commit after salvation.

  Believers really struggled with this question in the early church. Some people theorized that you only could sin three times after you became a Christian—sort of a "three strikes you're out" rule. Others postulated that only the sins you committed after you were baptized counted. Know what people did? They waited until they were really old to get baptized—feeling that maybe right before death you'd be too old to sin! None of these teachings is from the Bible; they were just ways that the church tried to deal with the undeniable fact that Christians sin after we are saved. The question is, How are *you* going to deal with that fact? Will you let it erode your faith and trust in God, or will you allow it to cause you to throw yourself in continued dependence on the mercy and grace of God?

  These questions find their answer in the assurances that God gives us about our salvation. If you look for assurance in yourself or your circumstance or your feelings, you'll find yourself filled with doubts. Assurance is found in the promises of God.

Discussion question 1 can be used here.

**There is a difference between the personal assurance of my salvation and the promised security of my salvation. While I may or may not have a *feeling* of assurance, security is a *fact* based on the promise of God. In this study, we're going to look at how God's promise of salvation can deepen our confidence in our salvation.**

I know that for some the idea of being secure in your salvation is a bit new and even frightening. We'll deal with some of those fears in just a moment. For now—I'd like you to sit back and fill in some foundations of our security with me. Even more, I'd like you to listen as we read verse after verse that point to God's promise of salvation. Let these verses, brick by brick, build a foundation of security in your life.

# The Promised Security of Salvation

Each member of the Trinity plays a part in our security as believers.

### *The sovereign decision of the* <u>FATHER</u>

- **God has declared us "not guilty" in his sight and canceled the punishment that should have been ours.**

  **I tell you the truth, whoever hears my word and believes him who sent me has eternal life and will not be condemned; he has crossed over from death to life.**

  **—John 5:24**

  **For God so loved the world that he gave his one and only Son, that whoever believes in him shall not perish but have eternal life. . . . Whoever believes in him is not condemned, but whoever does not believe stands condemned already because he has not believed in the name of God's one and only Son.**

  **—John 3:16, 18**

Look at John 5:24. We have eternal life; we will not be condemned; we have crossed over from death to life.

John 3:16 is perhaps the most familiar verse in the Bible. It is also one of the clearest verses you'll find about the security of God's promise of salvation. Circle the words "eternal life." That's the gift God gives to us. How long is eternal life? An eternity! And what do we need to do to receive this gift? John 3:16 tells us: believe in him.

Do you have any "garage-shelf" gifts? You know the kind I'm talking about. When you received each of these gifts you thought, "Exactly what I need." But at the time you couldn't find room for the gift or figure out exactly how it worked. So, eventually, the gift found its way to a shelf out in the garage. Oh, you still value it when you see it. You just can't figure out how to enjoy it.

It may surprise you to learn that the security in this great promise in John 3:16 often finds its way to a spiritual "garage shelf." How could that happen? Fairly simply, actually. We are immediately grateful for the promise of heaven when we become a believer, but soon begin to see it as something for later. The promise of heaven seems such a long way off. We're more interested in a promise for some rest today, or a peaceful night's sleep tonight, or some wisdom for the decision we have to make tomorrow.

Here's a sentence to change your thinking about this great promise. Your eternal life began the *moment* you trusted Jesus for your salvation! Oh, I freely admit that the quality of this life will take a great jump when we are in heaven. But that does not change the fact that you are given eternal life now. When you begin to see this truth on a daily basis, it changes the way you look at life. That business deal that isn't coming together is a little less stressful. The reality of the illness that you're facing becomes a little less fearful. The joy of knowing God is there to strengthen you becomes more real. So take the promise of eternal life off of the shelf. Rearrange everything else if you have to, but put this promise into the center of your daily life, where it belongs.

- **God is at peace with me; the war between us is over.**

  **Therefore, since we have been made right in God's sight by faith, we have peace with God because of what Jesus Christ our Lord has done for us.**
  —Romans 5:1 (NLT)

The Bible tells us that before we become Christians we are at war with God. Coming to Jesus is like raising the white flag, the one that means surrender. And when we surrender our lives to him, he gives us gifts. It makes you wonder what takes us so long to surrender. Because when we do, we have peace with God because of what Jesus did for us.

- **God has determined that nothing can ever separate me from his love.**

  **For I am convinced that neither death nor life, neither angels nor demons, neither the present nor the future, nor any powers, neither height nor depth, nor anything else in all creation, will be able to separate us from the love of God that is in Christ Jesus our Lord.**
  —Romans 8:38–39

Nothing can separate you from the love of God. God is the one who holds you in the grip of his love, and nothing is stronger than God.

Listen to these words written about God's hand.

> God's hand is not an open hand. It is a hand that holds. When a father or a mother holds the hand of a small child to lead him safely through some place of real danger, that father or mother will not let that little hand go, even though the child may want to pull away.[3]

Think about this for a moment. If you were waiting with a five-year-old to cross a busy street, what would you do? Reach out and grab the child's hand. If, as you waited for the light to turn green, the child began to squirm to get out of your grip, what would you do? Would you let go, thinking, "Well, it's your life—your choice. If you want to take it from here on your own, fine with me." Of course not! If that little boy or girl tried to get out of your grip, you would just hold on tighter.

Once you come to Christ, God becomes your Father. You are his child, and he will not loosen his grip on your life. There may be times when, because of temptation, you would like God to let go. But you are his child, and he will not let go.

## The high-priestly work of JESUS

### A Closer Look

**In the Old Testament sacrificial system, the high priest was the highest spiritual leader. He alone got to enter the Holy of Holies and put blood on the mercy seat once a year on the Day of Atonement. Jesus is our High Priest. When Jesus died on the cross, he was both the ultimate sacrifice and the ultimate sacrificer. He lives forever to do the work of a high priest—to be our intercessor and our mediator.**

• **Jesus lives to make INTERCESSION for me.**

The word *intercession* means "to plead on behalf of another." That's what Jesus does for us. Even now, even today, Jesus has prayed on your behalf.

> **Therefore he is able to save completely those who come to God through him, because he always lives to intercede for them.**
> **—Hebrews 7:25**

You see an example of Jesus praying for us in John 17.

> **I will remain in the world no longer, but they are still in the world, and I am coming to you. Holy Father, protect them by the power of your name—the name you gave me—so that they may be one as we are one. . . . My prayer is not that you take them out of the world but that you protect them from the evil one.**
> **—John 17:11, 15**

Jesus did not stop praying those kinds of prayers when he left this earth, and he continues to pray for us today. Jesus is praying for us, each one of us individually. He knows you by name. He knows every one of your weaknesses and every one of your strengths, he knows what gets you down and the struggles you're facing today.

As an example of this, remember what Jesus said to Simon Peter, "Simon, Simon, Satan has asked to sift you as wheat. But I have prayed for you, Simon, that your faith may not fail. And when you have turned back, strengthen your brothers" (Luke 22:31–32).

Jesus is praying for Peter. Knowing what will happen in his life, he prays for Peter even before he faces the trial that Jesus knows is coming. Knowing your heart and your circumstances, Jesus does the same for you. That sudden crisis that hits you—Jesus has already prayed for God to strengthen you through it. That temptation that is overwhelming you—Jesus is interceding for you, asking God to show you the way out.

This ought to give you an incredible sense of security. If there's anyone you want praying for you, it is Jesus!

- **Jesus lives to <u>MEDIATE</u> for me.**

  **My dear children, I write this to you so that you will not sin. But if anybody does sin, we have one who speaks to the Father in our defense—Jesus Christ, the Righteous One. He is the atoning sacrifice for our sins, and not only for ours but also for the sins of the whole world.**

  **—1 John 2:1–2**

  Remember the story of Job? Satan went before God to accuse this righteous man—and Satan is still the accuser of the faithful today. You can almost see the picture in heaven. Satan, our accuser, before Jesus, always our defender. Satan says, "Do you see what he just did? What she just did? How can they call themselves a Christian and do something like that?" Jesus stands on our behalf and says, "He or she trusted me for their salvation on January 23, 1985." And God says, "Not guilty. Case dismissed."

  Our salvation is based not on our performance but on what Jesus has done for us.

- **Jesus is <u>FAITHFUL</u> to me even when I am not faithful to him.**

  Would you read with me 2 Timothy 2:11–13.

  **This teaching is true: If we died with him, we will also live with him. If we accept suffering, we will also rule with him. If we refuse to accept him, he will refuse to accept us. If we are not faithful, he will still be faithful, because he cannot be false to himself.**

  **—2 Timothy 2:11–13 (NCV)**

When your children are unfaithful to you—when they do things you've told them not to do—do you disown them? Of course not. Discipline them? Yes. But they are still your children. Can you imagine God being any less committed to us than we are to our children?

One of the reasons that we struggle with accepting the depth of God's love for us is that we have so many definitions of love running around in our minds. Love is a feeling, love is romance, love is sentiment.

Let me give you one of God's definitions of love. It might surprise you.

Love is a contract.

This comes from the meaning of the Old Testament Hebrew word for love, *hesed*. God's love is a contract, but not the kind you may be thinking of. It's not a cold business agreement. It is a covenant contract, a relational commitment that is not to be broken. Even if one of the parties were to show unworthiness, a covenant contract would remain in force. Even when we are not faithful to God, he will not break his covenant of commitment to us.

I've heard some say, "That's not fair. It sounds like we can be as faithless as we like as Christians, can sin all we want, and God will love us just as much." Let me quickly say three things about that.

First, God will love you, but you will be miserable. It's a prodigal son existence to live a faithless life. There may be pleasure in sin for a moment, but then comes the depths of guilt, frustration, and loneliness. Christians who are caught up in sin almost always build lives of constant busyness and noise. They can't stand silence because the moment it becomes quiet they realize how terribly empty their lives are.

Second, God will love you but you will lose eternal rewards. The way you live your life does matter, both here and in eternity. We'll look at this more as we study heaven in a later session.

Third, never presume on the grace of God. If you think you are saved and yet are able to live any way you want with no sense of remorse, I would be deeply concerned about your salvation. While we all struggle with taking God's grace for granted, there are some who act as if it's a free ride to live however they want. "I have my gospel ticket punched. I'm headed for heaven no matter what, so what does it matter how I live in this life." I'd check the ticket again! Just because you can understand what salvation is and say the right words about salvation does not mean you are saved.

Look at Hebrews 10:23.

**Let us hold unswervingly to the hope we profess, for he who promised is faithful.**

—**Hebrews 10:23**

When I realize how faithful God is, I have the security that enables me to hold on to the hope that I have in him. This security of God's promise is hard for us to grasp. One reason is that we don't always keep our promises. I have some good news for you. God is not like us. God keeps his promises.

### A Closer Look

We live in a day of unfaithfulness. People cannot be trusted to keep their promises. That's true of both individuals and nations. Husbands are often unfaithful to the vows they made to their wives. Wives are often unfaithful to their husbands. Children are often unfaithful to the principles taught by their parents. Parents are often unfaithful to meet the needs of their children. Employees are often unfaithful to the promises they make to their employers. And employers are often unfaithful to fulfill their obligations and responsibilities to their employees. We also have to acknowledge that Christians are often unfaithful to God, although God is never unfaithful to them. Not one of us can claim immunity from the sin of unfaithfulness.

Only God is always faithful and keeps every promise in full. That fact is vital because everything we believe stands on the faithfulness of God. Our eternal destiny is at stake. In contrast to the unfaithfulness around us, it is refreshing to lift our eyes to our beloved God who is always faithful.

—John MacArthur

## The sealing power of the <u>SPIRIT</u>

In our study of the Holy Spirit, we saw that at the moment of salvation, the Holy Spirit performs several works on our behalf that secure our salvation forever.

- The Holy Spirit *regenerates* me (gives me new birth).
- The Holy Spirit *baptizes* me.
- The Holy Spirit *abides* in me as a gift from God.
- The Holy Spirit *seals* me.

And you also were included in Christ when you heard the word of truth, the gospel of your salvation. Having believed, you were marked in him with a seal, the promised Holy Spirit.

—Ephesians 1:13

Who is the Holy Spirit? He is God. God is living in us to secure our salvation.

A quick quiz from our study of the Holy Spirit. Do you remember what the "seal" was in the days that the Bible was written? It was a wax seal that was put on a scroll. The seal had two purposes.

Identification: each seal had a distinctive mark. A seal on a document was a guarantee that it had not been forged. It was a kind of notary stamp of that day.

Protection: it would be clear if the seal had been broken. And this was taken very seriously. One who broke the seal of a king would face the wrath of that king.

God's Spirit identifies you as God's child. There could be no more distinctive mark on our lives. And God's Spirit protects us in his love until the day we meet him in heaven.

**We can be certain of the security of our salvation because in the past, Christ made peace with God for each of us. Today, Jesus lives to make intercession for me, and the Holy Spirit guarantees that my future is full of glory. It is God's work that makes my salvation secure—I can do nothing to make him stop loving me or stop being faithful to his own promises.**

I'd encourage you to memorize this next verse, especially those of you who find yourselves filled with doubts about God's unconditional love for you.

**My sheep listen to my voice; I know them, and they follow me. I give them eternal life, and they shall never perish; no one can snatch them out of my hand. My Father, who has given them to me, is greater than all; no one can snatch them out of my Father's hand.**

—John 10:27–29

This is an amazing verse, overflowing with assurances. "I give them eternal life." That's an assurance. "They shall never perish." That's an assurance. "No one can snatch them out of my hand." That's an assurance. If God's promise of salvation were not secure, Jesus could not have spoken these phrases.

"My sheep listen to my voice." For many of us, that's where the secret to security lies. Sheep in Jesus' day learned to recognize the voice of their shepherd. (Still do today, in fact.) As they made their way home from the fields at the end of the day, a number of flocks of sheep would often converge at one watering hole. The flocks would become mixed to the point where it seemed there was no way to separate them. When they were ready to go, all of the shepherds would begin to call out at once for their flock to come to them. Amidst all of those voices, a sheep would be able to pick out the voice of its own shepherd and head straight toward him.

My encouragement to you is this. Listen for Jesus' voice in these words that we've just studied. There are a lot of other voices out there: your own doubts, human logic, past hurts. These voices say to you, "You can't trust God like that. No one could love you that much." Listen to Jesus' voice, to Jesus' words. And let him build a foundation of security in your life that cannot be shaken.

> Discussion question 2 can be used here.

> **Split Session Plan:** If you're teaching this study over two sessions, end the first session here.

## The Personal Assurance of My Salvation

God's promise of security and my personal inner assurance of salvation are different things. Just because God's promise is secure does not mean we always "feel" that security. Charles Stanley had lived for years without a sense of assurance of God's love. He came to believe that it was an assurance that we as humans cannot have. Listen to his words about the day that all changed.

> It was as if a light came on. Suddenly I saw it. I wanted to shout. I felt like a man just freed from prison. I began to thank God that I had been wrong all those years. I thanked Him for the restlessness that had kept me searching and praying. Then I was struck with the most awesome thought of all. I had been eternally secure since that day as a twelve-year-old when I prayed, asking Jesus to save me.
>
> That morning was a turning point in my life. It was far more than simply a shift in my theology. It introduced me to the true meaning of unconditional love. It was the beginning of my lifelong journey into the mystery of God's truly amazing grace. Terms such as peace and joy took on a whole new meaning. They became part of my experience, not just my vocabulary. . . . Security came to mean a great deal more than a guarantee of where I would spend eternity. It was the perfect word to describe the sense of intimacy I felt with Christ. I was secure. Secure in His love and acceptance of me. Secure in His daily will for my life. Secure in every promise He had made. And of course, secure in where I would spend eternity.[4]

For just a moment, think about the times in your life when you have had a sense of personal security. What are some of those?

### Teaching Tip

Let the group call out some ideas at this point. They may talk about times with their family when growing up or times of prayer as a new believer or times with a group of other Christians. It would be good at some point for you to say something like, "Some of you can't remember any times of real security—you weren't given that gift by your parents as you were growing up. The security in his love that God wants to give to you may be an entirely new and wonderful (although a bit unfamiliar) gift for you.

God wants to give us that sense of security in our relationship with him. If we are to have assurance, there are some tough questions we must answer honestly.

## How do I handle doubts about my salvation?

**Whenever a person is not sure if they are saved, there are several possibilities:**

- **They may not be saved.**

- **They may be disobeying God; disobedience causes us to lose the joy of our salvation and causes us to wonder if God still loves us.**

- **They may be experiencing temptation to doubt from Satan, who obviously does not want us to feel secure in our relationship with God.**

When it comes to salvation, there are three different kinds of security.

*False security* is believing you are saved when you are not. You may be counting on your good works or on some religious ritual. Jesus told us, in Matthew 7:21–23, that some suffer from false security.

> Not everyone who says to me, "Lord, Lord," will enter the kingdom of heaven, but only he who does the will of my Father who is in heaven. Many will say to me on that day, "Lord, Lord, did we not prophesy in your name, and in your name drive out demons and perform many miracles?" Then I will tell them plainly, "I never knew you. Away from me, you evildoers!"
>
> —Matthew 7:21–23

*Conditional security* is believing that something you do or do not do keeps you saved. It is the feeling that you must keep some law or avoid some sin in order to keep yourself in God's grace. It's amazing to consider the list of conditions that we've added to the Gospel over the years. We didn't put ourselves in the grace of God, and we cannot keep ourselves in the grace of God.

*Eternal security* is the third kind of security. This is the knowledge that your salvation is eternally secure in the hands of God. Eternal security is based not on your circumstance but on the promises we looked at in the previous section. Eternal security is unconditional hope based on Christ's sacrifice on the cross.

To break through doubts about your salvation you must first have the third kind of security, eternal security.

### What if I can't remember when I became a Christian?

**Though coming to Christ is often a process, at some point a person crosses "from death to life." No one gradually becomes "alive."**

Sometimes when you ask a person when they became a Christian they will say, "I've been a Christian all of my life." They say that because they've gone to church all of their life. But the truth is, none of us has been a Christian from the moment we were born. We all need the new life that only Jesus can give us by our being born again. And just as there is a moment when you were born physically, there is a moment when you are born spiritually. We talked earlier about the fact that some cannot remember exactly when that moment was. And it bothers you; it's bothered some of you for a long time. We can take care of that doubt right now.

**Prayer for assurance**

Just pray a prayer something like this.

*Jesus, I know I made this commitment before, but not being able to remember exactly when has caused me some real doubts. So right here and right now, on (say the date) I nail down in my heart the fact that my life is given to you. I trust in you and you alone to forgive the wrong things that I've done. I ask you to be the Lord—the leader and manager—of my life. Amen.*

Some of you aren't sure that you are a Christian. We can take care of that too.

**If you aren't sure that you are a Christian, make sure right now. Just ask Jesus to forgive you of your sins and to come into your heart.**

Write this date down in the front of your Bible or your notebook—do that right now. From now on, when you are tempted to doubt, you can open that book and look at the date—reminding yourself of the reality of your commitment to Jesus.

**And when Satan tries to hassle you and cause you to wonder about whether you really are a believer, you can point to this day and remember that you *did* ask Jesus to be your Savior.**

Discussion question 3 can be used here.

## *What happens to my relationship to God when I sin?*

When a Christian sins, fellowship with God is broken, but the relationship remains intact. God has said that we have been adopted into his family with all the rights and privileges of his Son, Jesus. He will never disown Jesus; he'll never disown us. But sin in our lives must be dealt with. Look at these diagrams to follow the process of what happens when a Christian sins.

Look at the diagram "Sin Barriers before Salvation." You see God and the person with their backs turned on each other—out of relationship with each other. You'll also see two lines, two barriers: one on God's side and one on our side. Before you became a believer you lived without a personal relationship to God, with barriers that kept you from getting to know him. On our side, those barriers were our sin and disobedience. On God's side, his holiness kept him from relating to us in our sin.

Now look at the next diagram. I want you to see what happens when a Christian sins. Notice that the believer's back is turned to God. Sin is deciding to do things our way, not God's way. Look also at the fact that we've put up barriers between us and God. You know what this barrier feels like. You feel distant from God even as a believer because you're caught up in yourself.

Then look at God's side. Is he turned away from us? No! Notice also that the barrier on God's side has been removed! Once you become a believer, God sees you in a new and holy way because of Jesus' death for you. While he knows that we sin, that sin is no longer a barrier because every time he looks at you he sees the forgiveness that Jesus poured out upon you.

This is hard for us to accept. We live in a world of reward and punishment. No matter how great your parents might have been, we all learned as children that it made mommy and daddy happy when we did good things and sad (or mad) when we did bad things. It's very easy to translate that into feeling that God somehow loves you more when you are being a good Christian, and loves you less when you are struggling with sin. Not true! God will never love you any more or any less than he does right now. God loves you as much on your good days as on your bad days.

Let me ask you, do you like to be around people who make you feel guilty? Do you look forward to talking with someone who you feel is really angry with you? Of course not! And when you think that God feels this way toward you, don't be surprised that you want to get as far away from thinking of him as possible.

Now look at the third diagram. This is the believer who has recognized in that moment what the cross of Christ really means. You realize, "Jesus paid for my sins." Because of this truth, all of the barriers are down. You don't feel fear in relating to God because you know that he loves and accepts you in Christ.

## Sin Barriers before Salvation

| Barriers on God's side | | Barriers on man's side | |
|---|---|---|---|
| God | 1. God's justice demands punishment of the guilty. | 1. Man's knowledge of his guilt brings fear of punishment. | Man |
| | 2. God's holiness demands rejection of the unholy. | 2. Man's knowledge of his lack of holiness brings fear of rejection. | |
| | 3. God's perfection demands devaluation of the imperfect. | 3. Man's knowledge of his imperfection brings loss of self-esteem. | |

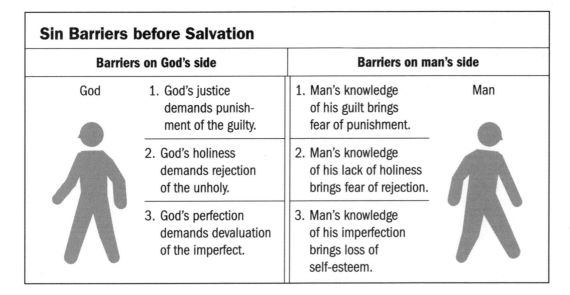

## Sin Barriers after Salvation When We Forget That God Totally Accepts Us

| Barriers on God's side | | Barriers on man's side | |
|---|---|---|---|
| God | Totally removed by Christ's death. | Expectancy of punishment, rejection, and loss of self-esteem all resulting from our early experiences with punishment. | Man |

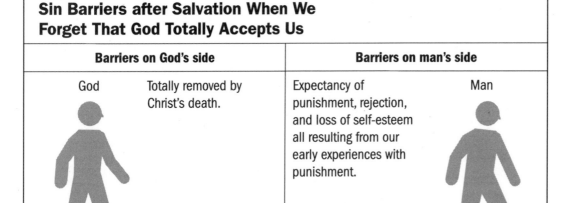

## Sin Barriers after Salvation When We Have Fully Applied the Results of Christ's Atonement

| Barriers on God's side | | Barriers on man's side | |
|---|---|---|---|
| God | Totally removed by Christ's death. | Totally removed by the knowledge of God's total acceptance and forgiveness and by the realization that God doesn't motivate by threats of punishment, rejection, and lowered self-esteem. | Man |

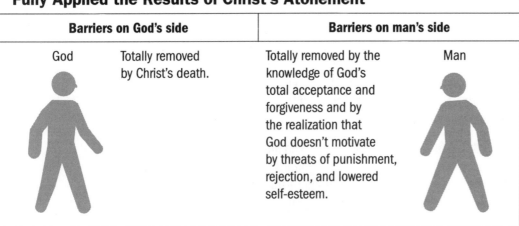

And so when you don't run from God, you run to him!

## Effects of Sin on the Christian

| What Sin Doesn't Do | What Sin Does Do |
|---|---|
| 1. Bring punishment from God. | 1. Brings loving correction and discipline from God. |
| 2. Make God angry with us. | 2. Interferes with our best personal adjustment, harms us, and eventually makes us unhappy. |
| 3. Cause God to reject us, even temporarily. | 3. Decreases our effectiveness in the world. |
| 4. Make us worthless or valueless to God. | 4. Damages the lives of others—especially those closest to us. |
| 5. Cause God to make us feel guilty. | 5. Brings loss of rewards in heaven. |
| | 6. Brings conviction from God. |

*Source:* Diagrams and chart adapted from Bruce Narramore and Bill Counts, *Freedom from Guilt* (Santa Ana, Calif.: Vision House, 1974), 83–85, 93.

Discussion question 4 can be used here.

## *Are there any proofs that I am a Christian?*

**While God alone can see into the hearts of individuals and determine who has honestly committed themselves to him, he has told us in his Word that there are some evidences that we are to judge ourselves (not others) by.**

The fact that you are a Christian is based on God's promise alone. There are, however, some evidences that you begin to see of God's salvation in your life.

Think of these evidences in this way. If a woman is told that she is pregnant, she and her husband will take the word of the doctor and rejoice. And they will both expect to see evidence of this pregnancy over the next several months. The new mom's abdomen will get bigger, she will feel the baby kicking inside her womb, she might have cravings for strange things like chocolate-covered pickles. She was just as pregnant before you could see all of these evidences, but if she is truly pregnant these are evidences that you will inevitably see.

I have to admit, the evidences that we are God's children are not quite as obvious. Of course God wants it that way—he wants us to live by faith. There are some very clear signs of the fact that you now are a Christian, signs that you, with eyes of faith, can see. As I read through this list and the verses, check the ones that you have seen evidenced in your life.

- **The <u>KNOWLEDGE</u> that God is our heavenly Father**

  All things have been committed to me by my Father. No one knows the Son except the Father, and no one knows the Father except the Son and those to whom the Son chooses to reveal him.

  —Matthew 11:27

- **A new reliance on <u>PRAYER</u>**

  Pray all the time. Ask God for anything in line with the Holy Spirit's wishes. Plead with him, reminding him of your needs, and keep praying earnestly for all Christians everywhere.

  —Ephesians 6:18 (LB)

- **A new ability to understand <u>SCRIPTURE</u>**

  But when he, the Spirit of truth, comes, he will guide you into all truth. He will not speak on his own; he will speak only what he hears, and he will tell you what is yet to come.

  —John 16:13

- **A new sense of the seriousness of <u>SIN</u>**

  For the grace of God that brings salvation has appeared to all men. It teaches us to say "No" to ungodliness and worldly passions, and to live self-controlled, upright and godly lives in this present age.

  —Titus 2:11–12

- **A new <u>LOVE</u> for lost people**

  Brothers, my heart's desire and prayer to God for the Israelites is that they may be saved.

  —Romans 10:1

- **A new love for <u>OTHER</u> <u>BELIEVERS</u>**

  We know that we have passed from death to life, because we love our brothers. Anyone who does not love remains in death.

  —1 John 3:14

How did you do? If you see no evidence at all, it may be that you are very young as a believer, still a baby Christian. Or it may be that you are one of the millions of people in our world who go to church but have yet to settle the issue of your salvation.

Let me ask you a question. It's a personal question, but it is one that needs to be asked. If I were to ask you, "Why should God let you into his heaven?"—what would you say?

Do you hope to get in based on the good things you've done? Not that you're that good, but you somehow hope that you're good enough. We expect that at least we're better than most people, and so we'll make the grade.

If that's what you've felt up until this point, there are one of two possibilities:

One—you may be a believer but have not as yet understood the significance of what Jesus did for you on the cross. Settle it tonight. Your salvation is not based on anything that you have done or can do.

Two—you may not be a believer. Oh, you may be religious. You may have attended church for years. But deep down, you've been depending on yourself for your salvation. The moment you recognize that will be one of the most significant moments in your life. Pride tells you, "I can't admit that. I'll just sit here and pretend, even to myself, that I'm not having these thoughts." But you are, and you know what it means. Your heart is tender right now, even vulnerable. Trust Jesus Christ with that tender heart.

---

### Key Personal Perspective

**Question: Why should God allow me into his heaven?**

**Only answer: Because I've trusted in Christ's work on the cross.**

**Not**
   **Because I'm a good person.**
   **Because I believe in God.**
   **Because I go to church.**

**If you can answer this question correctly, you can relinquish your doubts and fears about the security of your salvation. Begin to live in the freedom that comes from knowing your salvation is secure.**

**Let us go right in, to God himself, with true hearts fully trusting him to receive us, because we have been sprinkled with Christ's blood to make us clean.**

**—Hebrews 10:22 (LB)**

---

Let's pray together. Some of you need to trust Jesus with your tender heart right now. Say to him:

*Lord Jesus, I ask you to save me. Do for me what I cannot do for myself. I confess to you that I am a sinner and ask for your gift of forgiveness. Thank you that you paid the price for that gift by dying on the cross. I accept you, Jesus, as the new manager and director— the Lord—of my life.*

Others of you need to nail down the assurance of salvation that you have in Christ. Or just to be reminded again of that assurance. Would you pray this simple prayer:

*Father, I trust in you for the security of my salvation. Nothing can separate me from your love. Nothing can snatch me from Jesus' shepherding hands. I have eternal life and shall never perish because of my trust that you so loved the world that you gave your only begotten Son.*

*In Jesus' name, amen.*

**Finish memorizing memory card 6, "The Truth about Salvation."**

# Appendix

## *Scriptures Pointing to the Security and Assurance of Our Salvation*

There are an overwhelming number of Scriptures pointing to the security and assurance of our salvation. A few passages in the Bible seem to indicate that our salvation could be lost or taken from us. Here is a closer look at the meaning of those verses.

*Galatians 5:4:* "You who are trying to be justified by law have been alienated from Christ; you have fallen away from grace."

For many people, "falling from grace" is synonymous with losing salvation. This phrase is only used once in the New Testament. The apostle Paul defends himself and the gospel of Christ against a group called the Judaizers who arrived in the city of Galatia after he left.

The Judaizers taught that salvation was found through faith in Christ as well as keeping portions of the law. The main distortion they taught concerned circumcision; they believed that the Gentile believers must be circumcised to ensure their salvation (Gal. 5:2). It was not enough to put one's trust in Christ's death as payment for sin—they taught that a man must combine his faith with works in order to gain eternal life. They also observed many of the Jewish dietary guidelines and special Feast days.

Paul was heartbroken to see the Galatian Christians so easily led astray by the Judaizers (Gal. 1:6–7). He did not fear that they were going to lose their salvation—he was concerned that they would lose the joy of their salvation by adopting a form of religion that would severely restrict their freedom (Gal. 5:1).

He warned them that trusting circumcision as a means of salvation was a waste of time (Gal. 5:2–3) because it meant they would have to try to keep the whole law again. Combining Christ and the law wouldn't work because they were two entirely different systems. Law and grace just don't mix!

Paul then uses strong language to get his point across: "You . . . have been alienated [severed or nullified] from Christ" (v. 4). By trying to integrate the law into the Gospel they were nullifying the need for Christ's death for their sin. If salvation could be attained through the law, there was no reason for Christ to die. Then he says, "You have fallen away from grace" (v. 4). To fall from grace is to abandon the salvation-by-grace model for justification and to adopt the salvation-by-works model. He wasn't threatening them with the loss of their salvation, but a loss of freedom. He knew that to "fall" from God's system of grace would lead them right back into the frustration of living under the law.

*Hebrews 6:4–6* (NASB): "For in the case of those who have once been enlightened and have tasted of the heavenly gift and have been made partakers of the Holy Spirit, and have tasted the good word of God and the powers of the age to come, and then have fallen away, it is impossible to renew them again to repentance, since they again crucify to themselves the Son of God, and put Him to open shame."

The book of Hebrews probably was addressed to a group of Jewish Christians as indicated by the continual references to Old Testament scriptures, the theme that the old covenant was obsolete, and a concern the readers would turn away from their dependence on Christ and return to Judaism. None of these concerns would be an issue if the audience was primarily Gentile believers.

Evidently these Jewish believers were becoming disillusioned with Christianity. The writer sets out in his letter to persuade his brothers and sisters to keep the faith. These warnings are not given to people trying to make up their minds about who Christ is for the first time. They were people who at one time had expressed faith in God but were considering abandoning Christianity as a way of life.

This passage speaks of individuals who have "tasted the heavenly gift." Tasted is used in such a way as to mean "experienced," and they are said to have been "partakers" of the Holy Spirit. There's no doubt that these are genuine Christians. The author is afraid that they will return to their old ways of life, including their original form of worship (Judaism). They thought they would be returning to the God of their fathers, but actually they would be abandoning the God of their fathers.

The author used the word "repentance" in the sense of "changing one's mind." It is as though these believers have changed their minds about Christ and cannot be convinced otherwise. By turning their backs on Christ, these Jews were in essence agreeing with the Jews who had Christ arrested and put to death. Their public denial would lead outsiders to conclude that there must not be much to Christianity if those who at one time said they believed changed their minds and went back to their former religion.

This warning, though, in no way threatens the security of the believer. Instead, it is evidence for the believer's security. If a Jew, who was awaiting the coming of the Messiah, could find salvation through Christ and then walk away from him without the threat of losing his or her salvation, what do the rest of us have to fear?

*Hebrews 10:26–31 (NASB):* "For if we go on sinning willfully after receiving the knowledge of the truth, there no longer remains a sacrifice for sins, but a terrifying expectation of judgment, and the fury of a fire which will consume the adversaries. Anyone who has set aside the Law of Moses dies without mercy on the testimony of two or three witnesses. How much severer punishment do you think he will deserve who has trampled under foot the Son of God, and has regarded as unclean the blood of the covenant by which he was sanctified, and has insulted the Spirit of grace? For we know Him who said, 'Vengeance is Mine, I will repay.' And again, 'The Lord will judge His people.' It is a terrifying thing to fall into the hands of the living God."

If this passage teaches that willful sin results in the loss of salvation, it also teaches that salvation is lost over one willful sin. Furthermore, once it is lost, it is lost forever because there is no more sacrifice for sin.

The author of Hebrews is not writing about losing salvation. The context and details of the text rule that out as a valid interpretation.

Instead, he is warning his Jewish audience of the consequences of willful disobedience to Christ. They can no longer justify their sin in the light of the coming Messiah. He had already come. In their next encounter with the Messiah, he will stand as a Judge who will hand down decisions based on the new covenant. For believers who live for themselves with little or no thought for the things of God, it will be a "terrifying thing to fall into the hands of the living God."

*Revelation 3:5 (NASB):* "He who overcomes will thus be clothed in white garments; and I will not erase his name from the book of life."

These comments were directed to a group of faithful believers from the church in Sardis. Unlike the majority of people in the congregation at Sardis, these few believers had remained unsoiled by the world around them. Christ commends them for their consistent walk.

Five other times in Revelation the apostle John refers to the "book of life." In two of these passages it is clear that he did not believe that a person's name could be erased from the book of life.

*Revelation 13:8 (NASB):* "All who dwell on the earth will worship him, everyone whose name has not been written from the foundation of the world in the book of life of the Lamb who has been slain."

*Revelation 17:8:* "The inhabitants of the earth whose names have not been written in the book of life from the creation of the world."

John is using the word "world" in Revelation 17:8 to refer to the entire universe (see John 1:3; Acts 17:24). He indicates that the book of life was filled out before the first entry was ever born. If that is the case, God's foreknowledge has a great deal to do with who was written in and who was not. In anticipation of Christ's death on man's behalf, God wrote the names of those he knew from eternity past would accept his gracious offer. God wrote before we did anything. He filled out the book of life with what he knew we would do. Therefore, he did not write in response to what we actually did; rather, he wrote in response to what he knew we would actually do.

This distinction is very important. For if God wrote in the names as history unfolded, it could be argued that he erases them as history unfolds as well. But if God entered names according to his foreknowledge, it follows that it would be complete before the world began. In that case, no one needs to live with the fear that his or her name will be erased from the book of life sometime in the future.

In other words, God's pencil has no eraser! Before you were born God knew how you would respond to his offer of grace. According to his foreknowledge, he wrote your name in the book of life. And there it shall remain forever.[5]

## Discussion Questions

1. Look back at the three reasons why people lack assurance of salvation. Which one do you think most people struggle with? Has one of these been a struggle for you?

2. What is the difference between basing my sense of security in salvation on my faithfulness to God as opposed to basing it on his faithfulness to me? How does this impact our attitudes, motivations, and actions as believers?

3. What would you say to someone who said to you, "I've been attending church and praying and trying to read the Bible for years, but lately I've been feeling like I'm not really a Christian"?

4. If I believe in eternal security, where is my motivation to grow? Which of these three is the most significant for you?

- Grace

  For it is by grace you have been saved, through faith—and this not from yourselves, it is the gift of God—not by works, so that no one can boast. For we are God's workmanship, created in Christ Jesus to do good works, which God prepared in advance for us to do.

  —Ephesians 2:8–10

- Eternal rewards

  Whatever you do, work at it with all your heart, as working for the Lord, not for men.

  —Colossians 3:23

- Pleasing God

  So we make it our goal to please him, whether we are at home in the body or away from it.

  —2 Corinthians 5:9

## For Further Study

Graham, Billy. *How to Be Born Again.* Dallas: Word, 1989.

Lucado, Max. *In the Grip of Grace.* Dallas: Word, 1996.

Sproul, R. C. *Faith Alone: The Evangelical Doctrine of Justification.* Grand Rapids, Mich.: Baker, 1999.

Stanley, Charles. *Eternal Security: Can You Be Sure?* Nashville: Nelson, 1990.

Strombeck, J. F. *Shall Never Perish.* Grand Rapids, Mich.: Kregel, 1991.

Swindoll, Charles R. *Grace Awakening.* Dallas: Word, 1990.

Toon, Peter. *Born Again: A Biblical and Theological Study of Regeneration.* Grand Rapids, Mich.: Baker, 1986.

White, James R. *The God Who Justifies: A Comprehensive Study on the Doctrine of Justification.* Minneapolis: Bethany House, 2001.

# Sanctification
## Part 1

### Life Change Objectives

- To develop a deep conviction in you that, because of Jesus' love, you are holy.

- To build a foundation of truth that will lead to a lifetime of growth in Christ.

---

### Summary Teaching Outline

Sanctified means "set apart"

The Two Focuses of Sanctification

1. Sanctification is once and complete.
2. Sanctification is continual and progressive.

The Two Natures of the Christian

You express faith concerning your new nature when you see your-self as a new person.

You express faith concerning your old nature when you see your-self as dead to sin.

You express faith concerning your new and old natures when you see yourself with a new power to overcome evil.

---

Let me read you a letter that is typical of the feelings many of us have.

Dear Pastor,

I hope that you can help me with some of the feelings of frustration that I feel. I have to admit that when I hear others talk about growing as a Christian, it makes me feel somewhat guilty. They make it sound as if it is so easy, and it's just never been that way for me. Don't get me wrong—I attend church and even a Bible study, but I just don't see many changes happening in my life. I have a lot of the same struggles with myself that I had before I became a Christian, and I find myself falling into many of the same temptations. Sometimes I've wondered if this means

I am not a Christian at all—but deep down I know that isn't true. I guess I'm just tired of letting myself down—and God too. Do you have any hope for someone who feels like they're NEVER going to be able to get started?

If you've ever felt that way, I'm going to let you in on a little secret: you're not alone! One of the keys to breaking through these feelings we all face is for us to understand *how* God grows us. If we don't, we will be filled with frustration and will constantly wonder what God is doing.

Imagine for just a moment that a rose could think. What would it feel as it tried to grow into the best rose possible? With the sunshine and the gentle watering it received in the spring it would be thinking, "This is the life, this is what growth is all about. This is my exact idea of how growth should happen." However, just as the new growth starts to come out, along comes the gardener with some fertilizer. "That stinks!" the rose thinks. "That spoils my idea of how things should work." Then come the treatments to kill pests and to prevent disease—not at all what the rose had in mind for growth. Winter comes, and the rose loses all of its leaves. At the very moment that it feels most down because it has no leaves or flowers, along comes the gardener with pruning shears! What kind of timing is that? Why couldn't the gardener have done the pruning in the summer—when the rose had leaves and flowers to spare?

If only the rose could understand what was happening at each stage. What a difference that would make! Oh, the fertilizer would still stink, but the rose would understand why. Pruning would still hurt, but the rose would know that being pruned at the right time is the secret to next year's growth.

When we understand the ways that God grows us as believers, what a difference that makes! It doesn't make life perfect. It doesn't mean that growing will never hurt. It does enable us to understand what God is up to in our lives.

What's the real truth about growth in our lives as believers? How does growth become something that is happening in our lives and not just a subject that we talk about? The word in the Bible for God's process of growth is *sanctification*.

**As believers we have been:**

**Justified**

> **Declared eternally not guilty (Rom. 5:1; Gal. 2:16)**

**Sanctified**

> **The act of being set apart once for all to be holy (1 Cor. 6:11)**

The experience of growing in Christlikeness (1 Thess. 5:23)

**Glorified**

The completed act of our being with God for eternity (Rom. 8:30)

Justification happened the moment you were saved. Glorification will happen when we get to heaven. Sanctification is what is happening in our lives right now. That makes sanctification a subject that we all are very interested in!

**During the last two sessions we looked at what it means to be justified. In this study we begin a look at what it means to be sanctified.**

**Sanctified means <u>SET</u> <u>APART</u>.**

**In the Old Testament it was most often the places and objects of worship that were called "set apart" for God's honor and use:**

Holy priests (Ex. 28:41)

Holy garments (Ex. 29:21)

A holy altar (Ex. 30:10)

The Holy Land (Lev. 27:21)

**In the New Testament it is God's people who are "set apart" for God's honor and use.**

**If a man cleanses himself from the latter, he will be an instrument for noble purposes, made holy, useful to the Master and prepared to do any good work.**

—2 Timothy 2:21

In our house there are some dishes that are "common" and there are some that are "set apart" for special use. These set-apart dishes have a place of honor in our china cabinet and are placed on the table for holidays and other family celebrations.

Sanctified means we are set apart for God's use: put in a place of honor, used for his special purposes. And he doesn't use us only a few times a year. He has set us apart so he can work in and through us every day of our lives.

You are sanctified, set apart for God's use! God has put you in a place of honor as a believer that is much higher than you might imagine. In fact, the Bible says you are a saint!

**Sanctified comes from the same word as saint. In the Bible, all believers are called saints.**

**I am not trying to grow *toward* sainthood. I am a <u>GROWING SAINT</u> (2 Peter 3:18; 2 Cor. 10:15).**

Look at the person next to you and say, "Hi, I am Saint [fill in your name]."

That was hard for some of you. How can you be a saint? Most use this term for a person who they think rarely, if ever, sins. We use the designation "saint" for people who we feel are too old to sin. "Great old saints," we call them. You never hear anyone talk about "dear young saints." The Bible, however, teaches that every born-again believer is a saint. The New Testament refers to believers as saints fifty-six times! Even the people of Corinth, with all of their struggles with sin, were called saints.

Here is why it is important to know that you are a saint. Until you see who you are in Christ, you'll always be fighting your feelings as you grow. You'll think, "Of course I sinned again, I'm just a sinner anyway. Of course I can't understand the Bible. Of course that ministry failed—just who do I think I am anyway."

Accept it on faith that you have been sanctified. As a believer you are a saint. And listen to how your thoughts change. "Of course my prayers were anwered. Of course God's Word is changing me. Of course God used me in that situation."

"But you don't understand," you may be thinking, "I don't feel like some kind of saint." Join the club, we all feel that way! That's why growth can't be built on your feelings. Your growth as a Christian has its foundation in faith—faith in who God has made you to be and in the work that he is doing in your life.

**The doctrine of sanctification sets the foundation for our growth as Christians. One of the missing ingredients in our spiritual growth is an understanding of this doctrine. Without understanding the doctrine of sanctification, you can easily find yourself falling into the traps of**

> **trying to grow in Christ based on your own effort (legalism).**

> **presuming on God's grace to grow you no matter how you live (license).**

**While there are hundreds of things we can do to grow spiritually, all rest on the foundation of faith. To grow as a Christian, you must learn to see yourself by faith—the way that God sees you. As we study sanctification, we're going to look at five specific truths about you that can be accepted only by faith. These truths form the foundation for our growth as believers.**

In this session we'll look at two areas that require our faith:

1. The two focuses of sanctification
2. The two natures of the Christian

In the next session we'll cover three additional truths that require faith:

3. The power of grace over the law
4. The daily process of growth
5. God's promise to finish his work

# The Two Focuses of Sanctification

Sanctification refers to two things:

The <u>FINISHED</u> <u>ACTION</u> of being made holy

The <u>DAILY</u> <u>PROCESS</u> of becoming holy

Sanctification is both a finished action and a daily process. It's a lot like marriage. When you get married you say "I do," and then spend the rest of your life living out those two words. The finished action of the wedding ceremony then has to be lived out in the daily process of married life.

Let's look at that more closely.

1. **Sanctification is once and complete.**

   **And by that will, we have been made holy through the sacrifice of the body of Jesus Christ once for all.**
   —Hebrews 10:10

   **Because of God you are in Christ Jesus, who has become for us wisdom from God. In Christ we are put right with God, and have been made holy, and have been set free from sin.**
   —1 Corinthians 1:30 (NCV)

   In Hebrews 10:10 and 1 Corinthians 1:30 you see the same exact phrase: "have been made holy." It is past tense—God has *made* us holy. Because of our trust in Christ, we have been "set free from sin" and "put right with God."

   That doesn't seem to fit, does it? As we look at our lives, we know that none of us is perfect—we all still struggle with sin. How can God call us saints? How can he say that we've already been made holy?

   It's because of what his Son did for us all. When we trust in Christ, God sees us from that moment on as having the same holiness as his Son. It is not something we earn. It is a gift that God gives to us. The fact that

God has already made us holy in Christ is an unseen gift. Later in this study, we'll see how important a foundation that is for our continuing growth as believers.

Discussion question 1 can be used here.

Once God has made us holy we start on the path of growing into being the new people he wants us to be. That leads to the second focus of sanctification.

**2. Sanctification is continual and progressive.**

Growth is obviously a process in our lives, and that includes spiritual growth. There are no shortcuts to spiritual growth.

Look at 1 Peter 2:2. Just as a baby needs to grow step by step, we go through a process of growth as believers. It takes time to grow from spiritual infancy to spiritual maturity.

**Like newborn babies, crave pure spiritual milk, so that by it you may grow up in your salvation.**

—1 Peter 2:2

**Seek to live a clean and holy life, for one who is not holy will not see the Lord.**

—Hebrews 12:14 (LB)

**Grow in the grace and knowledge of our Lord and Savior Jesus Christ.**

—2 Peter 3:18 (NCV)

In these verses, circle "crave" in 1 Peter 2:2, circle "seek to live" in Hebrews 12:14, and then circle "grow in the grace" in 2 Peter 3:18. Notice that these are all things that we do, choices we make, actions we take. God has purposely decided to give us an opportunity to be involved in the process of our growth.

So, we have been made holy by God, and we are being made holy by God.

**One verse sums up both:**

**Because by one sacrifice he has made perfect forever those who are being made holy.**

—Hebrews 10:14

Circle "made perfect forever" and "being made holy." Made perfect forever—a finished act. Being made holy—a continuing process.

**You express faith concerning these two focuses when you say: "I am a sanctified person who is being sanctified."**

**This was done (finished, completed, settled) at the moment of salvation (1 Cor. 6:11; 2 Cor. 5:17).**

Let me sum up what this means.

Sanctification is not the process of me trying really hard to become something I am not. Sanctification is the process of beginning to live out what I *already am!* At the moment of salvation God changed our spiritual DNA.

## Teaching Tip

When you have a group say something all together, it often has a unifying and faith-strengthening effect. It's also a good way to focus the attention on something that you don't want them to forget. Often when you have a group say something together, they will speak fairly softly. If so, it's good to say something like, "Let's try that one more time, with great enthusiasm."

Take a moment right now and by faith say these two statements with me:

Lord, thank you that you made me holy!

Lord, thank you that you are making me holy!

Discussion questions 2 and 3 can be used here.

God has already made you holy, and God is making you holy. Do you feel the tension in those two statements? It seems like only one or the other should be true, but *both* are true! You may have noticed that much of the doctrine that we've studied is like that.

Jesus is both God and man.

God is both transcendent (above us) and immanent (near us).

God is sovereign and yet he gives us free choice.

It is often in the tension between two equally true but seemingly opposite truths that you find the real beauty of God's truth. It's like a guitar string—the beautiful note comes when you have just the right tension in the string. We sometimes tend to want to make doctrine like math: 1 + 1 = truth. Just the cold, hard, logical facts. But doctrine is much more than that, much more like music than math! In doctrine we hear the beauty of God's truth. Make no mistake, like music, doctrine must be exact, you cannot change its rules. As you begin to see the two truths of sanctification—our being holy and being made holy—in balance, it's as if you can hear the music of the truth in your heart.

God has made you holy. Do not let go of that truth!

God is making you holy. Do not let go of that truth!

It takes faith in both of these truths to see how God is sanctifying you.

**Split Session Plan:** If you're teaching this study over two sessions, end the first session here.

It is vital that we understand the doctrine of sanctification because it's easy to fool yourself when it comes to this issue of Christian growth.

Growth is not:

How many meetings you attend

How many verses you've memorized

How many books you've read

How many minutes you spent in your quiet time this morning

While these are all things that can produce growth in our lives as believers, it's easy to fool yourself, thinking that just because you're involved in a growth-producing activity you must be growing. You can be like a man who attends a health club and watches everyone else work out, then pats himself on the back for his involvement in exercise. Maybe he even rewards himself with a donut on the way home.

The doctrine of sanctification is a truth that reminds us that Christian growth is not just a matter of checking off the items on a spiritual "to do" list. Quiet time, check. Bible verse memorized, check. Went to church, check. What makes the difference is our faith in Christ as we do these things.

Since we are talking so much about faith, let me remind you of something. It takes just a mustard seed of faith to make an impact in your life and on this world. If you have just a tiny bit of faith in our great and awesome God, he will work in your life in ways that are beyond the boundaries of your imagination. Look around you in this room. There is not a person you are looking at, including me, who would not like to have more faith. But those of us who are growing, who are seeing God at work in our lives, are not waiting until we feel more faith to trust in God. We're taking the little faith we have and trusting in him, and we are watching that faith grow. Not as fast as we would like, but it is growing because that's God's promise.

We've looked at our need to have faith concerning the two focuses of sanctification. The second place to have faith is . . .

## The Two Natures of the Christian

If you don't get anything else from this study, I want you to see that sanctification is founded on faith—from start to end.

What are the two natures of the Christian?

**You have both an <u>OLD</u> nature and a <u>NEW</u> nature.**

What is this old nature, this new nature? This is extremely important to understand.

---

 ### A Closer Look

*The Old and New Natures of the Christian*

Your old nature, which the Bible also calls your "flesh," is your inner desire and tendency toward sin. It is not the feeling of being tempted; it is the inner part of who you are that inevitably will choose to say yes to various temptations. Before you became a believer, your old nature was your only nature. We all have this old nature—this natural propensity to sin—because of the fall of man that happened in the Garden of Eden.

Your new nature was given to you the moment you gave your life to Christ. The new nature is the new life and new power to live that have been given to you because of your trust in what Jesus did for you through his death and resurrection.

One of the most crucial aspects of growth in our lives as believers is learning how to trust God concerning both our old nature and our new nature.

---

- **You express faith concerning your new nature when you see yourself as <u>A</u> <u>NEW</u> <u>PERSON</u>.**

Would you read with me 2 Corinthians 5:17.

**When someone becomes a Christian, he becomes a brand new person inside. He is not the same any more. A new life has begun!**
— **2 Corinthians 5:17** (LB)

You are a new creation in Christ. The moment you believed in Christ as your Savior, a spiritual transaction happened that changed everything.

1. **I was "<u>IN ADAM</u>."**

   **All of us were born in sin because we are Adam's descendants. We choose to sin because that is our spiritual nature. The Bible refers to our condition as being in Adam, which means we are subject to judgment and death.**

   **For as in Adam all die . . .**
   — **1 Corinthians 15:22**

2. I am now "IN CHRIST."

Spiritual life is gained only through spiritual birth (John 3:6). The moment we were born again, our soul came into union with God because of Christ. We are now in Christ.

Praise be to the God and Father of our Lord Jesus Christ, who has blessed us in the heavenly realms with every spiritual blessing in Christ. For he chose us in him before the creation of the world to be holy and blameless in his sight.

—Ephesians 1:3–4

There are only two types of people in the world—those who are in Adam and those who are in Christ. You are in Christ if Christ is in you. An exchange of lives occurs: You give Jesus your life, and he gives you his.

This is a matter of faith, not sight. When you become a believer, you don't look in the mirror and see a different face—you see the same old you. You don't get a new house and a new car and a new job—that all stays the same. Even your personality pretty much stays the same. If you were a quiet person before you came to Christ, you don't all of a sudden become the life of every party. (God doesn't expect you to change—he wants to use the personality he gave you.)

So what does change? What is new? Only the most important things about you—things you can't see that will last forever.

## Who Is This "New Person?"

- I am a light in the world (Matt. 5:14).
- I am a child of God (John 1:12).
- I am Christ's friend (John 15:15).
- I am chosen and appointed by Christ to bear his fruit (John 15:16).
- I am a slave of righteousness (Rom. 6:18).
- I am a joint heir with Christ (Rom. 8:17).
- I am a temple, a dwelling place, of God (1 Cor. 3:16; 6:19).
- I am a member of Christ's body (1 Cor. 12:27; Eph. 5:30).
- I am a new creation (2 Cor. 5:17).
- I am reconciled to God and a minister of reconciliation (2 Cor. 5:18–19).
- I am a saint (Eph. 1:1; 2 Cor. 1:1–2).

- I am God's workmanship (Eph. 2:10).

- I am a citizen of heaven (Phil. 3:20; Eph. 2:6).

- I am righteous and holy (Eph. 4:24).

- I am hidden with Christ in God (Col. 3:3).

- I am chosen and dearly loved (Col. 3:12).

- I am a son/daughter of light and not of darkness (1 Thess. 5:5).

- I am an enemy of the Devil (1 Peter 5:8).

- I am victorious (1 John 5:4).

- I am born again (1 Peter 1:23).

- I am alive with Christ (Eph. 2:5).

- I am more than a conqueror (Rom. 8:37).

- I am the righteousness of God (2 Cor. 5:21).

- I am born of God and the Evil One cannot touch me (1 John 5:18).

- I am to be like Christ when he returns (1 John 3:1–2).

Let me ask you a very theological question. Can a butterfly go back into the cocoon and become a caterpillar again? Of course not! Once it becomes a butterfly it is what it is, a butterfly.

You are like a butterfly that has come out of the cocoon. It may take you some time to learn to fly spiritually, but once you become a new creation in Christ you are what you are, a new creation!

We're not talking about mere positive thinking. Positive thinking would be a caterpillar gluing on wings and trying to fly. Splat! God gave you a new nature when you became a Christian. Reminding yourself of who you are in Christ is "truthful thinking." My concern is that there are a lot of Christians out there who think, "I don't deserve to be a butterfly; look at the struggles in my life. I'm just a lowly caterpillar. I'll just strap on this old cocoon because I shouldn't be able to fly."

The greatest step of faith that we take in our lives is that of accepting what God says about Jesus.

The second greatest step may very well be accepting what God says about us once we believe in Jesus.

You are a new creation!

## Key Personal Perspective

*Truths to Help You Live Your New Life*

1. **You don't have to <u>ACHIEVE</u> your new life.**

   **Newness is a creation of God.**

   Colossians 3:10 says,

   **You have clothed yourselves with a brand-new nature that is continually being renewed as you learn more and more about Christ, who created this new nature within you.**

   **—Colossians 3:10 (NLT)**

   In the MESSAGE paraphrase it says, "Now you're dressed in a new wardrobe. Every item of your new way of life is custom-made by the Creator, with his label on it. All the old fashions are now obsolete." We don't have to make ourselves new; we are to live out the new life the Spirit has already given us! We're funny about this, often thinking we have to do it ourselves. It's as if God has given us this very expensive new suit (or dress) to put on. It's hanging in our closet and God has said, "This is my gift to you, wear it with joy." But we're over in a corner working with all our might to patch something together out of some scraps from the rag drawer. When we finally finish it, in our pride we say, "God, look at what I made!" I can see him shaking his head and smiling at us with a Father's love. "Just put on the suit I gave you."

2. **You don't have to work to <u>KEEP</u> your new life.**

   **Your new life is kept with Christ in God.**

   **Your old sinful self has died, and your new life is kept with Christ in God.**
   **—Colossians 3:3 (NCV)**

   Don't miss this picture in Colossians 3:3. Our new life is kept "with Christ"; that's certainly secure. But then it is put "in God"—that's security in security! That would be like putting your jewelry inside a safety deposit box inside an armored car inside an impenetrable vault—inside Fort Knox! *It's safe! It's secure!* God has taken care of that. If you were to try to hold on to your new life yourself, you'd try relying on rules (something you can see) rather than living in the security of his grace. Don't. You don't need to. God has already made your new life secure.

* **You express faith concerning your old nature when you see yourself as <u>DEAD</u> <u>TO</u> <u>SIN</u>.**

In Colossians 3:3, the Bible tells us that our old sinful self has died. Look at Romans 6:4.

> **Your old sin-loving nature was buried with him by baptism when he died, and when God the Father, with glorious power, brought him back to life again, you were given his wonderful new life to enjoy.**
> —Romans 6:4 (LB)

**One of the most discussed points of doctrine over the centuries has to do with what the Bible means when it tells us that this old nature is dead. Some have suggested that this means this old nature has disappeared—which obviously is not true from our daily experience! Others suggest it is a matter of self-discipline to say no to our old nature—yet self-discipline by itself is not enough to change us.**

**How do we choose to trust with faith what the Bible means when it says our old sinful nature is dead?**

> **You were taught, with regard to your former way of life, to put off your old self, which is being corrupted by its deceitful desires.**
> —Ephesians 4:22

**How do I "put off" the old nature?**

- **Not by <u>IGNORING</u> <u>IT</u>**

  Should I act as if I'm now somehow above temptation and sin—some kind of a perfect saint? Deep down, you know that's not true. Should I ignore these feelings in my life now that I'm a Christian—pretending that since I'm God's child all of these ugly thoughts and temptations are not there in my life? You can't deal with the old nature by telling yourself that what you know is real is not real. It does no good to come to church and pretend we are perfect.

- **Not by <u>HUMAN</u> <u>EFFORT</u>**

  Do I put it all on myself, believing that somehow my self-discipline and determination will suppress my old nature and allow my new nature to shine forth? The battle with sin *is* a battle we must fight. Our mistake comes in trying to fight it with our own energy. Some of us are more self-disciplined than others, but don't make the mistake of taking on this battle alone. You'll find that the harder you fight, the more sin grips you. It's like spiritual quicksand—the harder you kick the faster you sink. It is impossible for our human effort alone to win in the battle with sin. (Even if you are able by your own efforts to set aside a sinful habit, you end up feeling sinfully prideful about that achievement.) You need a power outside of yourself.

You can't deal with the old nature by ignoring it or by your own self-discipline. There is a third choice.

- **By faith in what <u>GOD</u> <u>HAS</u> <u>DONE</u>**

**And since your old sin-loving nature "died" with Christ, we know that you will share his new life.**

—**Romans 6:8** (LB)

You need to trust in what God has said about that old nature. And what does God say? The Bible says your old nature is dead. Wait a minute; what does that mean? I know by experience that the temptations and habits attached to that old nature are very much alive!

There is a very untheological picture that you often see in cartoons of this battle we have with our old and new natures. Remember what it is? The angel on one shoulder and the little devil on the other. How do you deal with these two conflicting voices? It doesn't work to pretend that the little devil isn't there; you're just lying to yourself. But human discipline isn't enough either; eventually you *will* give in to temptation. You're no match for Satan. The secret is to trust God's truth about both your new nature and your old nature. You look at your new nature and say by faith, "You're alive." You look at your old nature and say by faith, "You're dead."

---

 **A Closer Look**

*Don't Miss This!*

**What does dead mean? (It does not mean "no longer present or an influence in your life.")**

**It means:**

> **It no longer has the power to force you to sin—you have a choice.**
>
> **You no longer enjoy the sin in the same way—you have changed.**

---

For a moment there is pleasure in sin. Would you agree with me that there still is pleasure in sin after we become Christians? Why else would we keep doing it? Sin might have the same allure as it did before you came to faith in Christ, but it does not have the same sense of satisfaction. You are left feeling miserable. You have changed.

And you have a choice. A choice that is made daily in the process of growth. How often do you have to trust God that you are alive to him and dead to sin? Sometimes hundreds of times in a single day! All throughout the day you find yourself saying, "That sin looks very tempting, but the truth is I'm dead to sin. That's not where my joy is and that's not what I have to choose to do. The truth is, I'm alive to God. So, God, help me to live out the life you want me to have in you."

> Discussion question 4 can be used here.

- **You express faith concerning your new and old natures when you see yourself with a new power to overcome evil.**

  **Before salvation, I belonged to <u>SATAN</u>.**

  > **You belong to your father, the devil, and you want to carry out your father's desire.**
  >
  > —John 8:44

  **After salvation, I belong to <u>GOD</u>.**

  > **And you also are among those who are called to belong to Jesus Christ.**
  >
  > —Romans 1:6

  **Because I belong to God, Satan has no power to control me.**

  > **Be self-controlled and alert. Your enemy the devil prowls around like a roaring lion looking for someone to devour. Resist him, standing firm in the faith.**
  >
  > —1 Peter 5:8–9

Through God's power you can overcome Satan and the temptations of sin. Because the battle takes place in the routine of life, moment by moment and day by day, that is where we must have faith for victory, moment by moment and day by day.

First Peter 5:8–9 helps us to see how this victory happens. It's like resisting a hungry, roaring lion. You can't resist a roaring lion by running in fear; he will catch you from behind. Neither can you befriend the lion— not when you are its potential next meal! And I certainly wouldn't advise taking on a lion in hand-to-hand combat.

One of the techniques that lion trainers use is to nip the lion on the ear. It causes the much more powerful lion to follow the direction of the weaker trainer. Why? When the lion was a cub, this is what its mother would do to keep it in line. When the trainer is doing this, he is in essence appealing to a higher authority (the lion's mother) to communicate with the lion.

We don't resist Satan on our own authority, but on the authority of God and his Word. It's like nipping the lion on the ear—it works every time. Resist Satan, stand firm, knowing by faith that a victory you could never achieve on your own is yours in Christ.

Discussion question 5 can be used here.

**God has not left our growth to chance. The foundation of your sanctification is nothing less than the death and resurrection of Jesus Christ. This means two things:**

**First, because of the power of Jesus' crucifixion, you no longer have to be controlled by your old nature.**

> **I have been crucified with Christ and I no longer live, but Christ lives in me. The life I live in the body, I live by faith in the Son of God, who loved me and gave himself for me.**
> **—Galatians 2:20**

Did Jesus really die? Yes! Because he died, you no longer have to be controlled by your old nature.

**Second, because of the power of Jesus' resurrection, you have a new nature.**

> **In the same way, count yourselves dead to sin but alive to God in Christ Jesus. Therefore do not let sin reign in your mortal body so that you obey its evil desires. Do not offer the parts of your body to sin, as instruments of wickedness, but rather offer yourselves to God, as those who have been brought from death to life; and offer the parts of your body to him as instruments of righteousness.**
> **—Romans 6:11–13**

Was Jesus really resurrected? Yes! And by the power of his resurrection you can begin to live out the new life that God has made you for.

Romans 6 tells you to count yourself dead to sin. Count yourself? How do you do that? If I put two columns on a sheet of paper, one with the heading "Dead to sin" and the other headed "Alive to sin," where would you "count yourself?" Most people would put themselves in the middle. They haven't counted themselves as dead to sin because they still struggle with sin. (And, in our moments of complete honesty, we'd have to admit that we don't want to count ourselves as dead to sin because that means letting go of pet sins we selfishly hold on to. We think, "I don't want to put myself in this column because I still might want to do something in that column.")

If you're a believer

- You are dead to sin. Count on it!
- You are alive to God. Count on it!

I don't want to leave you with the impression that this process of making us holy is easy. God is building holiness into the lives of very imperfect human beings. So we struggle and we stumble and we wonder if we're making any progress at all. Let's close with the painfully honest words to a song by Chris Rice about the process of sanctification in our lives. It's aptly titled "Clumsy."

> You think I'd have it down by now
> Been practicin' for thirty years
> I should have walked a thousand miles
> So what am I still doin' here
> Reachin' out for that same old piece of forbidden fruit
> I slip and fall and I knock my halo loose
> Somebody tell me what's a boy supposed to do?
>
> 'Cause I get so clumsy
> I get so foolish
> I get so stupid
> And then I feel so useless
> But You're sayin' You love me
> And You're still gonna hold me
> And that You wanna be near me
> 'Cause You're makin' me holy
> You're still makin' me holy[1]

Let's pray together.

*Father, thank you that in the daily realities of life, where we often feel clumsy, you are making us holy. We praise you that our holiness does not rest upon what we do but on what you have done. Help us to see that because of Jesus' death and resurrection, you make each of us who trust in you a new creation in Christ. In Jesus' name, amen.*

**Begin working on memory card 7, "The Truth about Sanctification."**

## Discussion Questions

1. Do you think any Christian ever truly feels completely holy? Can you remember the times and places in your life when you have felt the most holy?

2. What are the inner attitudes that encourage and inspire your growth in Christ? What attitudes put up a barrier to your growth?

3. How has becoming a Christian changed your life? What new habits do you now enjoy as a Christian?

4. Have you been frustrated by the battle with sin? How do you think facing the battle through faith in God rather than with just personal willpower will make a difference in your daily life?

5. How would the truths we've talked about help you to answer someone who has the questions listed below?

   • I'm not really sure I'm a believer because of the way I sometimes act.

   • Why do I keep doing the same wrong things over and over now that I am a believer?

# Sanctification
## Part 2

## Life Change Objective

**To decide to trust grace rather than law for your growth, God's process rather than your plan for your growth, and God's promise rather than your willpower for your growth.**

## Summary Teaching Outline

The Power of Grace over the Law

  By faith you can say, "I am free from the law."

  By faith you can say, "I have a new master!"

The Daily Process of Growth

  By faith you ask God to renew your mind.

  By faith you practice the disciplines of growth.

  By faith you choose to trust God in the circumstances of life.

God's Promise to Finish His Work

  By faith you believe in God's ability to accomplish his work in your life.

## Teaching Tip

Remember that one of the keys to bringing doctrine to life discussed in the introduction was: "Teach knowing that the truth will set people free."

As you are preparing to teach this session and right before you start teaching, remind yourself, "Someone is going to be set free in a way that I may never know, but in a way that will have eternal impact." Jesus promises us that this will happen when he says, "The truth will set you free." The truth of Christ has the power to break through the lies that keep us locked up.

Suppose you get on a 737 jet going from Los Angeles to Dallas. You find your seat, buckle up, and get ready for the flight. You do everything the captain tells you. You even listen intently to the emergency instructions. After the flight gets up to speed and the captain turns off the "fasten seat belts" sign, you immediately stand up and say, "I'd better take it on my own from here." Then, standing in the middle of the aisle, you begin to slowly flap your arms like a pair of wings. "Excuse me," says a flight attendant, "what are you doing?" "I'm helping the plane to fly," you reply.

Of course you're not! No matter how gracefully you flap your arms, or how sincerely or energetically or joyfully you flap them, you look silly. Everyone knows the power for the flight of the plane comes from the engines, not from you.

Do you see the parallel for our growth as Christians? It's easy to get caught up in holy arm flapping, thinking that somehow it's all up to me now. But it's not. The power is God's alone! He's the only one who has the power to grow you to become like his Son.

In the last session we looked at the fact that we can grow in Christ; it's God's intention and plan. God has planted the seed. In this session we're going to talk more about how he cultivates and nurtures that seed to produce our growth. The exciting thing is he allows us to be a part of that process!

We don't get to create our growth, but we do get to cultivate our growth.

We don't provide the power that flies the plane, but we do get to choose what we do once we're on board.

Take a quick look at this review of what we learned last week.

**In the last session we learned that sanctified means "set apart" (saint comes from the same root word).**

**In the Old Testament it was most often the places and objects of worship that were called "set apart" for God's honor and use:**

> **Holy priests (Ex. 28:41)**
>
> **Holy garments (Ex. 29:21)**
>
> **A holy altar (Ex. 30:10)**
>
> **The Holy Land (Lev. 27:21)**

**In the New Testament it is all God's people who are "set apart" for God's honor and use:**

If a man cleanses himself from the latter, he will be an instrument for noble purposes, made holy, useful to the Master and prepared to do any good work.

—2 Timothy 2:21

And we looked at the first two of the five ways we put faith in God for our sanctification:

1.  The two focuses of sanctification
2.  The two natures of the Christian

You cannot create growth; that is God's job. But you can cooperate with the way that God grows us. In this session we're going to look at three additional ways that we have faith in what God is doing to grow us.

# The Power of **GRACE** over the **LAW**

Just as we are justified by faith and grace, we are sanctified by faith and grace.

> Remember, sanctification is a part of our salvation—part of the free gift that God gave us by Jesus' death and resurrection. Because God has allowed us to be involved in the process of sanctification it's very easy to stop seeing it as a gift, to begin to see it as something that we must work for or earn. You can't earn your sanctification any more than you can earn your salvation. Look at what Paul says in Galatians 3:3 and in Colossians 2:6.

**You began your life in Christ by the Spirit. Now are you trying to make it complete by your own power? That is foolish.**

—Galatians 3:3 (NCV)

**As you received Christ Jesus the Lord, so continue to live in him.**

—Colossians 2:6 (NCV)

> We received Jesus into our lives by grace, and we live our lives in him by grace.

> Chuck Smith writes in his book *Why Grace Changes Everything,*

>> Have you ever considered the vast difference between "works" and "fruit"? "Works" suggests a factory complete with pressures, deadlines and the constant need to produce. But "fruit" pictures a peaceful, tranquil garden, a place where we are inclined to stay and drink in the beauty while we enjoy each other's company.

>> It's important to realize that God doesn't come to His factory looking for products. He comes to His garden to enjoy its fruit. The gospel of grace invites us to leave behind the smog and pressure of a factory life of works and to instead bear the fruit that God desires to see in the garden of our lives.[1]

If we are to leave behind that life of serving God based on our own works, there are some practical faith decisions we need to make.

- **By faith you can say, "I am <u>FREE</u> from the law."**

**The law is not dead; it is not even "bad"—as the old nature is. The law is just not capable of bringing us salvation. It can show us our sin, but it cannot make us right before God.**

**Through Christ Jesus the law of the Spirit that brings life made me free from the law that brings sin and death.**

—Romans 8:2 (NCV)

**That old law had glory, but it really loses its glory when it is compared to the much greater glory of this new way.**

—2 Corinthians 3:10 (NCV)

What does it mean to be free from the law? It does not mean that we can just ignore the moral direction that God gives to us in the Old Testament. Obviously, being free from the law doesn't mean that murder and adultery, lying and stealing are now OK.

To be free from the law means that you no longer look to the law for salvation or for the power to grow as a believer. The law is powerless to save us or to grow us. When you depend on the law you find yourself getting up day after day seeking to pull yourself up by your own spiritual bootstraps—trying to find the power to do what is right in that which is powerless. It's a life where you feel that all the burden is on your shoulders, and the burden is too great to bear.

Say this with me slowly, "Rules cannot produce growth." The entire book of Galatians is written to emphasize for the believer, "Rules cannot produce growth." Rules can force us to behave in certain ways, especially if they come with enough reward or punishment. But they can't deepen our love or strengthen our relationships—the kind of growth that God is working to bring into our lives.

If you give your children only rules, never allowing them to make a decision on their own up until the time they're out of college, are they going to be "mature adults, ready for life?" Not a chance. Rules alone produce either unthinking compliance or (more often) rebellion, but not growth.

God wants us to grow in our relationship with him, and rules cannot deepen relationships. The law has a purpose in our lives before we become believers. It shows us how far we are from God. But the law is not able to bring us near to God. Only Jesus can do that.

Does the law have any purpose in our lives after we become believers? Jesus said in Matthew 5 that he came not to abolish the law but to fulfill it. He fulfills it by showing the meaning behind it and by giving us the power to live out that meaning. Grace produces growth, but much of what is in the law can show us the direction in which grace is going to grow us. Grace is the jet that powers us, but the law gives us some insight into God's flight plan for our lives. For instance, when we read in the Ten Commandments, "Do not accuse anyone falsely," we can see the integrity that God wants in our lives as believers.

Discussion question 1 can be used here.

- **By faith you can say, "I have a <u>NEW</u> <u>MASTER</u>!"**

**Now you are free from sin, your old master, and you have become slaves to your new master, righteousness.**

—**Romans 6:18** (NLT)

**In the past, the law held us like prisoners, but our old selves died, and we were made free from the law. So now we serve God in a new way with the Spirit, and not in the old way with written rules.**

—**Romans 7:6** (NCV)

None of us is our own master. Bob Dylan captured that truth when he sang:

You may be an ambassador to England or France,
You may like to gamble, you might like to dance,
You may be the heavyweight champion of the world,
You may be a socialite with a long string of pearls.

But you're gonna have to serve somebody, yes indeed
You're gonna have to serve somebody,
Well, it may be the devil or it may be the Lord
But you're gonna have to serve somebody.[2]

No one can be their own master. We all end up serving someone or something. The law is a wonderful teacher, but a terrible master. Because we cannot possibly keep the law perfectly, it becomes a constant source of pressure, discouragement, and guilt.

Victor Hugo gave us a vivid picture of what it means to have either grace or the law as our master in his famous work *Les Misérables*. How many have seen the play? The movie? Read the 1,200-page book? (These are the geniuses among us.) The main character, Jean Valjean, builds much of his life on one act of grace that was shown him—a stranger who did not hold him accountable when he stole a pair of candlesticks. Valjean finds freedom in the end, the freedom of grace. His pursuer, the policeman Javert, builds his life on the law. His entire life is ordered on exacting justice. In the end, he is put into a circumstance where he knows he must choose to break the law by letting Valjean go free. But he is unable to escape his life of rules and carries out his own punishment by taking his own life.

The terrible mastery of the law is simply this: it cannot allow for grace. To grow in Christ we accept by faith the truth that we have been released from the prison of keeping rules in order to satisfy God. Rules cannot produce growth, but grace received always brings multiplied growth.

Are you still in that prison—the prison of having to do the right thing to earn God's love? The prison of feeling that now that you're saved the rest of your Christian life is entirely up to you? The moment you became a believer, God unlocked that prison door and swung it wide open. Walk out into the light of God's grace!

## The <u>DAILY</u> <u>PROCESS</u> of Growth

Growth happens where you live life. It happens in your family, at your workplace, at your school, even in your car.

Because this is where growth happens, this is also where faith needs to happen: where you live and work and play, moment by moment and day by day.

Understanding how God works to grow us in the daily routine of life is vital. If you don't understand this you'll be like the rose we talked about in the last session: constantly confused and frustrated by the very things that God is doing to grow you.

Look with me at three faith decisions that you can make in the routine of life that put you right in the center of God's process of growth.

- **By faith you ask God to <u>RENEW</u> <u>YOUR</u> <u>MIND</u>.**

Listen to Ephesians 4:22–24.

> **You were taught, with regard to your former way of life, to put off your old self, which is being corrupted by its deceitful desires; to be made new in the attitude of your minds; and to put on the new self, created to be like God in true righteousness and holiness.**
>
> **—Ephesians 4:22–24**

**In the last session we looked at putting off the old and putting on the new. Being renewed in your mind is the often forgotten step in this process. Inner renewal is the key to outer transformation.**

**Do not conform any longer to the pattern of this world, but be transformed by the renewing of your mind. Then you will be able to test and approve what God's will is—his good, pleasing and perfect will.**

**—Romans 12:2**

**Therefore we do not lose heart. Though outwardly we are wasting away, yet inwardly we are being renewed day by day.**

—2 Corinthians 4:16

Unless you begin to think differently, you'll never begin to live differently. Change happens from the inside out, not from the outside in.

How does this work, this renewed mind? It works in the daily experiences of life. Ephesians 4 gives us a number of practical pictures.

**Ephesians 4:25–32 helps us to see that a key aspect of this inner renewal is the ability to see God's positive reasons for making a change. A renewed mind has the ability to see things the way that God sees them. It centers on the new way of viewing the world that has been our focus in this *Foundations* study.**

Look at how this works:

| Put off the old self | Put on the new self | Renewed in your minds |
| --- | --- | --- |
| Put off falsehood . . . | . . . speak truthfully to his neighbor . . . | . . . for we are all members of one body. |
| In your anger do not sin . . . | . . . do not let the sun go down while you are still angry . . . | . . . do not give the devil a foothold. |
| He who has been stealing must steal no longer . . . | . . . but must work . . . | . . . that he may have something to share with those in need. |
| Do not let any unwholesome talk come out of your mouths . . . | . . . but only what is helpful for building others up . . . | . . . do not grieve the Holy Spirit. |
| Get rid of all bitterness, rage and anger, brawling and slander . . . | . . . be kind and compassionate to one another, forgiving each other . . . | . . . just as in Christ God forgave you. |

Let's walk through a few of these together. You're in a situation where you are tempted to lie to someone—a family member or someone you know from church. Maybe it would bring you financial gain, maybe it seems that it would just make life easier—but you're tempted to lie. You know that God wants you to speak truthfully, but what is going to empower you to live out that truth? As long as all you're thinking is, "If I lie, my life will be better and easier," you're likely to lie. Who doesn't want their life to be better and easier! You need to start by thinking in a different way. "This person is a fellow member of the body of Christ. If I lie to them it will hurt the heart of God."

Let's look at another. Let's pretend that you sometimes struggle with your words. Anyone have a hard time pretending that? The unwholesome talk that we read about in Ephesians is not just swear words but the kind of words that tear other people down: critical or negative or sarcastic words. You know you should be a better encourager but think that just isn't you. You've always communicated with put-downs and sarcasm. You wouldn't know how to talk to people any other way. It's what everyone expects of you. What will get you to change? It will take a renewed mind. Paul's words are striking—it brings grief to God's Spirit when we speak words that tear down. Wow! That will start you thinking in a different direction! I've not only hurt another person with those words, I've brought grief to the very Spirit of God.

Discussion question 2 can be used here.

This renewing of our mind does not happen in a single day. It takes time. Think of your mind as one giant remodeling project.

Have you ever been involved in restoring or remodeling a building? (Or watched the movie *The Money Pit*?) When you're remodeling a house, some parts are in worse shape than others and they'll take longer to repair. And it's always the hidden things that take the longest—the plumbing and wiring behind a wall or under the floor. To repair these you have to tear into a perfectly good wall or floor, fix the hidden damage, then replace the wall.

Here's the point. Sometimes God has to tear down some walls before he can begin to redo your wiring. It's helpful to see why he's tearing down those walls. He is working to grow you, even in the hidden areas of your life.

Remodeling can be scary. When you tear into things it looks like a huge mess. You wonder if the work will ever be finished. As God grows us, it sometimes feels as if things get worse before they get better. It's a common feeling as he changes us from the inside out.

I encourage you to take a courageous step of faith right now. Tell God that you're willing for him to do this work in your life. Pray something like this, "Lord, I'll make myself available for your restoring work. Help me to not try to just patch over the problems or to try to do the job myself. And when I am afraid, help me to remember that the old, dilapidated shack that I've grown comfortable with will have to undergo some drastic changes as you're making a mansion of me."

**Split Session Plan:** If you're teaching this study over two sessions, end the first session here.

In the daily process of growth we look to God to renew our minds. But I want you to see that the process of growth is also a matter of the habits that we build into our everyday lives. Our habits control the way we think and the direction of our lives more than we imagine. You may remember that old poem,

> Sow a thought, reap an action.
> Sow an action, reap a habit.
> Sow a habit, reap a character.
> Sow a character, reap a destiny.
> —Anonymous

Want to know how important our habits are? We become identified by whatever we do habitually. If you stop by a coffee shop to get coffee every morning, people would call you a what? Right, a coffee drinker. If you are in the habit of cutting quickly in front of other cars as you drive, you are labeled a what? A bad driver. If you are in the habit of spending a lot of time with your kids, people tend to see you as a good parent.

## Teaching Tip

Get the group involved by pausing and letting them finish the above sentences with you. You'll likely hear some humor from them on these. Someone may say caffeine addict instead of coffee drinker, and who knows what they might say instead of bad driver. The point is not for them to get your right answer but for you to get their attention.

- **By faith you practice the <u>DISCIPLINES</u> <u>OF</u> <u>GROWTH</u>.**

**Spend your time and energy in training yourself for spiritual fitness.**
—1 Timothy 4:7 (NLT)

**Discipline yourself for the purpose of godliness.**
—1 Timothy 4:7 (NASB)

Growth takes time and energy. It is a matter of discipline. I say that with a caution. When you lean solely on your own discipline, it only results in pride. When you do the same things with the same energy, but lean instead on God to grow you through your obedience to him, you find yourself growing in ways you never imagined.

Richard Foster wrote in his book *Celebration of Discipline:*

> By themselves the spiritual disciplines can do nothing; they can only get us to the place where something can be done. . . . The disciplines allow us to place ourselves before God so that He can transform us.[3]

These disciplines place us before God, where he can transform us! It's amazing how we hope that God will transform us without ever putting ourselves in the place where he says he will do just that. If you wanted to try on and buy some clothes, you would go to a clothing store. You would put yourself in the place where you could buy clothes. If you wanted to play baseball, you would go to a baseball field. That's the place where baseball happens. How do you put yourself in the place where spiritual growth will happen in your life? It's not just a matter of going to church. Plenty of people attend church without ever growing spiritually. God tells us that there are certain disciplines that must become a part of our lives if we are to grow.

## A Closer Look

**Three of the most important disciplines of growth through which God sanctifies us are:**

**1. A daily quiet time—in God's Word and prayer**

**Jesus answered, "It is written: 'Man does not live on bread alone, but on every word that comes from the mouth of God.'"**

—Matthew 4:4

**Sanctify them by the truth; your word is truth.**

—John 17:17

To say "Lord, help me to grow" without making a life commitment to reading and studying and listening to God's Word is like praying for your flowers to grow without ever watering them.

**2. A weekly tithe to God**

**"Bring the whole tithe into the storehouse, that there may be food in my house. Test me in this," says the Lord Almighty, "and see if I will not throw open the floodgates of heaven and pour out so much blessing that you will not have room enough for it."**

—Malachi 3:10

**And they gave in a way we did not expect: They first gave themselves to the Lord and to us. This is what God wants.**

—2 Corinthians 8:5 (NCV)

We spend the majority of our lives making and managing and spending money. Anyone who thinks they can grow as a believer without making a disciplined commitment of their finances to God is just fooling himself or herself.

### 3. A regular commitment to a small group

**So now you Gentiles are no longer strangers and foreigners. You are citizens along with all of God's holy people. You are members of God's family.**

**—Ephesians 2:19 (NLT)**

Christians grow in bunches. You need the support, the challenge, and the encouragement that comes in your relationships to other believers to grow. And others need your support, challenge, and encouragement to grow.

Redwood trees grow to the tallest height of any tree in the world. The way they continue to stand at that great height gives us a good parable of how you and I grow as believers. The largest living things on earth, these trees can grow to more than 300 feet high. Yet their root system is surprisingly shallow, reaching no deeper than eight to ten feet. One way the trees are able to keep from falling over is by growing close to other redwood trees. Their root systems spread out and intermingle, providing more support together than they would have alone.

Redwood trees can't grow to a great height by themselves; they need each other. You need relationships with other believers to grow. Yet most of us get so busy we can't seem to find time to develop these kinds of relationships. You must *make* time. Joining a small group means you are deciding to make those relationships a regular part of your life.

---

Discussion question 3 can be used here.

In the daily process of life God grows us through a renewed mind and through spiritual habits. There is a third tool that he uses to grow us.

- **By faith you choose to trust God in the <u>CIRCUMSTANCES OF LIFE</u>.**

  **God has allowed our choice to be one of the key factors in our growth. One of the most important choices we make is our response to the difficulties and trials we all face as a part of life.**

  **Dear brothers, is your life full of difficulties and temptations? Then be happy, for when the way is rough, your patience has a chance to grow. So let it grow, and don't try to squirm out of your problems. For when your patience is finally in full bloom, then you will be ready for anything, strong in character, full and complete.**

  **—James 1:2–4 (LB)**

We also have joy with our troubles, because we know that these troubles produce patience. And patience produces character, and character produces hope. And this hope will never disappoint us, because God has poured out his love to fill our hearts. He gave us his love through the Holy Spirit, whom God has given to us.

—Romans 5:3–5 (NCV)

So even though Jesus was God's Son, he learned obedience from the things he suffered.

—Hebrews 5:8 (NLT)

Often the first step to growth in our lives is simply this: get a problem. Anyone having a difficulty with completing step one in this assignment? I didn't think so! We all have problems in our lives. They may seem relatively small or completely overwhelming—but they're the set of problems we're facing right now. Step two is the attitude that you and I have toward that problem. James says, "Be happy." Paul says in Romans, "Have joy." The happiness and joy are not about the problem. They are about what God is going to do in your life even through that problem.

The most patient people I've ever met are the people with the most enduring pain. The most loving people are the people who have faced the greatest rejection. The most giving people are those who have given when it seemed that there was nothing to give. It's not that every person who has had to endure becomes patient. Some become bitter. What's the difference? It is in our choice—the choice to recognize that God is at work even through the difficulties of life.

Wouldn't it be great if we could outgrow the need for trials to be one of the things that God uses to accomplish our growth? Not in this world. Hebrews 5:8 tells us that even Jesus learned obedience through suffering—and he was perfect. Trials are one of God's tools for teaching until we get to heaven.

## God's Promise to <u>FINISH HIS WORK</u>

**What is the ultimate goal that God is working toward in your life?**

**The goal is to be like Christ.**

We know that in everything God works for the good of those who love him. They are the people he called, because that was his plan. God knew them before he made the world, and he decided that they would be like his Son so that Jesus would be the firstborn of many brothers.

—Romans 8:28–29 (NCV)

We know that when Christ comes again, we will be like him, because we will see him as he really is.

—1 John 3:2 (NCV)

Look at Romans 8:28–29. It has always been God's goal to make us like his Son. First John 3:2 reminds us that this will happen when we get to heaven—when we see him we will be like him. But what about between then and now? God is also working to grow us to be more like Jesus in our daily lives each day. It is his primary goal for us— more important than any success or temporary happiness. Look at Ephesians 4:13.

**This work must continue until we are all joined together in the same faith and in the same knowledge of the Son of God. We must become like a mature person, growing until we become like Christ and have his perfection.**

—**Ephesians 4:13** (NCV)

When I say that we are to be like Christ, that sounds like a huge mountain to climb. The distance between where I am and who Jesus is seems so far—what hope is there for me? Let me give you a picture of how God grows us to become like Jesus that I hope will encourage you. Look at this picture of a bridge, illustrating how this growth happens step by step throughout our lives.

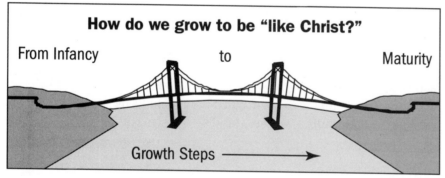

On the left you see the word *infancy* and on the right *maturity*. It's a process. We all begin the process as baby Christians, as infants in Christ. The goal we have is to cross the bridge, to get to the other side called maturity. A definition for maturity is "being like Christ."

How do you and I evaluate our growth toward being like Jesus? Here is how many of us do it. We're on the bridge, trying to move from one side to the other, and we look around us to see how everyone else is doing. If we're at the back of the pack, we feel we're not doing well. But if we're in the middle of the pack or even a little out ahead, we feel like spiritual giants. The problem with this is, we're just comparing ourselves with ourselves. What if none of us are growing? We can stay stuck on the infant side, feeling good about our growth because we're all at about the same place.

We need to learn from and encourage each other in our growth. But we must never set our standard on how other people are doing. The goal is to be like Christ. If you find someone who's a little further along in that goal than you, by all means let him or her help you to grow. Just remember our goal—to be like Jesus.

As you look at the goal of growing to be like Jesus, I know this can seem overwhelming. How am I going to do that for the rest of my life? It's tough to think about motivating yourself to grow every day for the rest of your life. I have some good news for you, some extraordinarily good news. You don't have to motivate yourself! The motivation comes from God who is at work in us. You just have to cooperate with what he is already doing.

Growth is not your work; it is God's work in you.

- **By faith you believe in God's ability to accomplish his work in your life.**

  **You are not alone. God is working for your growth. He is working to make you like his Son, Jesus.**

  **God is <u>COMMITTED</u> to your growth.**

  **And I consecrate myself to meet their need for growth in truth and holiness.**

  **—John 17:19 (LB)**

  **Long ago, even before he made the world, God chose us to be his very own, through what Christ would do for us; he decided then to make us holy in his eyes, without a single fault—we who stand before him covered with his love.**

  **—Ephesians 1:4 (LB)**

  Look at Jesus' prayer in John 17:19. He is committed to meet our need for growth. Ephesians 1:4 tells us that God has chosen to make us holy. God not only wants us to grow, he has committed himself to growing us.

  That's where the motivation to grow in our daily lives comes from. Our commitment to God is strengthened and energized by his commitment to us.

  **Our motivational power: God <u>WANTS</u> us and is <u>WORKING</u> for us to be sanctified.**

  Close your eyes, would you? I want you to listen to Philippians 1:6 as if it were the first time you ever heard it. Listen to this verse with every fiber of your being—as God's personal promise to you.

**He who began a good work in you will carry it on to completion until the day of Christ Jesus.**

—Philippians 1:6

Do you believe that? It's God's promise, a promise you can trust.

Discussion question 4 can be used here.

Let me tell you two stories as we close: one about an engine trying to climb a mountain and another about a disciple attempting to walk on water.

## Teaching Tip

If you have a copy of the book *The Little Engine That Could*, it will be more effective if you can bring that book and read from it. Then pick up your Bible and read the story of Peter walking on water.

You all remember the children's story of the little engine on the train that kept saying, "I think I can, I think I can" as it tugged and pulled its heavy load up the mountain until it finally reached the top.

It's a wonderful children's story, but we shouldn't get our philosophy of the Christian life from it.

The second story comes from the Bible, in Matthew 14. It's the story of the disciple Peter walking on water.

> Meanwhile, the disciples were in trouble far away from land, for a strong wind had risen, and they were fighting heavy waves.
> About three o'clock in the morning Jesus came to them, walking on the water. When the disciples saw him, they screamed in terror, thinking he was a ghost. But Jesus spoke to them at once. "It's all right," he said. "I am here! Don't be afraid."
> Then Peter called to him, "Lord, if it's really you, tell me to come to you by walking on water."
> "All right, come," Jesus said.
> So Peter went over the side of the boat and walked on the water toward Jesus. But when he looked around at the high waves, he was terrified and began to sink. "Save me, Lord!" he shouted.
> Instantly Jesus reached out his hand and grabbed him. "You don't have much faith," Jesus said. "Why did you doubt me?" And when they climbed back into the boat, the wind stopped.

—Matthew 14:24–32 (NLT)

How did Peter walk on water for those few seconds? Jesus didn't tell him to chant, "I think I can, I think I can!" He walked on water by focusing on Jesus. It was when his focus moved from Jesus to the waves that he began to sink.

These two stories are two different ways of living life. One is the "I think I can" life. The other is the "I know I can't, I know God can" life. The first life is entirely dependent on your own motivation and energy. The problem with the "I think I can" life is that there's always another mountain to climb. And one day you're going to run into a mountain that you can't climb. "I think I can" will not get us over the most important mountains of life: getting to know God and growing to become like Christ. One of the most refreshing and energizing moments in any life is the moment we say, "I know I can't, but I know that God can do in me what I cannot do for myself."

Here's the point. You can't walk on water by trying hard. It comes only through trust.

## Key Personal Perspective

Growth is not accomplished by <u>TRYING HARD</u>, but by <u>TRUSTING HIM</u>.

Trust means: We work out what God works in.

> Continue to work out your salvation with fear and trembling, for it is God who works in you to will and to act according to his good purpose.
> —Philippians 2:12–13

> And now—all glory to him who alone is God, who saves us through Jesus Christ our Lord; yes, splendor and majesty, all power and authority are his from the beginning; his they are and his they evermore shall be. And he is able to keep you from slipping and falling away, and to bring you, sinless and perfect, into his glorious presence with mighty shouts of everlasting joy. Amen.
> —Jude 1:24–25 (LB)

Look at Jude 1:24–25. It doesn't say, "And I am able to keep myself from falling away . . . to bring myself sinless and perfect into his presence." Of course not! But God is able. He is able!

Listen to Max Lucado's story of attempting to conquer a fifty-foot climbing wall at a family camp.

> My daughters and I chose to climb a wall—a simulated rock climb. The wall is made of wood with occasional rock-shaped fingerholds bolted into the surface. For safety, the climber wears a harness around his waist. The harness is attached to a rope that runs up through a pulley and then down into the hand of a guide who secures it as the climber climbs. I gave it a go. What's a fifty-foot wall for a middle-aged author? I gave the guide the "thumbs-up" and began. The first half of the trip I did well. About midway, however, I began to get tired. These hands and feet are not accustomed to climbing.
>
> With about twenty feet left to go, I honestly began to wonder if I would make it. I gave serious thought to telling the guide just to pull me up the rest of the way. My fingers were sore, and my legs were starting to tremble, and I was regretting every Big Mac I'd ever eaten, but the thought of surrender was lost in the cheers of my daughters who were already on the top. "Come on, Dad. You can make it!" So I gave it all I had. But all I had was not enough. My feet slipped, my hands slipped, and down I fell. I fell hard. But I didn't fall far. My guide had a firm hold on the rope. Because he was alert and because he was strong, my tumble lasted only a couple of seconds. I bounced and swung in the harness, suspended in midair. Everyone watching let out a sigh, and I gulped and resumed the climb. Guess what I did when I made it to the top? Do you think I boasted? Do you think I bragged about conquering the wall? No way. I looked down at the one who kept me from falling. "Thanks, pal," I told him. I didn't pat myself on the back or raise my fist in triumph. I didn't ask everybody if they'd seen what I did. I did the only thing that was right: I said thanks to the one who held me.[4]

Let's read Jude 1:24–25 together again as we close. Personalize it by using the words "me" and "my."

Read it with faith!

> And now—all glory to him who alone is God, who saved me through Jesus Christ my Lord; yes, splendor and majesty, all power and authority are his from the beginning; his they are and his they evermore shall be. And he is able to keep me from slipping and falling away, and to bring me, yes me, sinless and perfect, into his glorious presence with mighty shouts of everlasting joy.
>
> —Jude 1:24–25 (LB)

**Finish memorizing memory card 7, "The Truth about Sanctification."**

## Discussion Questions

1. Why do you think some get pulled into thinking we can measure our spiritual growth based solely on how we keep laws or rules?

2. What are two or three practical things that we can do to cooperate with God in his desire to renew our minds?

3. Which of the disciplines of growth do you find God using the most frequently and/or the most effectively in your life?

4. The goal of becoming completely like Christ will never be fully realized by any of us while on this earth. What are the practical and personal ways that you keep from getting discouraged as you reach for a goal you won't reach until you get to heaven?

## For Further Study

Bridges, Jerry. *The Practice of Godliness*. Colorado Springs: NavPress, 1983.

Cloud, Henry and John Townsend. *How People Grow*. Grand Rapids, Mich.: Zondervan, 2001.

Dieter, Melvin E., et al. *Five Views on Sanctification*. Grand Rapids, Mich.: Zondervan, 1987.

Foster, Richard J. *Celebration of Discipline*. Rev. ed. San Francisco: Harper & Row, 1988.

Henrichsen, Walter A. *Disciples Are Made—Not Born*. Wheaton, Ill.: Victor, 1980.

Nouwen, Henri J. M. *Reaching Out: The Three Movements of the Spiritual Life*. New York: Doubleday, 1986.

Ortberg, John. *The Life You've Always Wanted*. Grand Rapids, Mich.: Zondervan, 1997.

Willard, Dallas. *The Spirit of the Disciplines*. San Francisco: HarperSanFrancisco, 1991.

# Good and Evil
## Part 1

### Life Change Objective

To give you the truth you need to answer questions concerning the fact that we live in an evil world.

### Summary Teaching Outine

Why Does Evil Exist in God's World?

    Three truths

        1. God is good.

        2. God is all-powerful.

        3. The world is evil.

    How can all of these be true?

Three Reasons Why Evil Exists in Our World Today

God's Will: Because God Allows Evil

    1. He made a world in which evil could exist.

    2. God allows evil to continue to exist.

Satan's Influence: Because Satan Afflicts Evil

    Satan: a brief biography

Mankind's Choice: Because We Accept Evil

    1. Evil began with them.

    2. Evil is present in me.

The Questions That Remain

    Why does God continue to allow evil? Why doesn't God stop it?

Let's start with a little quiz. I'll mention some things, and you tell me if they are good or evil. Just shout out "good" or "evil."

For instance, God's love. Is that good or evil? Right, God's love is clearly good.

How about the Bible, good or evil? Again, it's easy to shout out that the Bible is good.

How about snow, is that good or evil? Now it starts to get a little more complicated. It's a good and beautiful creation of God, but sometimes evil things happen because of snow: avalanches and accidents.

How about computers? I heard a cheer of good from some of you and a groan of evil from the rest. The truth is, a computer is a tool that can be used for good or evil.

How about . . . you? Now it gets interesting, doesn't it? We know that every one of us is a creation of God, and yet we all struggle with the reality of evil in our lives.

This question of good and evil is the number one question that many people have about God. Why do bad things happen to good people? How could God allow this? It's not a question that you can answer in a few sentences. However, as we focus on this question over the next few sessions, we have a real opportunity to see our faith and our relationship with God built even as we look at this difficult question.

Let me remind you as we begin this study that it is good to ask these kinds of questions of God. Read even quickly through the book of Psalms, and you'll be amazed at the deep and searching questions that David asked God. He seems unafraid to ask anything—and David is called a man after God's heart. David's questions always led him to faith-filled answers.

**During these next two sessions we'll be looking at what the Bible says about the fact that good and evil exist alongside each other in the world today. There are many questions that are answered by understanding God's perspective on this truth.**

- **How could God allow such things as war and the death of children in the world today?**

This world is filled with good gifts from God. But right alongside those gifts is the presence of horrible evils. It does no good to pretend that evil does not exist—we know it does. The death of an innocent child is evil. Rape is evil. Famine is evil. Prejudice and hatred in their many forms are evil.

- **If God is all-powerful and all-loving, why can't he stop evil?**

  The thinking is: God must either not be loving enough to want to stop evil or must not be powerful enough to be able to stop evil. In this study we'll see the God-sized hole in that logic.

- **Why do bad things happen to good people?**

- **In light of what's happening in the world, am I just fooling myself to think that there is any hope?**

- **Will it ever end? When?**

  In *The Case for Faith,* Lee Strobel writes concerning our desire to know the answers to these questions.

  > I commissioned George Barna, the public-opinion pollster, to conduct a national survey in which he asked a scientifically selected cross-section of adults: "If you could ask God only one question and you knew he would give you an answer, what would you ask?" The top response, offered by 17 percent of those who said they had a question, was: "Why is there pain and suffering in the world?"[1]

  That is at the core of the question we are going to look at together these next two sessions.

**First we'll look at the overall problem of good and evil. Why does it exist in this world?**

**Next we'll look at the personal side of good and evil. How do I win the battle against evil in my personal life?**

One of the ways that we try to deal with the problem of evil is through denial. There are four classic false solutions to the problem of evil—solutions that start with denial. These all rest on our powers of logic—trying to figure out the answers on our own.

1. Deny that God exists.
2. Deny that God is great (his hands are tied). This was Rabbi Kushner's conclusion in his book *Why Do Bad Things Happen to Good People?* God would like to help, but sometimes he just doesn't have the power to do so. Comedian Woody Allen expressed this low view of God when he said, "If it turns out that there is a God, I don't think that he's evil. The worst that you can say about him is that basically he's an underachiever."
3. Deny that God is good.

4. Deny that evil exists. This, for instance, is what Christian Science believes, saying that the world is just an illusion. Christians who expect that they will live in a bubble of protection where God will not allow evil circumstances to invade are in reality struggling with a form of this type of denial.

None of these denials answers the problem of evil. Any answer to the problem of evil that begins with denial leaves you, in the end, disappointed and hopeless. As easy as it is to doubt God when faced with evil, let me remind you as we begin this study that facing the reality of evil in this world is also one of our greatest opportunities for faith. But that faith demands that we not be afraid to ask the honest questions. Let's start with: Why does evil exist in God's world?

Discussion question 1 can be used here.

# Why Does Evil Exist in God's World?

## *Three truths*

### 1. God is good.

The starting place of any discussion of evil in the world must be these three words: God is good.

There is just too much good in this world to deny the goodness of the Creator.

#### His <u>CHARACTER</u> is good.

**For the Lord is good and his love endures forever; his faithfulness continues through all generations.**
— **Psalm 100:5**

#### His <u>ACTIONS</u> are good.

**God saw all that he had made, and it was very good.**
— **Genesis 1:31**

Every time you take a breath of air, you experience God's goodness. He gave you life. We smell his goodness in a rose, see his goodness in a sunset, hear his goodness in a child's laughter, feel his goodness in a tender hug. We can taste God's goodness in a chocolate chip cookie.

### 2. God is all-powerful.

**Great and powerful God, your name is the Lord All-Powerful.**
— **Jeremiah 32:18 (NCV)**

All-powerful—that means exactly what it says. God has the power to do anything! However, and this is important, he is not going to act in a way that violates the goodness of his character.

That makes sense so far. God is good. God is all-powerful. It's the third truth that throws us for a loop.

**3. The world is evil.**

The Bible tells us this world is evil. Look at John 3:19 and 1 John 2:15.

**Their sentence is based on this fact: that the Light from heaven came into the world, but they loved the darkness more than the Light, for their deeds were evil.**

—John 3:19 (LB)

**Stop loving this evil world and all that it offers you.**

—1 John 2:15 (LB)

So the question then is,

## How can all of these be true?

If God is good, how could he allow evil to exist? If he is all-powerful, why doesn't he stop all evil?

**How could a good and all-powerful God create a world in which evil could exist and continues to exist? A lot of theological and philosophical jargon can be summed up in one simple sentence:**

**There is no <u>LOVE</u> without <u>CHOICE</u>.**

**God could have made a person who would never have chosen to sin, but then that person would have been denied the opportunity to choose to love.**

I would be a fool to even pretend to explain why all the bad things happen in this world. I don't know why God allows some evil to happen and prevents other evil things from happening. But I do know that there is no love without choice. We know that God wanted to give us the opportunity to love him. And to love someone you must be able to make the choice to love. Love that is forced cannot be true love. The choice that God gave us means we can say yes to a relationship with him. But it also means that we can say no to him, and yes to all kinds of evil in our lives. Choice gives us the opportunity to do the right thing—to love him. But it also gives us the opportunity to do the wrong thing, to not love him. To not love God is the ultimate evil. There is no greater evil than rejecting the love of the one who made us. And that ultimate evil results in all other kinds of evil.

### A Closer Look

*Two Truths to Remember*

1. **God is sovereign.**

2. **Mankind has free choice.**

**How do you reconcile those two? If God gives us choice, doesn't that put us in control rather than him? Our God is an awesome God! He is able to give us, as a part of his creation, a free will to decide and yet remain in complete control of his creation. How does he do that? He is God!**

As we walk through this study, listen for both of these truths. God has given us the ability to choose, but that does not mean that he has given up control. Listen for God's love in it all, listen for God's control in it all, listen for God's power in it all, listen for God's final answer in it all.

**One warning: be sure to keep these truths in balance. If you lean too far toward God's being in control, you come down on the side of fatalism: it doesn't matter what we do. If you lean too far toward man's free will, you come down on the side of humanism: we are in control of our fate.**

A talk about the presence of evil in our world can quickly turn purely philosophical. But this is not just philosophical, it is personal. The truth is, every one of us in this room have been and are being deeply impacted by the suffering that grows out of evil. I may not know what you're suffering through right now. But I do know that we all go through hard times. When we talk about good and evil, we're talking about a very personal subject! I encourage you not to minimize the struggles that you're facing. We know that the issue of evil is much bigger than what is happening to any one of us. But if you don't take an honest look at this through the filter of your own life, your answers to the problem of evil will always end up sounding more like something from a philosophy course than a personal word from the Father who loves you.

We need to have the sense, in light of our own struggles with evil, that we are sitting at God's throne and asking him the hard questions that are on our heart. Questions are a great thing when they drive us to God.

With that in mind, let's take a look at what the Bible has to say about why evil exists.

**There are three reasons why evil exists in our world today.**

# God's Will: Because God <u>ALLOWS</u> Evil

God is all-powerful. This means that evil could not exist in this world except for the fact that he allows it.

**The problem of evil and suffering is possibly the single greatest intellectual challenge to Christianity. It's hard for people to understand how a great and good God could allow evil to exist.**

Here is what God says in the Bible.

1. **He made a world in which evil <u>COULD EXIST</u>.**

   Notice, not must exist. God did not create evil. In Genesis, when God created, we're told that his creation was good. But he did create a world where evil could be our choice.

   **In Genesis 3:**

   - **God planted the tree of the knowledge of good and evil.**

   - **God let Satan as a snake into the garden.**

   - **God allowed Adam and Eve to eat of the fruit.**

   Look at how God allowed evil in Genesis 3. He planted the tree of the knowledge of good and evil in the Garden of Eden. He let the snake into the garden. He didn't stop Adam or Eve from eating the fruit of the tree.

   When faced with the truth that God allowed evil into this world, we have two great temptations.

   The first is the temptation to play God.

   It's natural for us to think, "If I were God, I would have certainly found another way to do it." For me, for all of us, this goes straight to the heart of our trust in God. It does not make sense to us, but we trust in the fact that God knows what he is doing even when we do not understand it. I trust in God's goodness and power, and so I choose not to play armchair quarterback with God. It's easy to say, "If I were God I would have figured out a way to give us choice without allowing evil into this world." The truth is, "If I were God I'd know instantly why he chose to do it as he did." But I'm not God. And neither are you.

   The second is the temptation to minimize God.

   Don't make the mistake of thinking that evil slipped into this world in spite of God's power. Evil didn't overpower God to make its way into that garden. God allowed it.

Here's where the hope and faith come in. Since evil is allowed in this world only by God's power, then we know that evil can be banished from the world by that same power. He has the power to stop evil at any moment. Why doesn't he? We'll look at what the Bible has to say about that toward the end of this study.

Discussion questions 2 and 3 can be used here.

### 2. God allows evil to <u>CONTINUE</u> <u>TO</u> <u>EXIST</u>.

God does not choose or cause evil, but he does allow it.

- **God allows us to make evil choices.**

  **So I gave them over to their stubborn hearts to follow their own devices.**
  **—Psalm 81:12**

  God allows people to make bad choices—evil choices. God allows you to make bad choices—evil choices.

  Picture it this way. God has filled this world with stop signs that tell us right from wrong. The laws we have as nations, the inner conscience we have, and his clear Word to us all give us those stop signs.

  The stop signs are clear. But God allows us to run the stop signs if we choose.

  If you start running stop signs it's easy to tell yourself that no harm will come of it. But every time you do so your heart is becoming harder. "Stop signs are a stupid thing to have," you tell yourself. "It saves me a lot of time to ignore them." In fact, some people even get a kind of thrill from running the red lights. But every time you run one of these stop signs it gets easier, which means your heart is getting colder. Every time you do it your way you get further and further from God.

- **God allows painful consequences for the evil choices we make.**

  **If someone sins and without realizing it does one of the things forbidden by Yahweh's commandments, he will answer for it and bear the consequences of his guilt.**
  **—Leviticus 5:17 (NJB)**

  God allows us to run the stop signs. And God allows that to result in crashes. Someday, inevitably, there will be a horrible crash.

  We run the red lights and flirt with another man or woman even though we're married. And then we have the audacity to tell ourselves, "I just couldn't stop," when we start an affair and experience disastrous consequences in our marriage.

We run through the stop sign and let our anger control us. After a while, we don't even think anymore about the hurt this is bringing to our family or coworkers.

We run the stop sign and decide to devote all of life to making money. "It's only for a few years," we tell ourselves. Don't be surprised when one day you wake up and realize that all you have is the money: no fulfillment, no relationships, no heart for God. Just things.

Wait a minute, some of you may be thinking, I thought this was a study about the philosophy of why there is evil in this world. Do you have to make it so personal—to talk about my sin? That's the place that an understanding of evil starts—with honesty about my sin. We've all run red lights. We've all crashed. That's why evil continues to exist in this world.

Sometimes evil comes into our lives because of what others do to us. They may do it knowingly, or it may be the action of someone who doesn't even know your name. But in honesty we have to admit that even more often we bring the consequences on ourselves. Our selfishness and sin end up hurting us and hurting those around us.

Allowing consequences for our evil choices is not malicious on God's part, it is loving. If there were no consequences to the choices we make that hurt our relationship with God and others, we'd keep making those choices. Here's a truth of human nature: we don't change when we see the light; we change when we feel the heat. The consequences we bring upon ourselves and our families can cause us to look to God's goodness.

Let me be clear. The fact that you are suffering does not always mean that you did something wrong or sinful or evil. Sometimes we suffer because of the actions of others. Sometimes we suffer because we live in a fallen, evil world. Whatever reason you're facing suffering, it helps to understand God's response to suffering.

 **A Closer Look**

*God's Response to Suffering*

**The fact that God allows suffering does not mean he enjoys suffering.**

1. He directly <u>CAUSES</u> some suffering. He is the punisher of evil (Isa. 13:11).

2. He has <u>COMPASSION</u> for all suffering (2 Cor. 1:3–4; Lam. 3:22–23; Matt. 14:14).

I'm so glad that God offers us compassion, not pat answers. That's the same thing that others need from us when they are going through suffering. They don't need to hear you say, "Here's why this is happening." They need to hear you say, "I'm here with you while this is happening."

3. **He is willing to <u>CARE</u> for us in our suffering (Ps. 46:1; Heb. 4:16).**

Elizabeth Styffe talks about her experiences with the reality of evil as she worked as a nurse in a children's intensive care unit.

> The unit that I worked on had kids with cystic fibrosis, the number one genetic killer of kids. There is no cure, every child that I worked with was going to die. God loved those children, more than I could ever fathom. There was one teenaged boy that I became very close to: John (not his real name). I received the call one day at home and heard the news, "It looks like John is going to die today." I went to the hospital and walked into the room to see John's parents standing there. His parents had two boys: one had already died from cystic fibrosis. John was their last son, and he was going to die today. What was so difficult for us all was that John was suffering, and moaning in pain. His parents looked at me and said, "Can't you do something." Of course, as a good nurse, I ran out to get more medication and to do all the nursing things. But nothing seemed to be working. His chest came off the bed as he struggled for every breath. We tried touching him and comforting him and his parents got in bed with him. There was only one thing that would cause John to stop moaning. I got next to his ear and did the only thing I could think of at the time. I sang in a whisper through my tears: "Jesus loves me, this I know. . . ." And that truth provided comfort.[2]

4. **He develops our <u>CHARACTER</u> through suffering (James 1:2–4; Heb. 2:10).**

That does not make the suffering good, by the way. God is good. So good that he is able to take even the evil that comes into our lives and use it to grow us to become more like him in our character.

5. **He will one day <u>CEASE</u> all suffering (Rev. 21:3–4; Rom. 8:18).**

The fact that God allows evil does not mean he does not grieve over the presence of evil in this world. The truth is, he hurts much more deeply over the reality of evil in this world than we do. God sees the reality of evil more clearly and feels the pain of evil more deeply than any of us could imagine.

When we're suffering we want to know that someone hears us. And God does.

When we're suffering, we want to know that someone will do something about it. *And God will.* He will one day cease all suffering.

Discussion question 4 can be used here.

**Split Session Plan:** If you're teaching this study over two sessions, end the first session here.

God has shown us three reasons for the existence of evil in our world. First, God's will: he allows evil. Second . . .

# Satan's Influence: Because Satan AFFLICTS Evil

**The influence of Satan is a second reason why evil exists in our world today. Evil is not some new creation of Satan—Satan does not have the power to create anything. All he can do is to try to twist or to withhold what God has created.**

### Is weather evil?

I love the fact that God made our world to have seasons, weather that we can enjoy. But remember the story of Job? Satan used the weather to kill Job's family.

### Is ambition evil?

There is nothing wrong with ambition for godly purposes. But remember the story of Ananias and Sapphira? Their ambition for honor led to the loss of their lives.

### Is sex evil?

Sex is a wonderful creation of God to give us unity in marriage. But Satan can twist that gift. Remember the story of David?

### Is our ability to talk evil?

Our words are a gift from God. However, remember the story of Peter, in Matthew 16:23. When Peter tried to keep Jesus from going to the cross, Jesus said to him, "Get behind me, Satan!"

**All of these are good creations of God. Evil is when Satan twists them into natural disasters, or war, or immorality, or slander.**

Satan is a powerful spiritual being, but he is just a created being. He cannot create anything any more than you or I could create something from nothing. Listen to these words written as though Satan were speaking.

I possess the will to create (hence my pride), but I am incapable of creating (hence my envy). And with an envy raised to such power as mortal minds can feel, I hate the Creator and his creation. My greatest masterpiece is never more than a perversion—an ingenious disordering of another's grand design, a perversion of order into chaos, of life into death. Why?... Perhaps, it is simply, as every craftsman knows, that nothing enduring, great or small, can ever be created without love. But I am as incapable of love as I am of goodness.[3]

**We as believers need to be able to understand and defeat the enemy without glorifying the enemy. Satan has power, but he is also stupid. (Why else would he have sinned against God?)**

## *Satan: a brief biography*

**Many of the ideas and pictures of Satan that we grew up with were influenced more by English literature such as Dante's *Inferno* and Milton's *Paradise Lost* than by the Bible. Here we're going to look at the straight story from the Bible about who Satan is.**

1. **He was an <u>ANGEL</u> in heaven (Rev. 12:3–9; 9:11).**

   Angels are not people who have died, they are spiritual beings made to serve God in heaven. Satan is a spiritual being, a creation of God.

2. **He <u>FELL</u> from heaven due to pride.**

   **And there was war in heaven. Michael and his angels fought against the dragon, and the dragon and his angels fought back. But he was not strong enough, and they lost their place in heaven. The great dragon was hurled down—that ancient serpent called the devil, or Satan, who leads the whole world astray. He was hurled to the earth, and his angels with him.**

   **—Revelation 12:7–9**

   **How you are fallen from heaven, O Lucifer, son of the morning! How you are cut down to the ground—mighty though you were against the nations of the world. For you said to yourself, "I will ascend to heaven and rule the angels. I will take the highest throne. I will preside on the Mount of Assembly far away in the north. I will climb to the highest heavens and be like the Most High." But instead, you will be brought down to the pit of hell, down to its lowest depths.**

   **—Isaiah 14:12–15 (LB)**

   How could that happen? I have absolutely no idea. You can find lots of conjecture about how and why Satan as an angel could have made a choice that resulted in his fall, but it's all just guesswork. Maybe we'll hear more about this story when we get to heaven. For now all we know is that it happened. Satan wanted to be like God in power, and that prideful attitude caused his fall.

3. He has been given <u>LIMITED</u> freedom to influence the earth.

   Satan's limit: he must ask <u>GOD'S</u> <u>PERMISSION</u>.

   Some examples:

   - **Job (Job 1:6–12; 2:1–6)**

   - **Peter: "Satan has asked to sift you as wheat" (Luke 22:31).**

Satan is on a leash! He cannot just do whatever he decides. He must ask for God's permission.

In Job 1:8 God says to Satan, "Have you considered my servant Job? There is no one on earth like him; he is blameless and upright, a man who fears God and shuns evil." Satan then accuses Job of serving God only because of the rewards. And God allows Satan to bring evil to Job's life to prove that Job's faith in God would not fail, regardless of the circumstances.

The truth that Satan's freedom is limited is troubling and comforting to us at the same time. This is not an easy truth to talk about.

It's troubling because we think of Satan asking for permission to bring into our lives some of our deepest hurts. "How could God have allowed that?" we ask. Let me give you a picture that I hope will help.

It is not as if we live in a great castle of protection, with God only letting a few problems through. This is an evil world, and we are all right in the midst of it. We are all on the battlefield called life, with the arrows of pain flying all around us. During our time in this world, we will all be hit by many of those arrows. Instead of thinking of God choosing which arrows will hit you, think of him determining which arrows will not strike. He sees an arrow headed straight for your heart and doesn't allow it to hit you because it would be too great for you to bear. He will not allow Satan to take your life before God's plan for your life on this earth is complete. Satan will never get permission to cause someone's death just seconds before they would have trusted in Christ for salvation. I think that we would be shocked if we were able to see all of the problems that God filters out of our lives. I say this not to minimize the problems you have but as a reminder that God is at work even in the midst of our problems.

That's where the comfort comes in. God knows about our problems and knows that he can give us the strength to face each problem even before it happens.

Faith reminds us that all of our problems are "Father filtered." Because God allows the problems, we know that his promise to give us the strength to face any problem is genuine.

One more thing about Satan:

4. **He is unalterably <u>CONDEMNED</u> to eternal destruction.**

**Satan will be thrown into the lake of fire, to be tormented forever.**

**And the devil, who deceived them, was thrown into the lake of burning sulfur.**

—**Revelation 20:10**

Satan is condemned to suffer God's judgment for eternity. He will not rule in hell; he will be judged in hell. He will not delight in inflicting suffering on others in hell; he will himself be suffering.

Satan is the Evil One. Although he will not get any pleasure out of others being in hell, he would rather have you suffering in hell with him than in heaven delighting in God's presence.

When King Herod (whom we read about in the story of Jesus' birth) faced death, history tells us that he ordered the execution of prisoners he held captive at the moment he breathed his last. He knew that no one would weep when he died; he had killed most of his own family in fear of their taking his throne. The deaths of these prisoners would guarantee tears at his death. That's a picture of Satan's attitude.

## Teaching Tip

One of the keys to good teaching is constantly asking yourself, "What are those listening to me thinking right now?" When you can anticipate their feelings or questions and then give answers to those questions, you will teach truth in a way that will be remembered. There is no better example of this than Jesus, who patiently waited for his disciples to have the questions before he taught them the truth.

As you are teaching about Satan's work in the world, it's likely that some who are listening may feel overwhelmed right now. Perhaps even frightened. Take a few moments to give them some encouragement.

Does all this talk about Satan scare you a bit? It doesn't have to. Some of you may be wishing you hadn't come today. You already have enough problems without hearing about all that Satan might throw at us! I have some good news for you. We don't have to be afraid of Satan because God's power is greater.

The reality of Satan and his work should make us alert, but never afraid. We are in a battle; no doubt of that. But we know that God will win the war! There are two lines of thinking that you and I must reject. Reject the thought that the battle does not involve you. Every Christian is on the front lines in the battle against evil, whether you want to be there or not. Satan will fight your growth and influence and faith and joy for the rest of your life. Second, reject the thought that you will be over-whelmed in this fight by Satan's force. God's power is immeasurably greater than Satan's, and he will inevitably win this victory.

> Discussion question 5 can be used here.

There is a third reason evil exists in the world.

# Mankind's Choice: Because We ACCEPT Evil

Evil is present in this world because we choose to do evil things. Don't blame God for that, and don't blame Satan either. You want someone to blame?

**Remember two truths:**

1. **Evil began with <u>THEM</u> (Gen. 3).**

Blame Adam and Eve.

We all enjoy pointing a finger at someone else, so let's do that for a moment. Evil began with *them*. Adam and Eve made the choice to sin. God said, "Do not eat from the tree of the knowledge of good and evil." And they ate the fruit of that tree.

**The choice that Adam and Eve made to sin had horrible consequences:**

- **If they ate of the tree they would "surely die." Sin brings death: spiritual and physical death.**

   **But you must not eat from the tree of the knowledge of good and evil, for when you eat of it you will surely die.**

   **—Genesis 2:17**

Adam and Eve suffered immediate spiritual death, separation from God. Eventually, they suffered physical death because of their sin. God had made them to live forever, but they would now face death.

- **Because they ate from the tree, they were banished from the Garden of Eden. Sin causes us to live in a fallen, imperfect world.**

    **So the LORD God banished him from the Garden of Eden to work the ground from which he had been taken.**
    —Genesis 3:23

    God made us to live in a perfect world, not in a world with all of the problems you see today. Sometimes you hear natural disasters referred to as acts of God. If you want to be biblically accurate, you would call them "acts of Adam."

- **Adam and Eve passed along to us as their children a sin nature. Sin became a part of all of us when they bit into that fruit. That's why we all inevitably sin. We cannot refuse the temptation of evil.**

    **This is called "original sin." We don't start with a clean slate. We all start with the knowledge of good and of evil and with a flawed heart that causes us to sin.**

    Original sin means that babies are not born spiritually innocent. We are all spiritually separated from God from birth, with a propensity to sin. Adam and Eve's sin affected the entire human race. You cannot choose not to ever sin. "For all have sinned and fall short of the glory of God" (Rom. 3:23).

    If you tell your three-year-old child, "You can play with everything else in this room except for this one small crystal vase that Grandma gave us," what will likely happen if you leave the room? Right—a beeline for the vase! It's our human nature that if a line is drawn in the sand, we desire to step over it.

    **Therefore, just as sin entered the world through one man, and death through sin, and in this way death came to all men, because all sinned.**
    —Romans 5:12

    Circle "because all sinned" in Romans 5:12. Not "all will sin," but "all sinned." Do you see what this is saying? In Adam we all sinned. He served as the representative of the entire human race—and did what every one of us would have done in the same situation.

As tempting as it may be to blame someone else for our sin problem, we all know that this is not where the story ends. We'd love to think that if we'd been in the Garden of Eden, we would have obeyed God. It's not true. The painfully honest truth is that whenever presented with this choice, man has always gone after the evil.

That leads us to a second truth. Evil started with them, but we must each honestly admit

## 2. Evil is present in ME.

**It's not just "their fault." We need to be able to admit that "evil is present in me."**

Paul writes in Romans 7:21 about a hard truth that he had learned.

**When I want to do good, evil is right there with me.**

**—Romans 7:21**

Have you learned that truth about yourself?

Listen as I read these verses from Romans 3.

**What shall we conclude then? Are we any better? Not at all! We have already made the charge that Jews and Gentiles alike are all under sin. As it is written: "There is no one righteous, not even one; there is no one who understands, no one who seeks God. All have turned away, they have together become worthless; there is no one who does good, not even one."**

**—Romans 3:9–12**

We need Jesus Christ! Without Jesus these verses are all we are left with. With Jesus you get the rest of the book of Romans. With Jesus Christ you get hope. With Jesus you get righteousness. With Jesus you get spiritual life. Only Jesus can deal with our sin problem.

Aleksandr Solzhenitsyn, who saw firsthand the evil that was done in the Soviet prison camps under Joseph Stalin, writes in *The Gulag Archipelago,*

**The line separating good and evil passes not through states, nor between classes, nor between political parties—but right through every human heart.[4]**

The fact that evil is present in me must lead me to confess my need for God! This is why we studied salvation before studying this issue of good and evil. It would have been very depressing if I had told you, "Now you'll have to wait three weeks to hear what God has done for you." I wanted you to hear the good news first—that Jesus came to free us from our sin.

Discussion questions 6 and 7 can be used here.

# The Questions That Remain

## Why does God continue to allow evil? Why doesn't God stop it?

These are the questions we really struggle with. There are things that happen in this world that I can't understand, that I can't explain. Why would God allow a child to suffer and die from cancer? I'd love to stand here and guarantee you that God would heal any suffering child, but I can't tell you that. I can guarantee you that he loves that child. I can guarantee you that God has an eternal plan for his or her life in heaven. I can guarantee you that God will work through this circumstance. I can guarantee you all of those things based on what God tells us in his Word, but I cannot guarantee you that he will work in exactly the way we ask in every circumstance. I cannot guarantee you that he will insulate us from evil while we are in this world.

Why does God allow it? Remember a couple of things.

1. **He already has defeated evil (1 Cor. 15:57; Col. 2:15).**

   **He defeated evil at the cross and will allow us to join him in that victory for all eternity. We are fighting a battle in which ultimate victory is assured.**

   We know as we struggle that we will be victorious in the end because we know that he will be victorious in the end. That gives me hope as I fight the battle. One day we will join him in a victorious eternity in heaven. And some of those questions that we all have about why things happen as they do on earth he will explain. If I have a question, it will be answered. But many of those questions, much of what taxes our understanding on this earth, will just melt away the moment we see Jesus. Those questions won't have the importance that they have in this world because we'll see him for who he really is.

   Why does God wait for that day? Why doesn't he end all evil now?

2. **He is PATIENT.**

   When you see a situation in this world that breaks your heart, that makes you cry out in pain, how do you think God feels about that? If it hurts your heart, what do you think it does to the heart of God? His heart certainly cries out more than ours. As I said earlier, his hurt over sin and evil is deeper than we could possibly imagine. Why, then, doesn't he stop evil? Because he is patient.

**God has provided for the salvation of all (1 John 2:2).**

**God desires for all to be saved (1 Tim. 2:3–4).**

**And he waits patiently, desiring all to come to salvation (2 Peter 3:9).**

He is patiently waiting for more people to come to him. God could have brought down the curtain on this world a long time ago, and a lot of the evil that has happened in this world would not have happened. But the millions of people that have been saved during those years would not have been saved. Millions of people would not have been rescued from an eternity of separation from God.

---

### Key Personal Perspective

**How do you answer someone when they ask you a question like: "How could a perfect, good, and all-powerful God allow wars and disease in the world today?" When faced with tragedy our first impulse is to ask, "Why? Why would God allow this to happen?" The study has reminded us of some of the answers, for ourselves and for others.**

1. **The world is evil, not because of God's creation, but because of mankind's <u>CHOICE</u>.**
2. **God <u>CARES</u> about those who suffer.**
3. **It is God's proclaimed purpose to one day do away with evil.**
4. **The reason he waits is so that more people might be <u>SAVED</u>, therefore not having to suffer eternal separation from him.**

---

In the end, the only solution to the problem of evil is trust. How much do you trust God?

When you trust God you're not afraid to ask the tough questions—you know that he can give answers when we can understand and can give assurance when we cannot.

When you trust God you're not afraid to admit that much of the evil in our lives is our own doing—trust releases you from the need to blame.

When you trust God you begin to get a glimpse of things in the light of eternity. You realize that those who seem to be getting away with evil are not, and that those who seem to go unrecognized for the good they do will be.

When you trust God you feel his compassion for you and me as we face the evil in this world. And every once in a while a truth will wash over you, the truth that whatever hurt you feel because of evil is multiplied countless times in the heart of God.

When you trust you realize that you may or may not get an answer for the questions you have, but that even without the answer you seek you can still trust the answerer.

Let's pray together. Why don't you hold hands around your table or with those on either side of you. We are all in this together.

> *Lord, I know that those who are holding hands with each other right now may have had the opportunity during this year to talk personally about the ways that evil is impacting their lives. It may be as obvious as someone who has clearly sinned against us, or it may be one of those circumstances that leave us asking, "Why?" Help us to be honest about the now but also hopeful about the future. We choose to remember what a good God you are, and what a loving God you are, and what a patient God you are. We choose to trust you as a good and loving God, to rest in the fact that you will one day bring justice to all evil. Thank you for forgiving me for the evil that I have done in my life. Father, lead us not into temptation and deliver us from evil. In Jesus' name, amen.*

**Begin working on memory card 8, "The Truth about Good and Evil."**

# Discussion Questions

1. Why do you think it's important that we be honest about the fact that we live in an evil world? What happens when we live in denial of the reality of evil?

2. Why do you think it was so important for God to give us free choice?

3. What is the difference between God allowing evil and God doing evil?

4. What is the thing that gives you the greatest hope and encouragement as you face personal suffering?

5. What has helped you to replace your fears of Satan and evil with faith in God?

6. Why is it unhealthy to always blame others for the evil in the world?

7. Jesus taught us to pray "deliver us from evil" (Matt. 6:13 NASB). In what circumstance would you like others to pray for you to be delivered from evil?

# Good and Evil
## Part 2

**Life Change Objective**

To enable you to live with victory over evil and Satan:

In one specific thought

In one specific habit

In one specific relationship

In one specific problem

**Summary Teaching Outline**

Set Your Mind on Victory

Be alert

Be humble

Be confident

Understand the Three Channels of Evil

The world

The flesh

The Devil

Overcome Evil in My Daily Life

Sin

Trials

Temptation

The Number 1 Principle for Overcoming Evil

**Teaching Tip**

The attitude of our heart has a tremendous impact on how we teach. How do you, as a teacher, keep your attitude full of enthusiasm and faith week after week? You need to find the things that prepare your heart to teach. For some it's listening to Christian music. For others it's a time of prayer. Some find their heart growing warmer as they, just before the study, meet and talk with those they'll be teaching. One of the steps of faithfulness that we take as teachers is to intentionally do the things that prepare our heart, not just our head, to teach.

It's not too difficult to think of a story that shows the reality of evil in our world. From natural catastrophes to national tragedies to personal crises, the presence of evil is a pervasive reality.

But the presence of evil is not the only story. Let me tell you a story of victory over evil.

Sam was a young man in a lot of trouble. He started drinking and taking drugs in junior high, and by the time he reached high school his life was completely controlled by these addictions. He felt nothing but emptiness and might very well have taken his own life if his sister had not found him putting a gun to his head. Through the encouragement of a family who showed him tough love but refused to give up on him, Sam came to faith in Jesus Christ. He got involved in a program called Celebrate Recovery, where he learned to trust God to live free from the control of his addictions. Sam now says,

> When I look back, I am thankful that I didn't have to go through years of wreckage before I realized that my life was out of control. I never would have thought that I would get sober before I was even old enough to drink. God had a different plan for my life.
>
> Today, my relationship with my family has been restored. God has used this trial in my life to bring my whole family closer together and now they all attend church. God gave me the desire to finish school and get my diploma and I am now attending college. The Lord has blessed me with a great job, as a teacher's assistant helping handicapped kids. One of the greatest blessings in my life is the relationships with real friends that love me for who I am and not what I have.
>
> The void in my life I was trying to fill with drugs and alcohol was finally filled when I surrendered my life to Christ. And as for my life being boring and not having fun, I can't tell you how many fun times and good memories I've had with my friends in Christ. Today, God has put a desire in my heart to help others. Now, God is using me, as a bridge, to help young people, like myself, get sober.

I am thankful to my family who never gave up on me and prayed for me continuously. I also thank my Lord and Savior, Jesus Christ, who has given me VICTORY over my addiction. He has given me a life worth living, a life of value and purpose. God has done for me what I couldn't do for myself.[1]

Make no mistake; the battle with evil will be a part of our lives as long as we live on this earth. But we can experience a large measure of victory in that fight. We can win a good number of the battles as we look forward to the day that Jesus will put an end to the war. Look at these verses and feel with me the excitement of victory.

---

**Key Personal Perspective**

**You are victorious over Satan!**

> Everyone who is a child of God conquers the world. And this is the victory that conquers the world—our faith.
>
> —1 John 5:4 (NCV)

> God stripped the spiritual rulers and powers of their authority. With the cross, he won the victory and showed the world that they were powerless.
>
> —Colossians 2:15 (NCV)

> But we thank God! He gives us the victory through our Lord Jesus Christ.
>
> —1 Corinthians 15:57 (NCV)

> Overwhelming victory is ours through Christ who loved us enough to die for us.
>
> —Romans 8:37 (LB)

---

Be sure to notice where that victory comes from. Circle in these verses the phrases: "child of God," "our faith," "with the cross," "through our Lord Jesus," and "through Christ who loved us." The victory is through Jesus Christ.

**In the last session we looked at the overall problem of evil. In this session we will focus on the personal battle that we all have with evil. As you see from the verses above, God has guaranteed us victory, but it does not come without a struggle. In this study we're going to look at how to win the battle with evil in your daily life.**

# Set Your Mind on Victory

## Be *Alert*

Blissful ignorance of evil is not the road to victory. Don't make the mistake of thinking that the victorious believer marches under the banner of an ostrich, with your head in the sand and tail in the air. It is impossible to gain victory by hiding your spiritual head in the sand and pretending that the enemy does not exist.

**The Bible gives us two powerful pictures to help us to be alert and aware:**

1. We live "<u>BEHIND</u> <u>ENEMY</u> <u>LINES</u>."

   **We know that we belong to God even though the whole world is under the rule of the Evil One.**
   
   —1 John 5:19 (GNT)

   When a soldier gets dropped behind enemy lines, he becomes very alert! He cannot grow comfortable in his surroundings because in every encounter there is the potential for discovery and disaster.

   In a spiritual sense, we as believers are behind enemy lines. That's not to say we cannot see the beauty of God's creation and his work in our lives while we are on this earth. But there is the potential for spiritual disaster in every circumstance and conversation.

   Some deal with this truth by hiding out from the world as much as possible. But that's like going spiritually AWOL! In John 17:15–18 Jesus prays for us, "My prayer is not that you take them out of the world but that you protect them from the evil one. They are not of the world, even as I am not of it. . . . As you sent me into the world, I have sent them into the world" (John 17:15–18).

   You're behind enemy lines. Stay alert.

2. Satan is a "<u>ROARING</u> <u>LION</u>."

   **Be self-controlled and alert. Your enemy the devil prowls around like a roaring lion looking for someone to devour.**
   
   —1 Peter 5:8

   First rule of lion trainers—never turn your back on the lion! By God's grace and strength we as believers can face this lion without fear, and we must face him. We must be aware of the fact that Satan is attacking us in an attempt to defeat us. As he attacks you may have noticed that Satan usually doesn't show up personally, pitchfork and all. In a few moments we'll look at the primary ways that these attacks come into our lives.

There is a second attitude that is vital for our eventual victory.

## Be _HUMBLE_

It's amazing how powerful an attitude humility is in defeating evil. As Proverbs 16:18 tells us, "Pride goes before destruction." One of the greatest and most famous military defeats in American history is that of General George Custer. Custer, the youngest man to ever be given the rank of general in the U.S. Army, serves as an example of the dangers of human pride. The day after his defeat, these words appeared in the _New York Times:_

> So far as an expression in regard to the wisdom of Gen. Custer's attack could be obtained at headquarters, it was to the effect that Custer had been imprudent, to say the least. . . . The movement made by Custer is censured to some extent at military headquarters in this city. The older officers say that it was brought about by that foolish pride which so often results in the defeat of men. It seems that a few days before Gen. Terry had offered four additional companies to Custer, but that officer refused them.[2]

—_New York Times,_ July 6, 1876

"That foolish pride which so often results in the defeat of men." Pride is even more dangerous on the spiritual battleground, where it always results in defeat. I need to recognize that I don't have the power in and of myself to defeat evil. Don't be a spiritual "General Custer," pridefully wanting the credit and honor for yourself and so losing the battle. Look at what God has to say to us in James 4:6–7:

**"God opposes the proud but gives grace to the humble." Submit yourselves, then, to God. Resist the devil, and he will flee from you.**

—James 4:6–7

### In every case, you start resisting Satan by SUBMITTING to God.

In _every_ case! You can either go against Satan on your power or submit to God and rely on his strength and power. On your own power it's like going up against an aircraft carrier in one of those orange fiberglass paddleboats you see on the pond in a city park. Try to battle Satan on your own and I have two words for you, "You're sunk." But in God's strength an entire fleet of ships joins your paddleboat—and Satan flees in the face of inevitable defeat.

Submitting to God is not a complicated process. It's simply a matter of admitting before him that you don't have the strength to handle something on your own and humbly asking for his help.

Be aware, be humble, and then . . .

## Be _CONFIDENT_

Can you be humble and confident at the same time? Of course. That's the description of the Christian life. Being humble means I'm not trusting in myself. Being confident means I'm putting trust in God.

- **Confident because of God's presence**

  **The one who is in you is greater than the one who is in the world.**
  —1 John 4:4

- **Confident because of God's promise**

  **The God of peace will soon crush Satan under your feet. The grace of our Lord Jesus be with you.**
  —Romans 16:20

- **Confident because of your prayers**

  **Jesus told us to pray with faith for personal victory over evil.**

  **Lead us not into temptation, but deliver us from the evil one.**
  —Matthew 6:13

Look at Jesus' prayer in Matthew 6:13 closely. Can you imagine Jesus lying to his followers? Of course not! Jesus taught us to pray victoriously about evil. Jesus would not have taught us to pray this way if it were not possible in our lives. His leadership and his deliverance are to bring about an entirely new direction and a completely different atmosphere in our lives.

> Discussion question 1 can be used here.

One of the reasons that we allow ourselves to get trapped by evil is a misunderstanding of how it makes its way into our lives. This is _vital_ information for every believer!

## Understand the Three Channels of Evil

**While Satan is the source of all evil, there are three different channels, or pipelines, through which evil has an opportunity to influence us as individuals. To live with victory, you must understand what these channels are and must know the biblical strategy for victory.**

The truth is, every battle requires a strategy. If you use the wrong strategy, you'll end up defeated.

Think about this for just a moment. Let me share with you a few everyday battles. I'll suggest some strategies for victory, and you tell me which ones will and will not work.

First, a young child who refuses to eat vegetables.

Would you:

- A. Give the child ice cream to eat instead.
- B. Tie the child to the high chair until they eat the carrots (or other vegetable).
- C. Pay $100 for every green been they eat.
- D. Stay at the table with the child and gently encourage them to eat.

Second, you learn that someone is gossiping about you at work.

Would you:

- A. Make up some juicy gossip about them.
- B. Hide Limburger cheese in their filing cabinet under "R" for revenge.
- C. Talk to the person who you know started the gossip.

Here's the point: in a battle, just doing something is not enough. You must do the right thing. Let's look at what God's Word has to say about how to be victorious over the three ways that evil comes into our lives: the world, the flesh, and the Devil.

## The **WORLD**

15

### Know your enemy

**In any battle, one of the keys to victory over an enemy is knowing and understanding that enemy.**

**The world means the philosophy and influence that reigns on this earth.**

The Bible uses the word *world* to refer to this planet that we live on. But it also uses the word to point to a "without God" philosophy of life. That's the meaning here—the idea of being "worldly."

Is the general philosophy of this world different from that of Christ? Without a doubt! Let me give you a few examples. The world says, "The more you have, the happier you'll be." "If you don't look out for yourself no one else will." "If it feels good, do it."

You get the idea. Read with me 1 John 2:16.

**For everything in the world—the cravings of sinful man, the lust of his eyes and the boasting of what he has and does—comes not from the Father but from the world.**

16

—1 John 2:16

Circle "cravings," "lust," and "boasting." Those are the big three. The craving for possessions, lust after our passions, and boasting in our pride are at the center of the way the world thinks.

## Strategy for victory

**What is the personal choice that I can make to begin to enjoy victory on this particular battleground?**

**LOVE the Lord.**

Look closely at 1 John 2:15–17.

**Do not love the world or anything in the world. If anyone loves the world, the love of the Father is not in him. For everything in the world—the cravings of sinful man, the lust of his eyes and the boasting of what he has and does—comes not from the Father but from the world. The world and its desires pass away, but the man who does the will of God lives forever.**

—1 John 2:15–17

The reason we fall into the world's way of thinking is because of our love for the things of this world. We love them because we think they will make us happy, will bring us contentment, will offer us security. The only way to escape the allure of our love for these things of the world is to find a greater love!

We all need a greater love in our lives. This longing is one of the reasons that there are so many love songs. A quick search through Internet pages devoted to love songs revealed entire websites devoted to:

Medieval love songs

Famous jukebox love songs

Love songs for those who have been in love more than once

Love songs for the harmonica

Love 'em and leave 'em love songs

The 100 best love songs

The 25 best love songs

The 10 best love songs

Romantic love songs

Silly love songs

Love songs to myself

There's nothing wrong with romantic love. But it cannot meet the deepest need in our lives. That is met through our relationship with the God who made us. Our love for God is not a romantic love, but a relational love. A depth of love for the Lord is not developed in an instant—no great love is. As you spend time with him, you'll see the things of this world becoming less and less important to you and the things of God becoming more and more important.

## The **FLESH**
**Know your enemy**

---

### A Fresh Word

Two meanings for flesh in the Bible:

1. Our physical bodies (1 Cor. 15:39; John 1:14)
2. Our spiritual "disposition to sin" (1 Cor. 3:3 NASB)

This is important stuff! There is a huge difference between saying, "Our bodies are evil" and "Our flesh is evil."

Remember our study of the Holy Spirit? Our bodies are meant to be temples of the Holy Spirit! First Corinthians 15 tells us that our bodies will one day be resurrected to eternal life. Sin starts in our unwilling hearts, not our physical bodies. Sin comes from the inside out rather than outside in. The heart is where the evil is. We don't think evil things because we live in an evil world; we live in an evil world because we think evil things (Matt. 15:10–20)!

---

### Strategy for victory

> You, my brothers, were called to be free. But do not use your freedom to indulge the sinful nature; rather, serve one another in love. . . . So I say, live by the Spirit, and you will not gratify the desires of the sinful nature.
> —Galatians 5:13, 16

**SERVE** one another in love.

**LIVE** by the Spirit.

The choice before us is made very clear in Galatians 5:13 and 16. Paul is writing to believers, warning them against the temptation to indulge our sinful nature. Here are the alternatives God gives us: indulge yourself or serve others. Live for yourself or live by the Spirit. If you don't choose to serve, you'll end up being selfish. If you don't live by the Spirit's guidance, your plan will always default to some means for pleasing yourself.

The secret to victory is not in trying to stop being selfish but in choosing to start serving others.

The secret to victory is not in trying to stop following the flesh but in choosing to start following the Spirit.

## *The Devil*

### Know your enemy

**See the last session's study.**

Quick quiz from last week:

> Does Satan always dress in red?
>
> Is Satan the ruler in hell?
>
> Does Satan ever tell the truth (just enough of it to draw you into the trap)?

Concerning knowing our enemy, Satan, J. I. Packer wrote:

> On the one hand, we can take Satan too seriously, as some in the early church and the Middle Ages did. This will cause us to fall out of the peace of God into morbid fears and fancies.... On the other hand, we can err by not taking the devil seriously enough.... Unwillingness to take the devil seriously has two bad effects: it fools men, by keeping them from the knowledge of their danger as objects of the devil's attacks, and it dishonors Christ by robbing the cross of its significance as a conquest of Satan and his hosts.[3]

Discussion question 2 can be used here.

### Strategy for victory

**Put on spiritual <u>ARMOR</u>.**

> **Therefore put on the full armor of God, so that when the day of evil comes, you may be able to stand your ground, and after you have done everything, to stand. Stand firm then, with the belt of truth buckled around your waist, with the breastplate of righteousness in place, and with your feet fitted with the readiness that comes from the gospel of peace. In addition to all this, take up the shield of faith, with which you can extinguish all the flaming arrows of the evil one. Take the helmet of salvation and the sword of the Spirit, which is the word of God. And pray in the Spirit on all occasions with all kinds of prayers and requests. With this in mind, be alert and always keep on praying for all the saints.**
> **—Ephesians 6:13–18**

**What is this armor? Don't focus so much on the picture of belts and breastplates in Ephesians 6; focus on what the picture is communicating. Paul discusses seven things that are armor against the Devil's schemes:**

1. **Truth**
2. **Righteousness**
3. **Readiness to share the Good News**
4. **Faith**
5. **Salvation**
6. **God's Word**
7. **Prayer**

When Paul talks about the helmet of salvation, he's not trying to communicate that the truth of salvation protects our head and not our heart. The point is, we need these seven things in our lives if we are to be victorious. Leave any one of them out and you have left yourself vulnerable to attack.

> Discussion question 3 can be used here.

Let me ask you some questions with admittedly obvious answers.

Knowing we are in a constant battle with Satan, what days are the best days to make sure you put on the armor: weekends, weekdays, or every day? Armor is no good unless you put it on!

Knowing that you are going to face a daily battle with evil, when do you think is the best time to put on the armor: at the beginning of the battle, halfway through the battle, or just before you are about to perish in the battle? You get the point. Put the spiritual armor on as the day begins! Why wait until you're full of Satan's darts?

Knowing that we are weak and vulnerable at many points, how much of the spiritual armor do you wear? Right. All of it!

How do you put on spiritual armor? Spiritually, of course! In your spirit, recognize God's protection of truth and the new righteousness you have in him. Some people do this mentally even before they get out of bed in the morning. It might be better for others to take this step before you go to sleep at night!

> **Split Session Plan:** If you're teaching this study over two sessions, end the first session here.

I love the title to a little out-of-print book on Christian growth: *How Come It's Taking Me So Long to Get Better?* It's a question we've all asked! The book's author, a Navy pilot during the Second World War, compares our growth as believers to the way the Marines would capture an island in the South Pacific. They would first establish a beachhead on the island, securing a relatively small piece of land. From that beachhead, successive waves of Marines would begin to fan out and take the island. The beachhead was taken very quickly, but winning the victory in the rest of the island might take weeks or months, sometimes even years.

There is an obvious parallel to how we, as believers, win the victory over evil in our daily lives. The moment we come to Christ, God establishes a beachhead in our lives. He sends his Spirit into our lives and gives us all of the promises in his Word. But the process of victory takes longer. Sometimes a lot longer. We have sudden victories, but more often victory comes in little steps in a painstaking process. God works to overcome evil in our lives one day at a time.

## Overcome Evil in My Daily Life

22

**There are many ways that we must face the reality of evil in the choices and circumstances of our daily lives. How do I enjoy God's victory when I face these different types of evil in my life?**

### *Sin*

23

**We face evil because of our personal choice to sin.**

> **Jesus replied, "I tell you the truth, everyone who sins is a slave to sin."**
> **—John 8:34**

Circle the words "slave to sin" in John 8:34. Sin enslaves us to the pride, passions, and possessions that we talked about earlier. It is a horrible feeling to wake up one morning and realize that the possessions you own have begun to own you. Even as believers in Christ, some know that a sin you have allowed into your life is slowly taking control of more and more of your life. You tell yourself you can stop anytime you want, but the truth is you're spending more and more of your time thinking about that sin and more and more of your energy trying to hide that sin.

**Want victory? Decide to <u>REPENT</u>.**

**But if we confess our sins to God, he will keep his promise and do what is right: he will forgive us our sins and purify us from all our wrongdoing.**

—1 John 1:9 (TEV)

A few weeks ago we looked at the definition of repent, which is to change your direction. Look at Acts 3:19.

**Repent, therefore, and return, in order that times of refreshing may come from the presence of the Lord.**

—Acts 3:19

Repentance equals refreshment!

Knowing that we will be refreshed by our repentance doesn't make it easier to repent. I know I am a sinner, but it is still a struggle to admit that I sin. We have an inner reluctance to repentance—our human pride. Parents, you see this in your children—am I right? Or do you all have perfect kids who, even before you discover a broken vase, say, "I was the one who broke the vase because I was being disobedient and throwing a football in the house." In your dreams! God sees the same kind of disobedience in you and in me as his children. We blame others, we excuse our sin, we pretend it's not a problem—anything but repent. And all the time God is promising from heaven, "If you'll only turn around, I can refresh your life in greater ways than you could imagine."

## *Trials*

**We face evil because we live in this fallen world. And we face the painful circumstances that are an inevitable part of living in this fallen world. We can bring those trials on ourselves, but they sometimes come through no fault of our own.**

Listen to C. S. Lewis's famous quote about how God uses the problems in our lives:

**God whispers to us in our pleasures,**

**speaks in our conscience,**

**but shouts in our pains:**

**it is His megaphone to rouse a deaf world.**[4]

—C. S. Lewis

We talked a couple weeks ago, as we were looking at sanctification, about the truth that God grows us through our problems. And we can't be reminded of this too often. God works in our lives, not in spite of, but even through the difficulties we face. How does he do this?

**Want victory? Decide to <u>REJOICE</u> (Matt. 5:12; Rom. 5:3–4).**

> **James, a servant of God and of the Lord Jesus Christ, To the twelve tribes scattered among the nations: Greetings. Consider it pure joy, my brothers, whenever you face trials of many kinds, because you know that the testing of your faith develops perseverance. Perseverance must finish its work so that you may be mature and complete, not lacking anything.**
> **—James 1:1–4**

You don't rejoice that you have trials—that would be crazy. You rejoice because you know that God is working even through the trials. We are thankful *in* all things, knowing that God is developing our character as we trust him with even the worst that the Evil One throws at us.

### Key Personal Perspective

**Two reasons God allows problems in our lives:**

1. **To develop maturity (James 1:1–4; Rom. 5:3–4).**
   **God can bring ultimate good out of temporary evil (Gen. 50:20; Rom. 8:28).**
2. **To enable <u>MINISTRY</u> (2 Cor. 1:3–7 LB).**

Second Corinthians 1:4 tells us that God "comforts us in all our troubles, so that we can comfort those in any trouble with the comfort we ourselves have received from God." You'll eventually be able to comfort someone else with the comfort that you receive from God as you face a trial. Your greatest ministry will likely come out of your greatest pain.

## *Temptation*

**We face evil because Satan tempts us to do wrong.**

Listen to Bruce Wilkerson's description of how temptation feels.

> You are tempted "when" something takes place—if it didn't take place, you couldn't enter into temptation. "Each is tempted when he is drawn away." The words "drawn away" are borrowed from the fishing and hunting context in which an unsuspecting fish is slowly drawn out of its original retreat under a bank or in a hole or when an animal is tracked into the area in which traps are set. The picture is of a person being distracted with something which draws their attention away from what it is currently focused on. . . .

Consider how this happens: a noise, someone walks past you, a telephone call, a "distracting thought" that seems to come from nowhere, a letter, a person who cuts right in front of you enroute to the office, a unique smell which instantly brings back old memories of previous sins, your neighbor puts in a beautiful new pool next to your ugly backyard, the cashier mistakenly gives you $20 too much change, someone shares a tasty piece of gossip, the married co-worker in the next office starts dropping hints about what could happen on the upcoming business trip. . . . Skillful temptation warriors learn how to discern almost instantly when they are being drawn away—and instantly draw back![5]

Temptation is different from sin! It's not a sin to be tempted; it is a sin to give in to temptation. You cannot keep from being tempted, but you can decide not to say yes to the temptation and sin. As Martin Luther used to say, "You can't stop birds from flying over your head, but you can stop them from building a nest in your hair."

### Want victory? Decide to <u>REJECT</u> (Luke 22:46; Luke 4:1–13).

32

It's interesting that the Bible never tells us to resist temptation, but instead calls for us to reject it outright. Don't get in a tug-of-war with temptation. It always tugs back and you find yourself getting pulled into the mud pit. Instead of resisting, reject. I'll say more about this tug-of-war in a moment.

Because temptation is so much a part of our daily battle with evil, let's spend a few more minutes on this. Temptation wilts in the presence of the truth. Here are . . .

### Four truths to remember about temptation:

33

1.  **Temptation will always be a part of our lives (Luke 4:2; 1 Thess. 3:5).**

    I don't care how much you grow as a believer; you'll always face temptation.

    **Jesus was perfect, and he was tempted.**

2.  **It is not a sin to be tempted; it's a sin to give in to the temptation.**

    **Jesus was tempted, but he never sinned (Matt. 4:1; Heb. 4:15).**

    Here's how Satan tries to trap you. You face a temptation. The Devil tells you that you're unholy just because you felt tempted and causes you to feel guilty. And then (can you hear the trap snapping shut?) he says something like, "You already feel guilty. You might as well go ahead and sin."

Erwin Lutzer said,

Temptation is not a sin; it is a call to battle.[6]

—Erwin Lutzer

### 3. We all face the same temptations.

**When the woman saw that the fruit of the tree was good for food and pleasing to the eye, and also desirable for gaining wisdom, she took some and ate it. She also gave some to her husband, who was with her, and he ate it.**

—Genesis 3:6

**These are the ways of the world: wanting to please our sinful selves, wanting the sinful things we see, and being too proud of what we have. None of these come from the Father, but all of them come from the world.**

—1 John 2:16 (NCV)

There they are again, the big three: Pleasure, Possessions, and Power. You can see them from the first sin in Genesis all the way to God's words to us in First John. Sin may come in a lot of different packages, but these are the only three flavors.

There is something about our human nature that loves to think our temptations are unique. "No one has ever faced the kinds of pressures that I'm facing," we tell ourselves. Don't flatter yourself. You're just not that creative! There is nothing new under the sun. We're facing the same temptations that people faced thousands of years ago. Folks used to covet their neighbor's horse; now it's our neighbor's Porsche. Same temptation.

### 4. There is <u>ALWAYS</u> a way of escape.

**No temptation has seized you except what is common to man. And God is faithful; he will not let you be tempted beyond what you can bear. But when you are tempted, he will also provide a way out so that you can stand up under it.**

—1 Corinthians 10:13

Always? Always! Let me emphasize that by saying it again. Always!

We can take the phrase "I just couldn't help myself" out of our vocabulary! God's promise in First Corinthians 10:13 tells us we'll never face a greater temptation than we can handle—never. For the Christian, there is no such thing as an irresistible temptation.

Let me give you a little spiritual exercise. When temptation comes your way, stare it down and say to it, "We both know that if I fall to you it isn't going to be your fault, it will be my choice. God has provided me a way out."

Maybe you've looked for God's way out—and couldn't find it. Does he hide it? No. He gives us specific directions for dealing with each type of temptation.

The way out of immoral passion is marked: *run*. Second Timothy 2:22 tells us to "flee youthful lust." Don't depend on your willpower. Get out of the situation as quickly as you can!

The way out of materialism is marked: *thanks* and *giving*. A thankful heart combined with the habit of giving will cause you to look at the things in your life with an entirely different perspective.

The way out of pride is marked: *serve*. Jesus himself is our example. Satan offered Jesus the world, trying to appeal to his pride. Jesus resisted this temptation with a decision to serve.

 **A Closer Look**

*An Often Asked Question*

**How do you deal with a "habitual sin"—the cycle of sin, confess, sin, confess?**

**Change the pattern to "sin—confess—*refocus*."**

**Sometimes we become our own worst enemy. The more we focus on what we're *not* going to do, the more we're tempted by it and drawn into doing it. If you get into a tug-of-war with Satan, you'll lose! The solution: Drop your end of the rope and walk away. Refuse to play Satan's game.**

**Here are four ways to refocus your thinking.**

**1. Worship.**

Worship is magnifying God. Anytime you can magnify God, you shrink the power of evil in your life. Draw near to God and he will draw near to you (James 4:8).

**2. Radical departure (Matt. 5:29–30).**

Cut off your right hand? Isn't that a little radical? Obviously Jesus is not speaking literally here—he is saying to do whatever it takes to get sin out of your life. For instance, wise Christian counselors advise those who are caught up in the sin of adultery to break it off and cease all contact. Even if that means changing jobs, churches, or moving to another town. Why? Because to break a sin pattern you often have to "radically depart" from a situation or circumstance that is causing you to stumble.

**3. Tell the truth; accountability with another person.**

This is the step that no one wants to take. This is the step that has the most power to change your life.

**4. Faithfulness over time.**

Don't be discouraged if you do not feel an immediate change. Think of it as balancing a scale. As you continue to put weight on the positive side, one day the scales will tip.

Discussion question 4 can be used here.

# The Number 1 Principle for Overcoming Evil

## Take the offensive!

- **When faced with inner accusation, picture the <u>CROSS</u>.**

One of Satan's names is "the Accuser." Through temptation or circumstances or the words of others, accusations will be thrown at you as a believer. You'll hear, sometimes just in your own thoughts, "You're not good enough." "How could God love someone like you?" "You'll never measure up." Instead of arguing with those inner thoughts of inadequacy, God invites us to focus on the cross of Christ. Whatever your inner turmoil over your faults and failures, Jesus died for you on that cross because of his love for you. And because of that death on the cross,

God took away Satan's power to accuse you of sin, and God openly displayed to the whole world Christ's triumph at the cross where your sins were all taken away.

—Colossians 2:15 (LB)

- **When faced with outer confrontation, picture yourself as <u>RESCUED</u>.**

The Lord will rescue me from every evil attack and will bring me safely to his heavenly kingdom. To him be glory for ever and ever. Amen.
—2 Timothy 4:18

[He] gave himself for our sins to rescue us from the present evil age.
—Galatians 1:4

Second Timothy 4:18 and Galatians 1:4 don't pull any punches. They talk about "every evil attack" we will face and the fact that we live in a "present evil age." They also talk about the greatest rescue operation ever completed. Jesus came from heaven down to earth to throw us a lifeline.

- **When faced with evil, do <u>GOOD</u>.**

Do not be overcome by evil, but overcome evil with good.
—Romans 12:21

This extremely significant verse tells us how important our focus is. You'll never defeat evil by focusing on evil: Satan and demons and the evil forces of this world. Evil is defeated by focusing on what is good and living what is good.

Romans 8:37 sums it all up. Read this verse with me.

We come through all these things triumphantly victorious, by the power of him who loved us.

—Romans 8:37 (NJB)

We face a daily battle, but we are being supplied with all we need for victory! No good thing will he withhold from us. He will give you what you need when you need it.

> World War II had been over for sixteen years, yet in the jungles, caves, and hill country of Guam a confused Japanese soldier was still in hiding. He defied capture and refused to surrender, mentally fighting a war that was over for his comrades almost two decades before. He did not know that World War II had ended, with his country going down in defeat....
>
> While Sergeant Ito Masashi was climbing over a rock near the American camp one day, the inevitable finally happened. He knew he was spotted. He froze. He thought he would be slaughtered when captured.... Ito braced himself for whatever might happen, but one of the men approached him gently and said, "You're all right now...."

The story of Sergeant Masashi reminds us of the condition of most of the people in the world today. They are unaware that a "spiritual war" was fought and that the battle was won when Christ went to the cross two thousand years ago.[7]

Evil is real. It impacts our lives every day. But you don't have to live in fear of Satan or of evil. God won the victory at the cross.

Let's think about some ways we can act on this truth as we close.

---

 **Acting on the Truth**

How can you overcome evil with good this week?

In one specific thought: how can you change your focus from what is evil to what is good in the way that you're thinking?

In one specific habit: how can you change a bad habit by instead committing to a good habit?

In one specific relationship: how can you begin to see what someone might have meant for evil as something that God can use for good?

In one specific problem: how can you rejoice in what God is doing in your life through a problem you're facing right now?

---

Discussion question 5 can be used here.

---

**Finish memorizing memory card 8, "The Truth about Good and Evil."**

# Discussion Questions

1. In what ways do you see God reminding you to put your confidence in him and not in yourself? Do any examples come to mind of how your confidence in Christ has been strengthened?

2. Through which "channel" does evil seem to exert its influence on you more often: the world, the flesh, or the Devil? Why do you think that is?

3. Which of the seven pieces of armor listed in Ephesians 6 have you found to be the most effective in giving you protection from evil? How do you put on this armor in your daily life?

4. What have you found to be the most effective way for you to deal with personal temptation? Do you struggle most with overcoming pride, pleasure, or possession (the temptation to be, to do, or to have)?

5. Talk together about how you would answer the four questions about our thoughts, habits, relationships, and problems in Acting on the Truth at the end of this study. Ask your group to pray for you in one of these areas this next week.

# For Further Study

Elwell, Walter, ed. *Topical Analysis of the Bible.* Grand Rapids, Mich.: Baker, 1991.

Geisler, Norman, and Ron Brooks. *When Skeptics Ask.* Wheaton, Ill.: Victor, 1990.

Lewis, C. S. *The Problem of Pain.* New York: Touchstone, 1996.

Little, Paul. *Know What You Believe.* Wheaton, Ill.: Victor, 1987.

Rhodes, Ron. *The Heart of Christianity.* Eugene, Ore.: Harvest House, 1996.

Yancey, Philip. *Disappointment with God.* Grand Rapids, Mich.: Zondervan, 1988.

Yancey, Philip. *Where Is God When It Hurts?* Grand Rapids, Mich.: Zondervan, 1990.

# The Afterlife

## Part 1

## Life Change Objectives

- To give you a deep understanding and gratitude for God's rescue from the certainty of an eternity without him.

- To change the way you think about yourself and others: from a focus on the here and now to a focus on eternity.

## Summary Teaching Outline

Is Hell a Real Place?

Why Was Hell Created?

Who Will Be in Hell?

What Happens to People in Hell?

    Emotional/relational torment

    Physical torment

    Spiritual torment

Where Do People Go Now When They Die?

    The progressive revelation of the afterlife in the Bible

    The intermediate state and the resurrection of the body

## Teaching Tip

Take a moment as you begin to teach today to remind yourself of the love you have for those you'll be teaching. As teachers, we need to love the truth and each person we are teaching. Leave out either one of those loves, and our teaching will be found wanting. There is no subject that begs to be taught with an attitude of love more than today's: the truth about hell.

Which section of the newspaper do you read first? (Front page . . . business . . . sports?)

I'd like to suggest that the most important section of the newspaper is the often ignored feature in small type buried in the back. The obituaries. I know one older man who reads this first, and if his name isn't there he knows he's going to have a great day! For most of us, death is something we'd rather ignore. Even as believers, we don't want to be thought of as pie-in-the-sky thinkers—we want to be firmly rooted in the here and now.

How many of you have called a friend over for coffee and started your conversation, "Let's talk about death." They might wonder what you put in their coffee! But the truth is, one of the keys to having a healthy perspective on life is knowing the real truth about death.

There is a great deal more interest in the afterlife today than there was only a few years ago. In the 1990s, 70 million Americans turned 50—there just might be a connection here!

Why are we studying this? First, the Bible has a lot to say about it. It is a subject that God obviously wants us to understand. Second, other people have a lot to say about it. Everyone has an opinion about death, and heaven, and hell. Many of the people you hear confidently talk about the afterlife have no clue as to what they're saying. They're just making it up.

Maybe you've gotten your ideas of the afterlife from the pop psychology of best-sellers and talk shows. Or it might just be ideas you've developed yourself—your own personal philosophy of death. The stark truth is, it doesn't matter what an actress like Shirley McClain or talk show host Oprah Winfrey or a person like you or me thinks. Who are you going to trust, Jesus Christ or a movie star? Your guesses or God's truth?

Only God, the creator of heaven and hell, can give us the real truth. Only Jesus, the one who died and rose again, is the genuine authority.

**All of us wonder about the end of our lives: how much time we have left, under what circumstances we will die, and just exactly what death will be like. The Bible gives us some clear truths about the end of our lives that we all need to understand. These truths affect the way we live today and the way we see the future.**

**In this session we'll look at what the Bible says about hell. We'll cover heaven in the next session (bad news first, then end on the good news!).**

Jot down the reference Ecclesiastes 7:4.

> Yes, a wise man thinks much of death, while the fool thinks only of having a good time now.
>
> —Ecclesiastes 7:4 (LB)

Now that's not a verse you'd put on next year's Christmas cards, but it does remind us of the wisdom of thinking about death. Only a fool would go through their entire life knowing they're going to die and never preparing for and thinking about that certainty.

> Discussion question 1 can be used here.

**The most frequently asked questions about hell include:**

**Is there really a literal hell?**

**Why was hell created?**

**Who will be in hell?**

**What happens to people in hell?**

**Where do people go *now* when they die?**

**How can I be sure that I won't go to hell?**

You might be thinking, this is a session I wish I'd missed! It's my prayer that by the end of our time together you will have a better understanding of this horrible place that has become nothing more than a casual swear word for many people, and that you'll sense a deepening, even overwhelming gratitude to the Lord for your salvation.

## Is Hell a Real Place?

Our opinions on the existence of heaven and hell are interesting. Listen to these answers to a national survey reported in *Time* magazine.

Do you believe in the existence of heaven, where people live forever with God after they die?

Yes: 81%

No: 13%

Do you believe in hell, where people are punished forever after they die?

Yes: 63%

No: 30%[1]

The fascinating part of this study is that even in our nonjudgmental age, 63 percent of people still believe in a place called hell! One of the reasons is that the Bible is so clear about hell. Jesus is very clear in his teaching about heaven and hell.

**Jesus taught that hell is a real place of judgment. (In fact, there are more verses in which he taught about hell than about heaven.)**

> **Then they will go away to eternal punishment, but the righteous to eternal life.**
>
> —Matthew 25:46

> **Most assuredly, I say to you, he who hears My word and believes in Him who sent Me has everlasting life, and shall not come into judgment, but has passed from death into life . . . for the hour is coming in which all who are in the graves will hear His voice and come forth—those who have done good, to the resurrection of life, and those who have done evil, to the resurrection of condemnation.**
>
> —John 5:24, 28–29 (NKJV)

**The Bible speaks of a time of judgment that all human beings will have to go through. It is referred to in several verses as being a time of "separating" or "sorting" the righteous from the unrighteous.**

| Verse | Metaphor |
|---|---|
| Matthew 13:47–51 | A dragnet catching fish |
| Matthew 25:31–46 | Shepherd sorting sheep and goats |
| Matthew 13:24–30 | Harvester pulling weeds and wheat |

The Bible pictures it for us. There will come a day when the good fish are sorted from the bad, the sheep and goats are divided, the wheat is separated from the weeds. That day is obviously not here yet—but it is coming.

**Who is the one who judges and does the separating? JESUS, the only righteous one.**

Jesus is at the center of everything we teach about heaven and everything we teach about hell. He is at the center of this moment of separation and judgment.

> **For he has set a day for justly judging the world by the man he has appointed, and has pointed him out by bringing him back to life again.**
>
> —Acts 17:31 (LB)

As I talk about the reality of hell, some of you may be wrestling with the feelings expressed in this article that appeared in *U.S. News & World Report:*

> Many modern Christians are simply ashamed of hell.... In increasingly secular American culture, adds (Al) Mohler, "hell has become about as politically incorrect a concept as one can find." ... (Martin) Marty of the University of Chicago was moved to remark a few years back that "hell has disappeared and no one noticed."[2]

We read that Jesus taught that there is a place called hell, and we believe his words. Yet there is something in us that is still bothered by the reality of hell. On the one hand we long for judgment and fairness—we could not accept a Hitler or a Stalin having the same reward in eternity as Billy Graham or Mother Teresa. On the other hand, we wonder how and why God could have created such a place. We ask ourselves if it wouldn't have been better if it just didn't exist. We're going to answer those questions as we walk through this study together.

There *is* a place called hell. But why? Nothing can be created apart from God.

Why would a loving God create such a place?

## Why Was Hell Created?

- **Hell was not created originally for any human being, but for <u>SATAN</u> <u>AND</u> <u>HIS ANGELS</u>.**

  **Then he will say to those on his left, "Depart from me, you who are cursed, into the eternal fire prepared for the devil and his angels."**
  **—Matthew 25:41**

  **These are the angels who followed Satan when he tried to lead a rebellion against God in heaven. They are also called demons.**

  Would you circle two words in Matthew 25:41. First circle "prepared." Hell is no accident, it is a place prepared by God. Circle also the word "depart." That tells you why God would prepare such a place. Satan and his angels originally lived with God in heaven, but left God's presence by their own choice. Satan chose to live outside of God's presence. His residence now is our earth, but it cannot always remain that way.

- **Contrary to popular opinion, Satan is not yet confined to hell. He now resides <u>ON EARTH</u>.**

Four times in the Gospels, Jesus called Satan the "prince of this world."

Now is the time for judgment on this world; now the prince of this world will be driven out.

—John 12:31

Satan can live apart from God on earth—even as many people in this world live a life separated from God. That's the choice Satan made. But what will happen when this earth is no longer a place where you can live separate from God?

- One day (according to the book of Revelation), God is going to cast Satan, death, and Hades into the <u>LAKE</u> <u>OF</u> <u>FIRE</u> (another name for hell).

And the devil, who deceived them, was thrown into the lake of burning sulfur, where the beast and the false prophet had been thrown. They will be tormented day and night for ever and ever.

—Revelation 20:10

Then death and Hades were thrown into the lake of fire. The lake of fire is the second death.

—Revelation 20:14

One day God will create a new heaven and a new earth. Nothing in this new creation will be separate from God! But Satan chose long ago not to be a part of this new creation. His choice to rebel against God condemned him to eternal separation from God. That's why hell was originally created, as a place of separation from God for Satan and his demons.

It's important to understand that Satan will not rule in hell; that's a picture we get from books and movies, but not from the Bible. Satan will be tormented in hell.

Discussion question 2 can be used here.

## Who Will Be in Hell?

Hell was created for Satan and the demons, but they, sadly, will not be the only ones in hell for eternity.

The facts of life and eternity that we must all eventually face are:

- We were all headed for an eternity without God in hell.

All have sinned and are not good enough for God's glory.

—Romans 3:23 (NCV)

Some people have more good in them than others have, but Romans 3:23 tells us that all of us "are not good enough" for God's glory.

Heaven is a perfect place. I'm not perfect. You're not perfect. If God let you as an imperfect person into a perfect heaven, it would no longer be perfect. It doesn't matter how good you are, God's standard is perfection, a standard we cannot meet. The truth is, I wouldn't want to live for eternity in a heaven that was anything less than perfect, would you?

We'd like to believe that everything will turn out all right in the end, that we'll all get to heaven, but that's just not true. Listen to this quote based on an extensive survey of American attitudes concerning the afterlife.

> The unquenchable confidence in a joyous afterlife is embedded deep in our history and psyche.... Americans believe it's our birthright to be happy. We guaranteed it in the Declaration of Independence. We feel we're entitled to it, and we'll sue somebody if we don't get it. Andrew Greeley, professor of sociology at the University of Chicago and a renowned author, supports the idea that Americans are increasingly optimistic about the afterlife. "Belief in hell has decreased," he says. "But belief in heaven has not. People have a conviction that God wouldn't do that to them."[3]

Lying to ourselves about how desperate our situation is if we continue to remain apart from God does absolutely no good. In fact, it does devastating harm; it keeps us from recognizing a second truth.

- **Jesus came to rescue us from this certainty of separation from God.**

**He is the one who has rescued us from the terrors of the coming judgment.**
**—1 Thessalonians 1:10** (NLT)

**Only Jesus can rescue us because only he can offer us forgiveness for the sin that is the reason we would spend eternity in hell.**

We needed rescue; God sent a rescuer! I don't know of a clearer way to state the real love that God has for each of us.

- **Those who trust Jesus _are_ rescued!**

**Therefore he is able, once and forever, to save everyone who comes to God through him. He lives forever to plead with God on their behalf.**
**—Hebrews 7:25** (NLT)

Billy Graham wrote:

> Will a loving God send a man to hell? The answer from Jesus and the teachings of the Bible is, clearly, "Yes!" He does not send man willingly, but man

condemns himself to eternal hell because in his blindness, stubbornness, egotism, and love of sinful pleasure, he refuses God's way of salvation and the hope of eternal life with Him.

Suppose a person is sick and goes to a doctor. The doctor diagnoses the problem and prescribes medicine. However, the advice is ignored and in a few days the person stumbles back into the doctor's office and says, "It's your fault that I'm worse. Do something."

God has prescribed the remedy for the spiritual sickness of the human race. The solution is personal faith and commitment to Jesus Christ. Since the remedy is to be born again, if we deliberately refuse it, we must suffer the horrible consequences.[4]

- **Those who do not trust Jesus are *not* rescued from hell and separation from God.**

  **And this is the testimony: God has given us eternal life, and this life is in his Son. He who has the Son has life; he who does not have the Son of God does not have life.**

  —1 John 5:11–12

To act as if God is at fault for people going to hell is the same as blaming the judge and jury when a guilty murderer is convicted.

This means that whenever you hear someone ask the question, "Why would God send people to hell?" you know that their perspective is upside down. God doesn't send anyone to hell. We do that to ourselves because of our sin. Based on our choice to sin, all of us are headed for an eternity separated from God. God would have been entirely just to allow us to suffer the consequences of our rebellion. But his love for us would not let him stand aloof and watch this happen. He sent his Son to rescue us!

## Key Personal Perspective

**What about the people I love?**

**After we ourselves have been rescued from hell by trusting in the grace and love of Jesus, our minds immediately turn to those we love. The thought of their spending eternity separated from God is almost too painful for us to bear.**

**If they're still living, <u>DON'T GIVE UP HOPE</u>!**

**Let those you love know the Good News that God can rescue them too. Many who initially reject God's invitation to life and forgiveness through Jesus end up accepting him. (The apostle Paul was one of those.)**

If they've already died, <u>TRUST</u> <u>THEM</u> <u>TO</u> <u>GOD</u>.

**Remember that God is the ultimate judge of eternity; you are not. Instead of getting caught up in worrying about changing what you cannot change, leave it with God. Let your concern motivate you to share with those who are still living the hope that Jesus gives. And make sure that those you love have no doubt about your faith in Christ and the fact that you know you are going to heaven when you die.**

Discussion question 3 can be used here.

**Split Session Plan:** If you're teaching this study over two sessions, end the first session here.

What's hell like?

In hell the mathematician who lived for his science can't add two and two. The concert pianist who worshiped himself through his art can't play a simple scale. The man who lived for sex goes on in eternal lust, with no body to exploit. The woman who made a god out of fashion has a thousand dresses but no mirror! Hell is eternal desire—eternally unfulfilled.

But there's another side. G. K. Chesterton once remarked, "Hell is God's great compliment to the reality of human freedom and the dignity of human personality." Hell, a compliment? Yes, because God is saying to us, "You are significant. I take you seriously. Choose to reject me—choose hell if you will. I will let you go."[5]

C. S. Lewis said it this way,

There are only two kinds of people in the end: those who say to God, "Thy will be done," and those to whom God says, in the end, "Thy will be done." All that are in hell, choose it. Without that self-choice there would be no hell. No soul that seriously and constantly desires joy will ever miss it.[6]

God does not want us to be separated from him. That's why he sent his Son to die for us, taking our place. That is why he so clearly warns us concerning what will happen to those who are separated from him in hell.

# What Happens to People in Hell?

 15

In this world even the worst sinner enjoys the benefits of God's presence. Even though this world is stained by sin, we still experience the joys of God's creation and his work. It will not be that way in hell.

What is hell like? The most horrible thing to be said is, "It is a place totally apart from God." No love, no creativity, no kindness, no forgiveness, no beauty, no light—no God.

As a place totally apart from God, hell is a place of torment.

**The Bible clearly teaches that hell is a place of never-ending torment, torture, and anguish.**

**Then they will go away to eternal punishment, but the righteous to eternal life.**

—Matthew 25:46

Look at what hell is like: not to delight in the fact that evil people will suffer but to have compassion and love for people who need the Lord and to praise God for rescuing us from hell.

## Emotional/relational torment

**But the subjects of the kingdom will be thrown outside, into the darkness, where there will be weeping and gnashing of teeth.**

—Matthew 8:12

**Do not be afraid of those who kill the body but cannot kill the soul; rather be afraid of God, who can destroy both body and soul in hell.**

—Matthew 10:28 (GNT)

Hell is not going to be a big party. You may have heard it said, "I'd rather party with my friends in hell than sit on a boring white cloud in heaven." There are no friends in hell. There are no parties. It's a place of separation and eternal disappointment and torment.

Look at Matthew 8:12: *Eternal* weeping and gnashing of teeth. When you make a decision that you regret, you grind your teeth in anger at your choice. That's what it means to "gnash" your teeth. Hell is a place of eternal regret.

Matthew 10:28 tells us that hell is a place of death, eternal death. People exist forever in hell, but it would be wrong to say they live forever there. It is a place of death.

## Physical torment

**So if your hand makes you lose your faith, cut it off! It is better for you to enter life without a hand than to keep both hands and go off to hell, to the fire that never goes out. And if your foot makes you lose your faith, cut if off! It is better for you to enter life without a foot than to keep both feet and be thrown into hell. And if your eye makes you lose your faith, take it out! It is better for you to enter the Kingdom of God with only one eye than to keep both eyes and be thrown into hell. There "the worms that eat them never die, and the fire that burns them is never put out."**

—Mark 9:43–48 (GNT)

Fire—this is what we usually focus on when we talk about what hell is like. Fire is a picture of the torment we face in this place of separation from God. Hell is not a place of cold nothingness. It is torture to be separated from all that God is. As horrible as the physical torment may seem, the spiritual suffering is even deeper.

## *Spiritual torment*

**Then he will say to those on his left, "Depart from me, you who are cursed, into the eternal fire prepared for the devil and his angels."**
—Matthew 25:41

**They will be punished with everlasting destruction and shut out from the presence of the Lord and from the majesty of his power.**
—2 Thessalonians 1:9

Look at these words in Matthew 25:41 and Second Thessalonians 1:9: depart from me . . . cursed . . . eternal fire . . . punished . . . shut out.

Jill Briscoe writes:

> I was talking about the realities of hell to a bunch of lively junior high kids. I wondered if they would be interested. They were! What's more, they came up with some definitions for me. "What do you think hell is really like?" I asked. "I think it's being allowed to take one good look at God and then never being allowed to look again," a 13-year-old boy announced seriously. I think he had one concept of hell right. It is the idea of exclusion from the very presence of God.[7]

Looking at this truth causes us to think twice before we callously think, hear, or say the words "go to hell" ever again. We wouldn't wish this on anyone! And God doesn't either. I want to come back to that in a moment, but there is a question we need to take some time to answer first.

Discussion question 4 can be used here.

# Where Do People Go Now When They Die?

At this point we're going to begin a very in-depth look at a number of things that have to do with the afterlife. Put on your spiritual scuba gear, because we're going to be diving very deep in the next few minutes. The truths we're going to look at take some thought, but the thought is worth it. Failing to understand the truths we'll be looking at leads to all kinds of false teachings and personal doubts.

For instance, some teach that we as believers don't go to heaven immediately when we die—that our souls "sleep" in the grave until Jesus comes again. That's not what the Bible teaches. Others teach that believers, before they go to heaven, are punished for their sins in a place called purgatory. Again, that's *not* what the Bible teaches, and we'll see why. These are just a couple examples of the confusion and false teaching on the afterlife. We're going to clear up the confusion in the next few minutes.

**According to New Testament teaching, believers go immediately into the presence of God to await resurrection of the body and the eternal joy of heaven. Unbelievers go to Hades for punishment and to await the resurrection of the body and final punishment in hell.**

That's the simple truth—and we could end it there. But then I'd be leaving you without the assurance that you need. I don't want you to think that I assured you that you will immediately be with Jesus when you die. I want you to know that "*God* assures you" you'll be with him. To have that assurance, let's jump into that in-depth Bible study.

**This simple statement brings up a *lot* of questions! These include the growth in New Testament and Old Testament teaching concerning the afterlife, the intermediate state between now and Jesus' final judgment, and the future resurrection of the body. Because a great deal of false teaching and unfounded fears grow out of a misunderstanding of these truths, we'll take an in-depth look at them.**

## *The progressive revelation of the afterlife in the Bible*

The Bible often gives us greater insight into a subject in the New Testament than in the Old Testament. This is called progressive revelation—which is God revealing more and more truth on a subject as we read through the Bible from beginning to end.

A friend says to you, "You aren't with the Lord when you die. I read in the Old Testament that we all go to a dark shadowy place called Sheol."

Your answer is, "But God didn't stop with the Old Testament. He gives us a lot more light on this!" It's easy to get confused about what the Bible teaches concerning the afterlife if you look only at the Old Testament.

1. **In much of the Old Testament, the afterlife was seen as shadowy and unknown.**

   You can see this through a study of a word that was most often used of the afterlife in the Old Testament: *Sheol.*

**Sheol**

**The Hebrew word *Sheol* is used sixty-six times in the Old Testament. The Old Testament consistently refers to the body as going to the grave, and the soul of man as going to Sheol. The earliest thought of Sheol indicates there was no distinction made in the minds of people between the morally good and the bad; all went to Sheol (Gen. 25:8; 37:35). As time went on, people began to believe that Sheol had sections; there is a contrast between the "lowest part" and the "highest part." While not clearly stated, it seems like the wicked are in the lowest part, while the righteous are in the highest part (Deut. 32:22).**

> Sheol is the beginning of our understanding of the afterlife, but God reveals much more! We come to know more and more about the afterlife as God reveals more throughout the Old Testament and into the New Testament. It's somewhat like a Polaroid picture, slowly developing before your eyes. The picture of the afterlife is a little clearer in Psalms than it is in Genesis, a little clearer in Daniel than in Psalms, and *much* clearer in the New Testament than in the Old. Just as we must understand what Leviticus says to us about the need for sacrifices of animals in light of what the New Testament tells us about the sacrifice of Jesus, we must understand what the Old Testament tells us about the afterlife in light of the New Testament's further revelation.
>
> So your answer to your friend who is telling you we don't go to heaven when we die is, "God tells us in the New Testament that we'll immediately be with Jesus when we die. What believers were unsure of in the Old Testament we can be sure about today!"

---

 **A Closer Look**

**While the Old Testament saints did not have a clear and precise understanding of what happens after death, this lack of understanding did not keep them from enjoying eternal rewards. They may not have known they were going into God's presence, but they certainly did go there.**

---

2. During the intertestamental period (the 400 years between the final events of the Old Testament and the first events of the New Testament) the Jewish concept of Sheol had progressed to the stage where it was believed that Sheol had two distinct compartments.

One section was a place of torment for the wicked, called <u>HADES</u>.

The other was a place of conscious bliss, often called <u>ABRAHAM'S BOSOM</u> or <u>PARADISE</u>.

Jesus told a story in which he talked about both Hades and paradise: the story of the rich man and Lazarus.

Now there was a rich man, and he habitually dressed in purple and fine linen, joyously living in splendor every day. And a poor man named Lazarus was laid at his gate, covered with sores, and longing to be fed with the crumbs which were falling from the rich man's table; besides, even the dogs were coming and licking his sores. Now the poor man died and was carried away by the angels to Abraham's bosom; and the rich man also died and was buried. In Hades he lifted up his eyes, being in torment, and saw Abraham far away and Lazarus in his bosom. And he cried out and said, "Father Abraham, have mercy on me, and send Lazarus so that he may dip the tip of his finger in water and cool off my tongue, for I am in agony in this flame." But Abraham said, "Child, remember that during your life you received your good things, and likewise Lazarus bad things; but now he is being comforted here, and you are in agony. And besides all this, between us and you there is a great chasm fixed, so that those who wish to come over from here to you will not be able, and that none may cross over from there to us." And he said, "Then I beg you, father, that you send him to my father's house—for I have five brothers—in order that he may warn them, so that they will not also come to this place of torment." But Abraham said, "They have Moses and the Prophets; let them hear them." But he said, "No, father Abraham, but if someone goes to them from the dead, they will repent!" But he said to him, "If they do not listen to Moses and the Prophets, they will not be persuaded even if someone rises from the dead."

—Luke 16:19–31 (NASB)

Here you get the idea of two distinct compartments. The rich man can see Lazarus in paradise, but he cannot cross over to the other side.

**A Closer Look**

Jesus' story in Luke 16 teaches us two hard-to-hear truths:
1. There is <u>NO REST</u> from torment.
2. There are no <u>SECOND CHANCES</u>.

You see how our God is increasing our understanding? First, people viewed all of the dead as going to a shadowy place called Sheol. Then God gave further light, and people understood Sheol as a place with two compartments: Hades for the wicked and paradise for the righteous. There is a clear line between the two that cannot be crossed.

After Jesus' resurrection, the picture gets even more clear.

3. **After Christ's resurrection, the New Testament teaches that believers who die enter immediately into the presence of Christ and that unbelievers enter immediately into a place of punishment and separation from God.**

**I am torn between the two: I desire to depart and be with Christ.**
—**Philippians 1:23**

Philippians 1:23 tells us that when we depart from this earth we are "with Christ."

Why am I taking you into this deep water of doctrine? Because false ideas about the afterlife grow out of not knowing that we go immediately to be with Jesus when we die, because of doubts that get planted in our minds about God's eternal plan for us. All believers of all times are now with the Lord in heaven, and that is where you and I will immediately go when we die. No waiting period. No purgatory. No soul sleep. Immediately in the presence of the Lord!

## The intermediate state and the resurrection of the body

**Therefore we are always confident and know that as long as we are at home in the body we are away from the Lord. We live by faith, not by sight. We are confident, I say, and would prefer to be away from the body and at home with the Lord.**
—**2 Corinthians 5:6–8**

The "intermediate state" is the phrase used by theologians to describe the state that those who die are in between now and the time that Jesus comes again.

Why the difference? Because while our souls go immediately to be with God or to suffer in Hades, our bodies have not yet been resurrected as Jesus' body was resurrected.

> They found the stone rolled away from the tomb, but when they entered, they did not find the body of the Lord Jesus.
> —Luke 24:2–3

Now that you've probably gone as deep as you'd like to go, I'm going to take you a little bit deeper!

We know that when we die it is our spirit that goes to be with Christ. But what about our body? Is it just thrown aside?

When Jesus was resurrected, what happened to his body? It was no longer in the tomb. Jesus' body disappeared from the tomb because his body was resurrected. His physical body was transformed to become a resurrected body that would live forever. When we as believers die, what happens to our bodies? Our spirits go to be with the Lord, but our bodies remain here on earth. Why the difference? Let's take a look at what the Bible has to say.

The Bible tells us clearly that:

- When Jesus was resurrected he had a resurrected body (John 20:19–20).

- We too will one day have a resurrected body (1 Corinthians 15:42–44).

- We receive that resurrected body when Jesus returns (1 Thessalonians 4:16–17).

Do not fear. Although the body awaits resurrection, when you die your spirit immediately goes to be with the Lord.

**Picture it like this:**

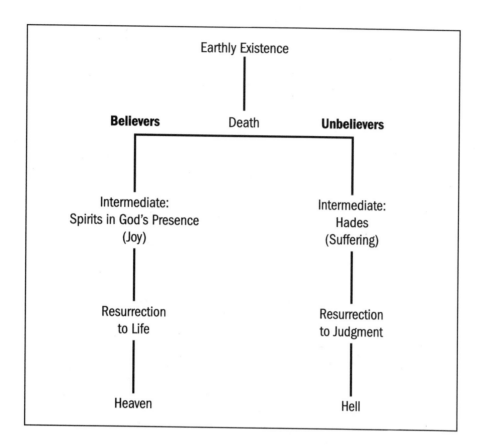

So, what do you look like in heaven while you're with him in spirit and have not yet received your resurrected body? The four-word theological answer: "We do not know." The Bible doesn't tell us.

By the way, there are a *lot* of things we don't know about the afterlife. God has told us just enough to help while we're here on earth. He doesn't burden us with things we don't need to know until we get there. Honestly, sometimes the questions we ask God are somewhat like your five-year-old walking up to you and saying, "Tell me what's going to be on my college entrance exam—I have to know today!" God's answer to us would be something like the answer we'd give our kindergartner, "If I told you now you wouldn't understand a word I was saying, and you have different things to be concerned with right now. Like cleaning your room!" In the midst of this study it's good to take a moment to admit something about us. We haven't even mastered spiritual finger painting (things like "love God" and "love people") and we're asking God to teach us calculus. The simple and straightforward question that we *can* all answer now is this:

### Key Personal Perspective

*How Can I Be Sure I Won't Spend Eternity in Hell?*

**What kind of crime does a person have to commit to be sent to such a horrible place? The crime that will send a person to hell is:**

<u>REJECTING</u> **Jesus Christ as the Son of God, the Savior we all need.**

For God so loved the world that he gave his one and only Son, that whoever believes in him shall not perish but have eternal life. For God did not send his Son into the world to condemn the world, but to save the world through him. Whoever believes in him is not condemned, but whoever does not believe stands condemned already because he has not believed in the name of God's one and only Son.

—John 3:16–18

*Remember:* **If you decide (by desire or by neglect) to live separate from God in this life, you'll live separate from him in the next life! But if you accept God's offer of a relationship with him through Jesus in this life, you'll live with God in the next life!**

In the end we will either say to God, "Thy will be done," or God will say to us, "Thy will be done."

At a church in the Los Angeles barrio, the youth pastor stood up to speak after a Christian concert. The singers had invited everyone there to make a commitment to Christ. Not only did no one respond, it was evident that no one was listening. The pastor looked at the back rows of the outdoor tent the concert had been held in and said, "All of you back there, . . . come up here. Andrew, José—I'm talking to you too—up here with me." As he called each of these teenagers by name, it was evident that this was no fly-by-night evangelist—he knew and loved these kids. The kids tried to look as cool as possible as they walked up the aisle, but this pastor knew them too well. "Before you leave tonight," he said, "listen to me. The message in this music tonight, this is serious business. You know what I'm talking about—in this neighborhood this might be the last time some of you hear this. This is about heaven and this is about hell—it's serious business about you."

We try our best in our society not to take hell "too seriously." We throw the word around as a casual swear word, and jokes about hell are all too common. But somewhere deep down we know we're whistling in the dark, that this is serious business.

Let's settle some serious business right now:

If Jesus has rescued you—thank him as you never have before.

If you're depending on yourself for that rescue and have neglected God's love for you, turn to him now. Cry out to him for the salvation that only he can give.

If you have friends or family who have died and you're frightened may be separated from God in hell, trust God as the perfect and just judge. Leave it in his hands.

If you have friends or family who are alive and who have not yet called upon Jesus to rescue them, ask God for a new boldness to tell them the Good News of Christ's love—the Good News that Jesus came to forgive our sins if we will trust him.

Let's pray together.

*Father,*

*As we study the truth about hell, it brings a hush over our soul. It is a truth that makes the right things seem so much more important. There is a place called hell—and that tells us how great our salvation truly is. There is a place called hell—and that impels us to tell others the good news of your life. There is a place called hell—and that motivates us to live the holy lives to which you've called us. Father, it's our prayer that one person could see in us and hear from us the difference that Jesus can make—and that they will be drawn to trust in you. Thank you, Father, that you sent Jesus to die on a cross—that you invite all people of all places and all times to find their hope in you.*

*In Jesus' name, amen.*

Discussion question 5 can be used here.

**Begin working on memory card 9, "The Truth about the Afterlife."**

## Discussion Questions

1. What do you think most strongly influences most people's beliefs and opinions about the afterlife?
   - The Bible
   - Other world religions
   - New Age thinking
   - Wishful thinking
   - Movies and television
   - Other _____

2. We've learned that there is a hell. What is it that most clearly reminds you that hell is a real place? Why is it important that there is a hell?

3. Take some time together as a group to pray two things:
   - Prayers of praise for Jesus' willing sacrifice on the cross to save us from hell.
   - Prayers for those you know who have not yet trusted Christ to save them.

4. Why do you think the Bible so clearly and graphically tells us that hell is a place of suffering?

5. How does it make you feel to realize that you, as a Christian, will never have to stand before God to be judged on whether you'll be in heaven or hell—it's already settled! Talk together about the confidence and the joy of knowing that we've already made the most important decision in our lives.

# The Afterlife
## Part 2

**Life Change Objectives**

- **Joy!!**

- **To decide to live in the light of eternity in one significant way the next week.**

---

**Summary Teaching Outline**

Where Is Heaven?

Who Will Be in Heaven?

How Will I Be Judged as a Believer?

   1. The great white throne judgment

   2. The "bema" judgment

What Will Heaven Be Like?

How Can Heaven Affect My Life Now?

---

I want to talk to you about a goal for your life that will change everything about your life. This is not one of those personal goals that we set and strive for, hoping that we will be able to reach them. I want to talk to you about one goal that you can be certain you will reach. This single goal is so important that just knowing we will reach it can change everything for you.

That goal is a place . . . called heaven. *Wait.* Don't tune me out. We have three boxes that we put things in as we set priorities: urgent, not urgent, and after I'm dead. Since heaven is in the third box, we all tend to not give it much attention—myself included.

And that's a big mistake. There is no greater truth to build your life on—to reduce your anxieties, to motivate in you genuine greatness—than this goal of heaven.

Listen to what the apostle Paul, who made a more-than-slight impact on this world, had to say about this goal in his life.

**I strain to reach the end of the race and receive the prize for which God, through Christ Jesus, is calling us up to heaven.**
—Philippians 3:14 (NLT)

The goal you should have your eye on, Paul says, is heaven. He compared it to a finish line. Paul often compared life to a race. (Not a bad picture.) What if I said to you, "I want you to run a race, but I'm *not* going to tell you where or when the finish line is." That would be pretty strange! One of two things happens when we aren't sure of the finish line:

We run a frantic race: we run as fast as we can, all of the time, just in case the finish line is around the next corner.

We run a frustrated race: since we don't know where we're headed, we slow down—maybe even stop—and hope that someone will come along to give directions.

We need finish lines—and the hope and reward of heaven is the ultimate finish line of life. Not that there is anything wrong with having other goals: for business or family or school. We should have goals. We need goals in life. But if you see them as the ultimate finish line, you'll be deeply disappointed! They're just not enough. We need the hope of heaven.

Look at Ecclesiastes 3:11. We're all born with an inner sense of what we're going to talk about in this study. We have an intuition that there is something greater and grander—that we were made for more than life on this earth.

**God has created men and women with a sense that this life is not all there is. The Bible says,**

He has also set eternity in the hearts of men.
—Ecclesiastes 3:11

**All of us know instinctively that the grave is not our final destiny. In the last session we explored what the afterlife will be like for unbelievers.**

Many questions remain about the specifics of the afterlife for believers:

Where is heaven?

Who will be in heaven?

How will I be judged as a believer?

What will heaven be like?

How can heaven affect my life now?

# Where Is Heaven?

If I told you you didn't have to be afraid of giving a wrong answer, then asked you to point to heaven, where would you point? Point with me. Yes—not down, not sideways—you would point *up*.

## Heaven is UP

About now some of you are saying to yourselves, "Wow, you're really a deep thinker! Heaven is up, I could have come up with that one."

The fact that a four-year-old points up when we say "where is heaven" may sound simplistic, but it is also deeply significant. The word *heaven* has always had the connotation of up.

LORD, I look up to you, up to heaven, where you rule.

—**Psalm 123:1** (GNT)

This grows out of the three ways that the word was used in Old Testament times.

In the Old Testament, heaven is spoken of figuratively in terms of layers of sky. The heavens are where the birds fly, the trees breathe, and the rain falls. This was referred to as the FIRST HEAVEN.

The heavens are also where the moon and stars move in their orbits. This was referred to as the SECOND HEAVEN.

The THIRD HEAVEN, or highest heaven, was said to be where God dwells in a special way.

That third heaven is not "up" in the sense that it is out there somewhere beyond the orbit of Pluto. The Bible does not tell us an exact location of heaven; it indicates that it is a place above anything we now know. It is higher than what we now experience, more than we could imagine, beyond all of the pain and confusion of this world.

The fact that heaven is God's dwelling place leads to the second deeply emotional picture that the Bible gives us of where heaven is.

### Heaven is <u>HOME</u>

The word *home* is such a powerful word. There is no more important "place." Although you may have grown up in a home that was far from what it should have been, every one of us has in our minds a picture of an idyllic home. It's a picture of deep personal fulfillment, unshakable security, rich and meaningful relationships, and lasting joy.

**Heaven is God's <u>DWELLING</u> <u>PLACE</u> and the <u>FINAL</u> <u>DWELLING</u> <u>PLACE</u> of believers.**

> I heard a loud shout from the throne, saying, "Look, the home of God is now among his people! He will live with them, and they will be his people. God himself will be with them."
>
> —Revelation 21:3 (NLT)

**One of the names given to heaven is the <u>HEAVENLY</u> <u>CITY</u>.**

> But they were looking for a better place, a heavenly homeland. That is why God is not ashamed to be called their God, for he has prepared a heavenly city for them.
>
> —Hebrews 11:16 (NLT)

Some stories are worth repeating. One of those is this experience of a husband and wife returning from the mission field that has made its way into many sermons and emails and has even been written into a song by Steven Curtis Chapman.

> An old missionary couple had been working in Africa for years and were returning to New York to retire. . . . Their health was broken; they were defeated, discouraged, and afraid. When they went down to the wharf to board the ship, they discovered they were booked on the same ship as President Teddy Roosevelt, who was returning from one of his big-game hunting expeditions.
>
> When they boarded the ship, no one paid any attention to them. They watched the tremendous fanfare that accompanied the President's arrival, . . . with passengers stationing themselves at vantage points to catch a glimpse of the great man. As the ship moved across the ocean, the old missionary said to his wife, "Something is wrong. Why should we have given our lives in faithful service for God in Africa all these many years and have no one care a thing about us? Here this man comes back from a hunting trip and everybody makes much over him, but nobody gives two hoots about us."
>
> His wife replied, "Dear, you shouldn't feel that way."
>
> But he said, "I can't help it; it doesn't seem right."

When the ship docked in New York, a band was waiting to greet the President. The mayor and other dignitaries were there. The papers were full of the President's arrival.

No one noticed this missionary couple. They slipped off the ship and found a cheap flat on the East Side, hoping the next day to see what they could do to make a living in the city.

That night the man's spirit just broke. He said to his wife, "I can't take this; God is not treating us fairly." His wife replied, "Why don't you go in the bedroom and talk to the Lord about the whole thing?"

A short time later he came out from the bedroom, but now his face was completely different. His wife asked, "Dear, what happened?"

"The Lord settled it with me," he said. "I told him how bitter I was that the President should receive this tremendous homecoming, when no one met us as we returned home. And when I finished, it seemed as though the Lord put his hand on my shoulder and simply said, 'But you're not home yet!'"[1]

Heaven is home—a home far above and beyond anything that we can imagine on this earth. Even on our best days, there is something in all of us that knows that this world is not all there is, that we are longing and waiting to be home. I love what Vance Havner said in his later years about our longing for heaven, "I'm homesick for heaven. It's the hope of dying that has kept me alive this long."[2]

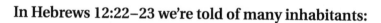

Discussion question 1 can be used here.

# Who Will Be in Heaven?

**In Hebrews 12:22–23 we're told of many inhabitants:**

> But you have come to Mount Zion, to the city of the living God, the heavenly Jerusalem. You have come to thousands of angels gathered together with joy. You have come to the meeting of God's firstborn children whose names are written in heaven. You have come to God, the judge of all people, and to the spirits of good people who have been made perfect.
>
> —Hebrews 12:22–23 (NCV)

**This passage tells us that in heaven there will be:**
**Angels**
**God**
**The church**
**Old Testament believers**

Let's take a moment here to be clear about a few things:

First, notice that people and angels are different. You don't become an angel when you die—angels and people have always been different creations of God.

Second, believers from both New Testament times and from Old Testament times will be in heaven. As you'll remember from our study of salvation, we're all there in heaven because of what Jesus did for us on the cross. Those in the Old Testament had faith in a Messiah who they knew would one day come. And all who've lived after Jesus have faith in that same Messiah, the Son of God who gave his life on a cross.

**As we saw in the last study, the only people who will spend eternity with God are those who choose him in this life.**

**That if you confess with your mouth, "Jesus is Lord," and believe in your heart that God raised him from the dead, you will be saved.**

**—Romans 10:9**

Just think of it. When you tell someone the good news of Jesus' love for him or her, you're not only offering a strength for living everyday life in this world, you are showing them the way to eternal life! Billy Graham talks about the new urgency that this puts into the sharing of our faith:

> A woman who had just experienced a death in her family told me she felt such an urgency to share Christ with someone that when a repairman came in to fix the furnace she backed him up against the wall and said, "If that furnace had blown up in your face and you had died, would you know for certain where you would spend eternity?" The repairman was so startled he forgot to leave a bill.
>
> Why do some people believe they have a paid ticket to heaven? They give many answers, but most can be classified within three basic attitudes. The first is, "Just look at what I've done on earth. My record is pretty good, compared to some. I'll be in heaven because I lived such a good life."
>
> . . . The second answer might be, "I really don't know and I'm not sure that I care. I gave it some thought for a while, but there were so many other things that seemed more important."
>
> Only one answer will give a person the certain privilege, the joy, of entering heaven. "Because I have believed in Jesus Christ and accepted Him as my Savior. He is the One sitting at the right hand of God and interceding for me."[3]

## A Closer Look

Will babies or children who die go to heaven? *Yes!* Although they are not old enough to be saved, they are kept safe by God's grace. A child (or someone who is mentally handicapped) who dies before reaching the age that they can understand their sin and need for Christ will not be held accountable for what they cannot understand. That would violate both God's justice and God's grace. Although the Bible does not directly answer this question, we can see two specific indications that the answer is yes.

1. God is just and righteous in everything he does.

   > The LORD is righteous in all his ways and loving toward all he has made.
   >
   > —Psalm 145:17

   He will not make a mistake in any of his judgments.

2. David believed that he would be reunited with his baby who had died (2 Sam. 12:23).

# How Will I Be Judged as a Believer?

Those of you who are very "test" oriented are likely thinking, "This is one final exam that I want to make sure I pass with flying colors."

The Bible tells us of two times of judgment at the end of the world:

1. The <u>GREAT WHITE THRONE JUDGMENT</u>

   At this judgment those who do not believe in Christ will hear their final judgment and sentencing of separation from God. Those who trust in Christ will not face this judgment.

   The picture that some of us have in our minds is not a true biblical picture. You know the picture I'm talking about. You're in a line with tens of thousands of others, and the line is snaking behind you as far as the eye can see. In front of you are the pearly gates and Saint Peter with a clipboard. As you get closer and closer to the front of the line you're saying to yourself, "I hope my name is on that list. I hope my name is on that list."

Look at me. Listen to what I'm about to say. Because of what Jesus has done for us, you won't even be in that line! The moment you asked Christ to be your Savior, that was settled. You have already passed from death to life! Listen to what Jesus promises in John 5:24.

> I am telling you the truth: those who hear my words and believe in him who sent me have eternal life. They will not be judged, but have already passed from death to life.
>
> —John 5:24 (GNT)

There is, however, a judgment for believers that is different from the "Great White Throne" judgment. It is called

## 2. The "BEMA" JUDGMENT

### In speaking to the believers in Corinth, Paul writes,

> For we must all appear before the judgment seat of Christ, that each one may receive what is due him for the things done while in the body, whether good or bad.
>
> —2 Corinthians 5:10

### *Bema* is the Greek word translated "judgment seat" in these verses.

Would you circle the word "all" in 2 Corinthians 5:10. That means me, and that means you—and every believer who has ever lived.

This is not a judgment as to whether or not you will be in heaven for eternity. This judgment is all about rewards—or the loss of rewards.

I saw a great illustration of this judgment seat in a third grade elementary school class. It was the last day of school, and the parents had joined the children and their teacher in the classroom. It was Awards Day, the day that each child would be given an award for the learning they had accomplished and the character they had exhibited during that year. Mrs. Rhodes, the teacher, pulled out a stool and put it in front of the class. Each child would come one by one to sit on that chair to receive their rewards from their teacher. As she placed the stool Mrs. Rhodes said, "This is our awards chair. Actually, it is the same chair that was our 'test chair' for your children's final oral tests last week—but today it is the awards chair."

What a picture of this moment when we stand before Jesus. We will be tested in the presence of Jesus—and what we have built into our life that does not last will be lost. Our works will be tested. And then, in the presence of all, we will be rewarded for what we have done—for what *does* last. And just as every child in that class made their way to that chair on that day, every one of us will be rewarded for our faith.

First Corinthians 3 gives the clearest description of how this judgment for believers works.

## The nature of the bema judgment

> By the grace God has given me, I laid a foundation as an expert builder, and someone else is building on it. But each one should be careful how he builds. For no one can lay any foundation other than the one already laid, which is Jesus Christ. If any man builds on this foundation using gold, silver, costly stones, wood, hay or straw, his work will be shown for what it is, because the Day will bring it to light. It will be revealed with fire, and the fire will test the quality of each man's work. If what he has built survives, he will receive his reward. If it is burned up, he will suffer loss; he himself will be saved, but only as one escaping through the flames.
>
> —1 Corinthians 3:10–15

Write down with me three truths that we see in this passage, and then I'd like to walk through them with you.

1. **What we've built into our lives that will last will be <u>REWARDED</u>.**

2. **What we've built into our lives that will not last will be <u>LOST</u>.**

3. **Whatever our rewards or loss, our salvation is <u>SECURE</u>.**

This judgment is pictured as a fire, a fire that tests the quality of what you and I have built into our lives. Some things in our lives are like wood, hay, or straw. They may look nice, even impressive, but they will not stand the test of eternity. There are a lot of things in this world that will not last beyond this world—would you agree with that? Absolutely! You have a lot of things that won't last even this year. We all need a house over our head and certain things to survive, but if I spend all of my time and energy in getting a bigger house or more and more things, all I'm doing is adding wood to the bonfire as I head into eternity. In the end, we will see what is truly important. In the end, we will be rewarded for what we've built into and through our lives that lasts.

Discussion question 2 can be used here.

You may remember the moving scene from the Stephen Spielberg's movie *Schindler's List*. Oskar Schindler, the Polish businessman who had used a portion of his fortune to have the names of Jews put onto a work list that would prevent their being sent to a concentration camp, faces those who had escaped certain death because of his actions. As he looks into their faces he has a moment of clarity, of seeing what is really valuable. In a conversation with his Jewish friend Itzhak Stern about what could have been he says,

Schindler: I could've got more . . . I could've got more, if I'd just . . . I could've got more . . .

Stern: Oskar, there are eleven hundred people who are alive because of you. Look at them.

Schindler: If I'd made more money . . . I threw away so much money, you have no idea. If I'd just . . .

Stern: There will be generations because of what you did.

Schindler: I didn't do enough.

Stern: You did so much.

Schindler: This car. Goeth would've bought this car. Why did I keep the car? Ten people, right there. Ten people, ten more people . . . (He rips the swastika pin from his lapel.) This pin, two people. This is gold. Two more people. He would've given me two for it. At least one. He would've given me one. One more. One more person. A person, Stern. For this. I could've gotten one more person and I didn't.[4]

He was asking the question that all of us will ask in the end. Why didn't I invest more of my life in that which is truly important? The good news is: you don't need to wait until you get to heaven to ask. You can start asking now! God doesn't want us to be motivated by the guilt of what we have not done. The motivation is in the reward—in what our lives can count for. And there will be genuine and unimaginable rewards! First Corinthians 3 calls them gold, silver, and precious stones. People who've come to know Christ, character that has been developed, sacrifices that have been made, prayers that have been prayed: gold, silver, and precious stones that will last for eternity!

**Therefore judge nothing before the appointed time; wait till the Lord comes. He will bring to light what is hidden in darkness and will expose the motives of men's hearts. At that time each will receive his praise from God.**

—1 Corinthians 4:5

**A Closer Look**

We're told in Scripture that believers will be rewarded based on three specifics:

1. <u>ACTIONS</u>

> For the Son of Man is going to come in his Father's glory with his angels, and then he will reward each person according to what he has done.
> —Matthew 16:27

2. <u>THOUGHTS</u>

> I the LORD search the heart and examine the mind, to reward a man according to his conduct, according to what his deeds deserve.
> —Jeremiah 17:10

3. <u>WORDS</u>

> But I tell you that men will have to give account on the day of judgment for every careless word they have spoken.
> —Matthew 12:36

Every time I act in a Christlike way, that has eternal impact. Every time I think in a Christlike way, that has eternal impact. Every time I speak in a Christlike way, that has eternal impact. And there will be a day when Jesus looks us in the eye and says to us for each faithful act, thought, and word, "Well done."

**Split Session Plan:** If you're teaching this study over two sessions, end the first session here.

# What Will Heaven Be Like?

## Six truths to bring you joy

Let me read to you a portion of an article about heaven from a very unlikely magazine: *Entertainment Weekly.* Considering the explosion of movies about heaven and hell, the article asks the question in its title, "Whose Afterlife Is It, Anyway?"

> Secular visions of heaven and hell are becoming as commonplace at the multiplex as three-hour running times. Yet as the movies move toward the light, they're creating their own peculiar cinematic catechism.

Hollywood's answers add up to a touchy-feely, shrewdly all-inclusive, slightly warped version of spirituality featuring to-die-for angels and special effects that have a Pottery Barn burnish.... Perhaps as a result of the namby-pamby pluralism, shaky metaphysics, and do-it-yourself salvation, these films have a way of troubling some theologians.[5]

I guess so! Here's a little tip that will serve you well in life: don't get your theology from movies. Oh you'll find a kernel of truth from time to time, but they're few and far between.

Want to know something? The real truth about heaven is more amazing than anything Hollywood could ever dream up and put on film. Even if it were written right, the best we could display on a movie set would be a very pale imitation of the truth about the afterlife. It's the reality of heaven that's the real blockbuster!

Heaven is not some ethereal place where you stand on a cloud all day long and play a harp. It is a very material place—filled with a beauty that you and I can only begin to imagine.

> Heaven is not dull; it is not static; it is not monochrome. It is an endless dynamic of joy in which one is ever more oneself as one was meant to be. Heaven ... is reality itself; what is not heaven is less real.[6]

Read Psalm 16:11 with me.

**You have made known to me the path of life; you will fill me with joy in your presence, with eternal pleasures at your right hand.**
— **Psalm 16:11**

Among the dozens and dozens of joys that we could talk about that will be a part of eternity in heaven, let's take a few moments to look at just six. We've looked at many of these in earlier studies. I want to touch on them again simply as a reminder of what heaven will be.

### 1. Holiness

**And now, all glory to God, who is able to keep you from stumbling, and who will bring you into his glorious presence innocent of sin and with great joy.**
— **Jude 1:24** (NLT)

Circle "innocent of sin."

**Dear friends, now we are children of God, and we have not yet been shown what we will be in the future. But we know that when Christ comes again, we will be like him, because we will see him as he really is.**
— **1 John 3:2** (NCV)

Circle "be like him."

We will not be the same people in heaven as we are on earth. We'll still be human beings—we do not become gods—but we will be like Jesus! In our heart and character, we will be completely like him. I don't know about you, but as much as I might have grown as a Christian, that still is very different from the person I am today. I am looking forward to that day—when I will be a new person!

## 2. A glorified body

**Now we know that if the earthly tent we live in is destroyed, we have a building from God, an eternal house in heaven, not built by human hands.**

**—2 Corinthians 5:1**

**For while we are in this tent, we groan and are burdened, because we do not wish to be unclothed but to be clothed with our heavenly dwelling, so that what is mortal may be swallowed up by life.**

**—2 Corinthians 5:4**

We talked about this a few sessions ago, but it's good to be reminded that we are one day going to have a glorified body. You might need that reminder when you look in the mirror tomorrow morning!

## 3. Immortality

**He will wipe every tear from their eyes. There will be no more death or mourning or crying or pain, for the old order of things has passed away.**

**—Revelation 21:4**

Circle "no more death."

**For our earthly bodies, the ones we have now that can die, must be transformed into heavenly bodies that cannot perish but will live forever.**
**—1 Corinthians 15:53 (LB)**

Aren't you glad I told you some of the other things first? Who would want immortality if heaven were a boring place, a place where we suffered as we do on this earth, or a place where our bodies wore down with the years. Circle the two words "live forever." Heaven isn't just forever. It is a place where we *live,* truly live, forever.

In heaven you'll never hear the words "been there, done that." No boredom there. Everything is continually and eternally new. Always fresh. Always vibrating with life.

### 4. Satisfaction of all needs

**Never again will they hunger; never again will they thirst. The sun will not beat upon them, nor any scorching heat.**

—Revelation 7:16

I wonder what we'll eat in heaven? I suppose we wouldn't have to eat if we didn't want to or it wouldn't be heaven. But we know that Jesus sat down to a couple of meals while he was in his resurrected body—so there's at least a possibility that we'll eat in heaven. If so, it'll be much more than just angel food cake for me!

More seriously, to never hunger and never thirst is a picture of the fact that all of our needs will always be met. It's not just that we'll be filled; we will never get hungry!

### 5. Sharing of Christ's glory

**Now if we are children, then we are heirs—heirs of God and co-heirs with Christ, if indeed we share in his sufferings in order that we may also share in his glory.**

—Romans 8:17

Circle "heirs of God."

You and I will share in the inheritance of God's Son, Jesus Christ. That has to be one of the most surprising joys of heaven. For all of us, it would be more than enough just to be in heaven with Jesus. I've never met a person who had the attitude, "I'm not going to heaven unless I get a cut of Jesus' inheritance." Yet for all of us who would be overwhelmed even at the privilege of being in heaven, God adds the lavish grace of sharing in the glory of his Son.

### 6. Intimate fellowship with God and other believers

**Now we see but a poor reflection as in a mirror; then we shall see face to face. Now I know in part; then I shall know fully, even as I am fully known.**

—1 Corinthians 13:12

Circle "fully known." We'll be fully known and fully loved. You already are fully known and loved by God, but in heaven you'll see that truth clearly.

> Discussion questions 3 and 4 can be used here.

One of the ways to make it through the realities of everyday life is to remember that this life is not all there is—and that it is not the best that can be. We watch a bunch of smelly middle-aged men sitting around a campfire clicking their beer bottles and saying, "It doesn't get any better than this." *I hope it does!*

It does get better than this! Say that with me. "It does get better than this!" I encourage you to write these words on a card to put in your wallet or purse—ready to pull out at just the right moment. On the freeway in a traffic jam. Waiting in line at the airport. When your day is unraveling at the seams. When you've just received some terrible news from the doctor. It does get better than this—God will one day take us home. We will be like Jesus. There will be no more death. Our bodies will be immortal. Every need will be met. We will be fully known.

One more thing: pick the best day you'll have next year—the one where everything goes perfectly. On that day remember: "It will get better than even this!"

## Teaching Tip

The most personal way to say something is the most powerful way to say it. It is difficult for many to speak personally, to reveal ourselves. Our emotions well up, and the words don't come out as we would like them to. One way to break through this is to be honest with the group you're teaching. Tell them that you are about to talk about a subject that is very personal. "You'll forgive me if I don't get the words exactly right, but I hope you'll hear my heart on this one." As you talk about the joys of heaven, make your expression of hope a personal expression of joy.

# How Can Heaven Affect My Life Now?

Philip Yancey writes:

> A strange fact about modern American life: although 91 percent of us believe in an afterlife (says George Gallup), no one much talks about it. Christians believe that we will spend eternity in a splendid place called heaven. . . . isn't it a little bizarre that we simply ignore heaven, acting as if it doesn't matter?[7]

He's right, you know. We often act as if heaven is for "later. I have to find the strength to get through today."

Our mistake is forgetting (or never knowing) that the truth of heaven is essential to making it through the realities of everyday life. Paul Minear said,

> Delete the thought of heaven from man's lexicon and he is soon reduced to a one-dimensional environment, living without any invisible means of support.[8]

C. S. Lewis wrote:

> If you read history, you will find that the Christians who did most for the present world were those who thought most of the next. . . . It is because Christians have largely ceased to think of the other world that they have become so ineffective in this one.[9]

So, how can thoughts of heaven impact my life today?

**Let's look at five specific areas that can affect our lives now by being heavenly minded.**

### 1. Motivation for <u>EVANGELISM</u>

**Jesus answered, "I am the way and the truth and the life. No one comes to the Father except through me."**
—John 14:6

**This is what God told us: God has given us eternal life, and this life is in his Son. Whoever has the Son has life, but whoever does not have the Son of God does not have life.**
—1 John 5:11–12 (NCV)

The truth of heaven is one of the ways that we break through the natural discomfort most of us have when it comes to sharing our faith. For many of us, it is difficult to talk about deeply personal and very important issues—and there is nothing more important than the truth of our salvation. To break through that reticence, remember what you are offering people. An eternity of joy!

Suppose with me for a moment that you have a friend who suffers from cancer. Reading in a magazine, you come across an article that says that a new cure has been found for that form of cancer that is 100 percent effective. What would you do?

Would you fail to tell your friend for fear that he or she might not believe you?

Would you keep it to yourself because you couldn't answer all the questions they might have about this new treatment?

Would you wait to tell them until a more convenient time?

Would you pray that they might stumble across the same article?

Would you hesitate to tell them because they might think you were being judgmental about their cancer?

None of the above! You would run, not walk, to the nearest phone. You wouldn't be able to wait to tell them the news.

One of the reasons that all of us, including me, fail to tell the Good News is that we've forgotten how good the Good News really is! You are sharing with people God's offer to give us eternal life!

### 2. Wise use of <u>FINANCES</u>

**Don't store treasures for yourselves here on earth where moths and rust will destroy them and thieves can break in and steal them. But store your treasures in heaven where they cannot be destroyed by moths or rust and where thieves cannot break in and steal them. Your heart will be where your treasure is.**

—**Matthew 6:19–21** (NCV)

How do you store treasure in heaven?

Invest as much as you can in the things that will last: people's salvation, growth in Christian character, life-changing ministries—the things that will endure beyond this life. Remember that old saying, "You can't take it with you, but you can send it on ahead!" Sometimes investing in eternity means giving away what you have to serve others. Other times it means using what you have—your house, your car, your possessions—to serve others.

### 3. Serving the <u>NEEDY</u>

**Then the King will say to those on his right, "Come, you who are blessed by my Father; take your inheritance, the kingdom prepared for you since the creation of the world. For I was hungry and you gave me something to eat, I was thirsty and you gave me something to drink, I was a stranger and you invited me in, I needed clothes and you clothed me, I was sick and you looked after me, I was in prison and you came to visit me." Then the righteous will answer him, "Lord, when did we see you hungry and feed you, or thirsty and give you something to drink? When did we see you a stranger and invite you in, or needing clothes and clothe you? When did we see you sick or in prison and go to visit you?" The King will reply, "I tell you the truth, whatever you did for one of the least of these brothers of mine, you did for me."**

—**Matthew 25:34–40**

It is striking that in Matthew 25 the rewards in heaven are handed out to those who care for the unnoticed in this world.

It is our unfortunate habit to talk and plan and strategize more about meeting these needs than to actually take the step to *do* something and meet a need.

In the light of eternity, who do you and I need to notice this week?

# Listen, Christian

I was hungry, and you formed a humanities club and discussed my hunger. Thank you.

I was imprisoned and you crept off quietly to your chapel in the cellar and prayed for my release.

I was naked and in your mind you debated the morality of my appearance.

I was sick and you knelt and thanked God for your health.

I was homeless and you preached to me of the spiritual shelter of the love of God.

I was lonely and you left me alone to pray for me.

You seem so holy, so close to God. But I am still very hungry, and lonely, and cold.

Thank you.[10]

## 4. Endurance in SUFFERING

> So we do not give up. Our physical body is becoming older and weaker, but our spirit inside us is made new every day. We have small troubles for a while now, but they are helping us gain an eternal glory that is much greater than the troubles. We set our eyes not on what we see but on what we cannot see. What we see will last only a short time, but what we cannot see will last forever.
>
> —2 Corinthians 4:16–18 (NCV)

The early believers *often* looked to the hope of heaven for the strength to endure the suffering and persecution they faced on a regular basis. Instead of feeling that God owed them freedom from suffering on this earth, they recognized that any pain that we face here is minuscule compared to the glory that God is preparing for us.

Listen to the MESSAGE paraphrase of 2 Corinthians 4:16–18:

> So we're not giving up. How could we! Even though on the outside it often looks like things are falling apart on us, on the inside, where God is making new life, not a day goes by without his unfolding grace. These hard times are small potatoes compared to the coming good times, the lavish celebration prepared for us. There's far more here than meets the eye. The things we see now are here today, gone tomorrow. But the things we can't see now will last forever.
>
> —2 Corinthians 4:16–18 (MESSAGE)

5. Easing of <u>ANXIETIES</u>

**Since you became alive again, so to speak, when Christ arose from the dead, now set your sights on the rich treasures and joys of heaven where he sits beside God in the place of honor and power. Let heaven fill your thoughts; don't spend your time worrying about things down here.**

—Colossians 3:1–2 (LB)

William Barclay said it this way,

> It is easy for a man to be so busy with things of time that he forgets the things of eternity, to be so preoccupied with the things which are seen that he forgets the things that are unseen, to hear so insistently the claims of the world that he cannot hear the soft invitation of the voice of Christ.[11]

Discussion question 5 can be used here.

Let's get practical for a moment. How in the world do you set your eyes on what you cannot see? How do I fit this big a truth into my daily life? Go around having "heavenly visions" all day?

If you had the vacation of a lifetime planned for next July, would you wait until July to think about it? Of course not. You would make preparations to go, and you would look forward to your trip. That's exactly how we look forward to heaven: make preparations to go and look forward to that day.

As we close, here are some practical ways to let heaven fill your thoughts.

## Acting on the Truth

**God's Word repeatedly instructs us to shift our focus from earthly matters to focus on God's perspective. Take seven minutes at the beginning or the end of the day for a week to focus on these seven truths:**

1. **His plan for me will never change.**
2. **My salvation is safe and secure in heaven, where nothing can destroy it.**
3. **When he comes for me I will go with him to the home he carefully and lovingly has been preparing for me.**
4. **Nothing can ever separate me from his love—no pain, no suffering, no tragedy, no hardship, no demon, no horrible mistake on my part, nothing!**

5. I am to spend my days learning to love him and to trust him.

6. I am to be his arms and hands of compassion to fellow human beings.

7. And someday, I will join millions of other believers at his throne, and together we will worship him. We will sing with the angels,

Worthy is the Lamb, who was slain, to receive power and wealth and wisdom and strength and honor and glory and praise!
—Revelation 5:12

Let's pray together:

*Lord, I don't want to live one moment longer with doubt about whether I'll be in heaven. Thank you for sending Jesus to tell me the Good News that you love me and you want to welcome me into your eternal home. Instead of trusting in what I can do to get me to heaven, I trust in the way you provided—through Jesus' death and resurrection. I trust you to forgive me and to lead me.*

*I ask today that you would help me to see the problems and worries of this life in light of the hope of heaven. I trust that there will come a day when you will remove our suffering and when you will right every injustice and when you will multiply every joy.*

*As I look forward to the promise of heaven, I'm deciding today to invest my life in eternity this next year. I want to use the gifts and abilities that you've given me to do more than build a good life for myself and my family in this world. I want to live for that which lasts.*

*In Jesus name, amen.*

**Finish memorizing memory card 9, "The Truth about the Afterlife."**

## Discussion Questions

1. Do some brainstorming together for a few moments about how great heaven will be by giving one-line completions to the following statements. Have fun with this!

   The greatest thing about heaven will be that I won't have to . . .

   The greatest thing about heaven will be that I will be able to . . .

   A picture that helps me to think of the greatness of heaven is . . .

   In heaven there will be an abundant supply of . . .

   In heaven there will be no . . .

   Someone I'm looking forward to meeting in heaven is . . .

   Something I'm looking forward to doing in heaven is . . .

2. First Corinthians 3:10–15 says that believers who build the wrong things into their lives will "suffer loss" but will be saved. What do you think are some of the things that we build into our lives now that will be "burned up"? What are some of the things that will last? What kind of loss do you think we will suffer?

3. Look again at the list of six things that describe "what heaven will be like." Which two sound the most attractive to you right now? Which one is difficult to understand?

4. How would you like your glorified body to look? What would you like it to be able to do?

5. In what way would you like the truth of heaven to have a greater impact on your daily life?

## For Further Study

Elwell, Walter, ed. *Topical Analysis of the Bible.* Grand Rapids, Mich.: Baker, 1991.

Evans, Louis H., Sr. *Your Thrilling Future.* Wheaton, Ill.: Tyndale, 1982.

Gilmore, John. *Probing Heaven.* Grand Rapids, Mich.: Baker, 1989.

Habermas, Gary R. *Immortality: The Other Side of Death.* Nashville: Nelson, 1992.

Hybels, Bill. "Your Everafter: Heaven." Audiotape. Carol Stream, Ill.: Preaching Today, n.d.

Morey, Dr. Robert A. *Death and the Afterlife.* Minneapolis: Bethany, 1984.

Rhodes, Ron. *Heaven: The Undiscovered Country.* Eugene, Ore.: Harvest House, 1995.

Toon, Peter. *Heaven and Hell.* Nashville: Nelson, 1986.

# The Church
## Part 1

**Life Change Objectives**

- To deepen your love for and commitment to the church.

- To see in a new or deeper way your part in living out all five purposes of the church.

**Summary Teaching Outline**

The Beginning of the Church

    Envisioned by God

    Established by Jesus

    Energized by the Spirit

The Nature of the Church (What is it supposed to be?)

    The church is an *ekklesia*.

    The church is a *koinonia*.

    The ordinances of the church

The Mission of the Church (What is the church supposed to do?)

What do you think of when I say the word *church*. Some people think of an organization—the Baptist denomination of churches. Others think of a building—the church on the corner. Some think of it as an event—I went to church this weekend.

Let me tell you about a family that went to church for the first time in a long time: Mom, Dad, their eleven-year-old daughter, and seven-year-old son. It was the little boy's first time in church—so he watched everything intently. He kept his eye on his parents to figure out when to stand up, when to sit down, when to sing, and when to listen. As the offering plate was passed he was amazed to see people putting money in, but no one taking any out. He saw his dad carefully take a dollar bill out of his wallet, crease the bill down the middle and put it in the offering. On their way home Dad began to complain about the service—the music was too loud, the preacher went too long, the piano was off key. "But Dad," piped up the little boy from the back seat, "you have to admit it wasn't a bad show for a buck!"

More than we'd care to admit, that's the way many people think of church. It's an hour-long event that happens on Sunday. The Sunday worship service may be an important event in the life of every church—but the church is more than an event. The building may be where the church meets—but the church is not the building.

This is one of the most important studies we do in *Foundations*. Why? Because *you are the church*. You and I, as followers of Jesus Christ, make up the church of Jesus. And if we don't understand what the church is, we won't be able to be all that God calls us to be.

**As we begin this study of the church of God, some may ask, "Why is the church so important? Why can't I just have a relationship with Jesus and forget about the church?" We all know people who consider themselves Christians but seldom attend church. Is the church really necessary?**

**Absolutely! To have faith in God means we cannot live the Christian life in isolation, like a spiritual Robinson Crusoe. The truth is, we cannot live out the Christian life without belonging to the church. The New Testament knows nothing of unattached Christians.**

We need to change our picture of the church.

## Our Need for the Church

| God's Ideal | Our Actual Practice |
|---|---|
| Church is a spiritual necessity | Church is an optional activity |
| Interdependence is valued | Individualism is valued |
| Spirituality takes place in community | Religion is a private matter |
| Active involvement in social concerns | Aloof from the real world |
| All people fully accepted together | Segregation practiced (racial, social status, etc.) |
| Authentic behavior, with the public and private lives matching | Hypocrisy; saying one thing but practicing another |

To recapture the role God intended for us as his church, we must gain an understanding of how the church began, what its nature is, what its mission is, and explore the implications for *our* church.

# The Beginning of the Church

## *ENVISIONED* by God

**The Bible makes it clear that God has always desired to create a people for himself; a people who would love him with all their hearts, and a people for whom he could prove himself to be a faithful God.**

> For you are a people holy to the LORD your God. The LORD your God has chosen you out of all the peoples on the face of the earth to be his people, his treasured possession.
>
> —Deuteronomy 7:6

Deuteronomy 7:6 reminds us that God chose a people back in Old Testament times who were to follow him. We know them as the nation of Israel. What group makes up God's people in the world today? God's church! We are God's people.

Findley Edge, author of the classic renewal book *The Greening of the Church,* writes:

> What does it mean to be the people of God? They are a people who believe, certainly. They are a people who are "good" in terms of personal morality, certainly. But these things do not constitute the heart of the matter. The uniqueness of God's people is that they are called to a mission. This is clearly understood. They have joyfully accepted this mission and have given their lives to its fulfillment. . . . The people of God believe that what God is seeking to do in the lives of people and in the world is what is desperately needed. They believe this so deeply and with such commitment that their lives are joyfully given to God as instruments in seeking to cause the will of God to be "done on earth as it is in heaven."[1]

## A Closer Look

When Adam turned away from the blessing of being in harmony with God, God turned to creating a people for himself. He called Abraham, Isaac, and Jacob to be the forefathers of these people—Israel. When Israel proved to be unfaithful to God's covenant promises, God continued his plan through a "remnant" of people, who also became unfaithful to him. God's plan came to fruition when he sent his Son, Jesus, to bring together finally a people who would belong totally to God. These people would be an "elect race, a royal priesthood, a holy nation, a people of God's possession." This is the church.

> Look at 1 Peter 2:9. I want you to notice that as a people chosen by God we belong to God.

**But you are a chosen people, a royal priesthood, a holy nation, a people belonging to God, that you may declare the praises of him who called you out of darkness into his wonderful light.**

**—1 Peter 2:9**

> God alone has the property rights to the church. Because it is God's, He alone proposes, composes, imposes, and disposes. Never will He surrender His right as owner and possessor of the church.... All that the church is, has, does, and becomes is due to the fact that it is divine in origin and possession and that the Holy Spirit is at work. It is the church of God.[2]

## *ESTABLISHED* by Jesus

In Matthew 16:18, Jesus says, "I will build my church, and the gates of hell will not prevail against it." This indicates that the church was still in the future when he spoke. He was making a prediction concerning his future building of the church.

> These words of Jesus come right after Peter's great confession of faith. Jesus had asked his disciples, "Who do you think that I am?" Peter's reply to Jesus was, "You are Christ, you are the Son of the living God." In response to that faith, Jesus said, "I will build my church."

> Let's not go too fast here. That one little phrase, "I will build my church," is as crucial as anything we'll talk about in understanding what the church is.

> Whose church is it?

Jesus said, "I will build." It is Jesus' church.

Who builds Jesus' church? Jesus!

No doubt we are a part of his church and he involves us in building that church. But the moment it becomes ours rather than his, it's no longer a church. A social club maybe, a service organization possibly—but not the church. "Whoa," you might be thinking, "that means there are a lot of organizations that call themselves a church that may not really be a church." Exactly. And there are many times when our personal perspective can get skewed—as we start to think of the church we're in as *my* organization rather than Jesus' church.

The place where this confession of Paul and response of Jesus occurred is important to know. It was in Caesarea Philippi, to the far north of Israel. This area above the Sea of Galilee is far different from the desert picture you often get of Israel. It's a beautiful mountainous area—with streams flowing through lush green foliage. Here's what is most fascinating for us about this spot. Carved into the face of and within the caves of those mountains were images and statues of many of the gods that were worshiped in that day. Caesarea Philippi was said to be the birthplace of the Greek god Pan and was filled with ancient pagan temples. Here—in this place—Peter boldly stated his trust in Jesus as the true way to God. Here—in this place—Jesus said he would build his church.

What a picture of the church today! We stand in the midst of a world where there are many ideas about who God is and what he wants to do in the world. Some say, "This is God"; others say, "No, that is God"; still others say, "We should accept everyone's idea of God." And we as believers are still saying today what believers said in New Testament times, "Jesus is the Christ, he is the way to God." And Jesus is still saying today, "That's what I build my church on—that faith in me and that decision to follow me."

## *ENERGIZED* *by the Spirit*

**How is the church built? It is the work of the Holy Spirit baptizing believers into the body of Christ.**

Read with me 1 Corinthians 12:13.

**For we were all baptized by one Spirit into one body—whether Jews or Greeks, slave or free—and we were all given the one Spirit to drink.**
—1 Corinthians 12:13

What is the birthday of the church? Not our church—*the* church. The church was born on the Day of Pentecost. When the Holy Spirit came into the lives of the believers who were meeting in an upper room that day, the church became alive.

W. A. Criswell, who for fifty years was the pastor of First Baptist Church in Dallas, wrote:

> The church founded during [Jesus'] earthly ministry had waited to be brought to life. It was a potential church before Pentecost. The members were amazed by the events of the preceding months. They knew intellectually some of the things that had happened, but they had not appropriated the power and the authority Jesus had conferred on them. They had not yet received the Holy Spirit. . . . Surely no power on earth could have made this frightened collection of leaderless people into the bold witnesses who changed the history of the world. Only God could have done it, and it was their testimony that he had. The gift of God that empowered the early church was the Holy Spirit.[3]

The Holy Spirit is the power behind every bit of growth and any effective ministry in the church. For a church to make a difference in the world without being plugged in to the power of the Holy Spirit is as impossible as turning on a lamp without first putting the electric plug into the socket.

God envisioned, Jesus established, the Spirit energized. The whole of God is involved in the whole of what the church is in this world.

It is *his* church, so one of the questions we need to ask is, "What does he tell us his church is supposed to be?"

## The Nature of the Church (What is it supposed to be?)

### *The church is an* <u>EKKLESIA</u>.

**The primary Greek word used for the church in the New Testament is *ekklesia*, which has the meaning "to call." It was used to describe an assembly of people (secular or spiritual), but it came to mean an assembly or community called by God. So the assembling was not the key. The key was the fact that God called them together.**

This word, *ekklesia*, occurs 114 times in the New Testament, but only three times in the Gospels because Jesus did not establish the church until after his resurrection. Any word that shows up that often in the Bible is obviously an important word for us to understand.

*Ekklesia* refers to both the <u>UNIVERSAL</u> church and the <u>LOCAL</u> church.

**The universal church is composed of people from every tribe and race and culture (regardless of their denominational affiliations) who have accepted Jesus Christ as their Lord and Savior.**

**In the universal church the emphasis is on the <u>UNITY</u> of the church.**

> You and I have a unity with all believers. That means a unity not only with those who live in every place but also those who live in every time. You have a unity with the young pastor who is meeting in a house church in the far north of China, with the believer in India who is suffering persecution for her faith, with the small group of believers in France who are trying to break through years of spiritual apathy.
>
> Let me tell you about a moment when that unity was strongly felt. A group from Saddleback Church had traveled to Taiwan for a meeting with a large group of young church leaders. As we were driving from the airport to Taipei, our translator for the meeting, Philip, began to tell us of his heart for his country. With one of the lowest percentages of believers to total population in the world, the Christians often felt alone and discouraged. During the conference that followed, Philip did a wonderful job of translating—in the dry, matter-of-fact tone that fit his personality as an engineer. Rick Warren, speaking in the last session of the seminar, looked out on the group that had packed into the large worship room and encouraged them with the words, "Don't give up." As Philip began to translate those three words his voice broke—in compassion for those without Christ and those church leaders in his country. "Don't give up," Rick said again, and again Philip's voice broke as those words fell softly from his lips. You could have heard a pin drop in the room— all of our hearts were gripped by his love for his people. The unity that we all felt with him, with those believers, was deep, was real, and lasts even to this day.
>
> This unity that we feel as a part of the body of Christ in this world needs to be expressed in a way that people can see and feel. That's where the local church comes in.

Discussion question 1 can be used here.

**The local church is a group of believers who meet together for worship, instruction, fellowship, and ministry.**

Paul wrote many letters to local groups of believers. You know the names of some of them. The church that is in . . . (fill in some names with me).

**In the local church, the emphasis is on the <u>MINISTRY</u> of the church.**

The local church is how the body of Christ ministers to our community. We are Jesus' hands of compassion to those around us. We are his feet to carry the Good News of Jesus' love to our homes and workplaces and schools. As we minister to one another and to those in our community, the local church brings light to a dark world. Let me ask you, how much light do you have to have for it to be noticed in a dark room? Just a tiny light! Churches all over the world, large and small, bring more light to their communities than you or I could imagine.

## *The church is a <u>KOINONIA</u>.*

 13

Another important Greek word that relates to the church is *koinonia.* Difficult to translate into English, it carries the idea of communion, fellowship, sharing, and participation. It is used to describe the life that the *ekklesia,* or church, is to share in Christ.

*Koinonia* is our participation together in the life of God through Jesus Christ.

*Koinonia* is:

- more than the congenial relationship of "buddies."

- more than participating in a potluck dinner.

- more than "I can get along with you because you're so much like me."

*Never* reduce the word *fellowship* to mean a programmed meeting we have after church or a good relationship with someone you would have liked whether or not you were a Christian.

### Teaching Tip

When you teach, it's important to look at the "pace" of your words. If you always speak at one speed, those who are listening will begin to tune you out. Whatever your natural pace, at times you need to speed it up a little to add energy, and at times you need to slow down your words to add emphasis. For instance, the next paragraph is one where you could slow down your words to let them sink it. Slowing down your words and pausing between the phrases will allow people to feel the historical and relational depth of true fellowship.

As the church began, fellowship meant Jews and Gentiles, who had been enemies for centuries, becoming one in the body of Christ. Breaking through thousands of years of separation, they came together to worship together. Those who before would not speak to one another now worshiped together in one church. That is the depth of what fellowship is.

**Koinonia is a oneness that is possible only through God's supernatural work.**

We're going to look at some words that characterize the fellowship of the church. These words grow out of the passages where the Greek word *koinonia* is used in the New Testament. Let me make this practical. These are words that should be lived out in any small group that you are a part of in the church. These are words that should characterize our relationship with any other believer. These are words that should be seen in the way that I serve in the body of Christ.

**Koinonia is characterized by:**

- **LIGHT** (1 John 1:6–7)

  The light of God's presence characterizes our relationships as believers—we see things more clearly. This doesn't mean we're perfect! It means we can choose to walk together in the light rather than stumble around in the darkness.

- **UNITY** (Phil. 2:1–2)

  Unity is not uniformity. Say that with me. "Unity is not uniformity." Did you notice that although we all have different-sounding voices, it sounded louder and stronger when we said it together? We don't have to all be the same to have unity. If fact, the exciting thing about Christian unity is that God gives us the ability to work as one with so many that are so different from us.

- **ACCEPTANCE** (Philem. 1:17)

  Look at Philemon 1:17.

  > So if you consider me a partner, welcome him as you would welcome me.
  >
  > —Philemon 1:17

  Paul is writing to his friend Philemon about another friend named Onesimus—asking one friend to welcome another. This sounds fairly simple until you realize that Onesimus was a runaway slave who had been owned by Philemon! In a world where men treated their slaves as property, Paul said, "Welcome him as a Christian brother. Accept him as a part of the family." That's radical!

I wonder, who do you need to accept as a part of the family of God?

- **SHARING OF MATERIAL GOODS (Acts 2:44–45)**

When others have a need in the body of Christ, that means you have a need. It is true that later in the New Testament Paul had to warn the Thessalonians about some who were taking advantage of the fellowship—not working at all and expecting others to take care of them. But that's not usually the case. If you see a fellow Christian with a genuine need, and you know that God has given you the ability to meet that practical need, then meet their need!

- **GIVING MONEY (2 Cor. 8:4)**

The offering in the church is one expression of our fellowship as believers. Not only does it meet the needs of others but we are working together in trust as we give together to reach the world for Christ.

The next word may be a word that you don't want to write in, but write it in anyway. Fellowship is characterized by:

- **SUFFERING (Phil. 3:8–10)**

Suffering. That's a long way from potlucks, isn't it? Paul writes in Philippians 3:10,

> I want to know Christ and the power of his resurrection and the fellowship of sharing in his sufferings.
>
> —Philippians 3:10

As believers in the United States, we'd have to honestly say that we don't know much about the fellowship of his sufferings. We don't know what our brothers and sisters in Russia know about the fellowship of his sufferings. We don't know what our fellow believers in China know about the fellowship of his sufferings. You and I must admit that we just do not know what many of our fellow believers in the world know about suffering.

But that doesn't mean we don't know anything. That doesn't mean we never suffer loss or prejudice because of our relationship with Christ. And that *does not mean* that we should forget about what so many in the church around the world are facing. When one part of the body suffers, the whole body suffers along with it. Your prayers for persecuted believers around the world have more impact than you can imagine.

Maybe you're frightened of suffering. I am! Who wants to face times of suffering? But the apostle Paul, who went through more suffering than you or I will ever face—he was whipped to near death three different times, he was beaten with rods, he had huge rocks thrown on him—the apostle Paul writes and tells us that with every suffering his sense of closeness to Jesus only deepened.

- **LORD'S SUPPER** (1 Cor. 10:16)

    The Greek word for fellowship, *koinonia,* is used in describing the Lord's Supper. In the Lord's Supper (Communion), we fellowship with Jesus and with other believers. It is such an important expression of our fellowship that it is one of the two "ordinances" that Jesus gave to the church.

> Discussion question 2 can be used here.

## A Closer Look

### *The Ordinances of the Church*

The word *ordinance* comes from the word *ordained.* It refers to the events that Jesus specifically ordered us to make a regular part of our worship as a church. The two ordinances that Jesus gave to the church are baptism and the Lord's Supper.

*Baptism* demonstrates <u>PHYSICALLY</u> what took place <u>SPIRITU-ALLY</u> when we accepted Christ. Through baptism, our participation in his death, burial, and resurrection is portrayed, and we rise up out of the water, symbolizing the new life we now have in Christ.

Why is it important for you to be baptized as a believer in Christ? First and foremost, because Jesus commanded it! He "ordained"—he commanded—baptism to be a step we take as we follow him. In his Great Commission in Matthew 28:19 and 20, Jesus told us to "Make disciples of all nations, baptizing them in the name of the Father and of the Son and of the Holy Spirit."

When you are baptized, you are picturing to the world what happened in your life when you became a believer. Look at Romans 6:4:

> We were therefore buried with him through baptism into death in order that, just as Christ was raised from the dead through the glory of the Father, we too may live a new life
>
> —Romans 6:4

When you go down into the water it is a picture of the fact that Jesus forgave your sins, put them to death. When you come up out of the water it is a picture of the new life that you now have in Christ.

*The Lord's Supper,* or Communion, also is a physical reminder of deep, spiritual realities. We remember that through his broken body and spilled blood a <u>NEW</u> <u>COVENANT</u> has been established between God and man.

> And when he had given thanks, he broke it and said, "This is my body, which is for you; do this in remembrance of me." In the same way, after supper he took the cup, saying, "This cup is the new covenant in my blood; do this, whenever you drink it, in remembrance of me." For whenever you eat this bread and drink this cup, you proclaim the Lord's death until he comes.
>
> —1 Corinthians 11:24–26

When we take the Lord's Supper we remember that Jesus really died, and that Jesus really lives for us. I've taken the Lord's Supper many, many times—as some of you have—and I'd have to say to you that it never gets old or routine. This moment of recognizing all that Jesus did for you and me never loses its meaning. There is always a deep sense of how much he loves me. And not just me. He loves everyone who is in that room as we take the Lord's Supper together.

Sometimes the ordinances are called "sacraments," from the Latin *Sacramentum,* which was an oath of allegiance a Roman soldier took to his emperor. Christians took over the term and meant that it bound them in loyalty to Christ. In the ordinances, Christ's grace and forgiveness are depicted—they are sermons acted out. We are allowed the opportunity to express our allegiance and loyalty to Christ when we are baptized and when we eat the Lord's Supper together. The ordinances do not give us "more" of God's grace. They are a way to praise God for the grace we've already received.

## Teaching Tip

If you are good at answering questions from the audience, you may want to take a few questions about the Lord's Supper and baptism at this point. Because so many come from different backgrounds in your church, there are likely many questions about how and when and why you practice these ordinances of Jesus.

**Split Session Plan:** If you're teaching this study over two sessions, end the first session here. (If you're teaching this study in two sessions and plan to share the Lord's Supper, it may be better to do so here after you've just taught about it rather than at the end of the next session.)

# The Mission of the Church (What is the church supposed to do?)

What is the church supposed to do? It is amazing how easily we neglect the specific answers to this important question. Without those answers, we all too quickly find ourselves acting without a clear sense of our purpose. We may have a lot of activity, but no direction or priorities. The Bible is filled with teaching concerning what the church is to do. Understanding what the Bible says about the church's mission enables us to focus our heart and energies as a church on God's priorities.

In his book *The Purpose-Driven Church,* Rick Warren writes,

> A clear purpose allows concentration. Focused light has tremendous power. Diffused light has no power at all. For instance, by focusing the power of the sun through a magnifying glass, you can set a leaf on fire. But you can't set a leaf on fire if the same sunlight is unfocused. When light is concentrated at an even higher level, like a laser beam, it can even cut through steel.
>
> The principle of concentration works in other areas too. A focused life and a focused church will have far greater impact than unfocused ones. Like a laser beam, the more focused your church becomes, the more impact it will have on society.... If you want your church to make an impact on the world, you must major in the majors. It is amazing to me how many Christians have no idea what the main objective of their church is. As the old cliché says, "The main thing is to keep the main thing the main thing!"[4]

So, what is the main thing? What does God tell us in the Bible is the mission of the church? Let's take a biblical look at God's five purposes for us as a church.

## *The five purposes of the church*

**The five purposes of the church are given in two statements of Jesus: the Great Commandment and the Great Commission.**

### The Great Commandment

Let's all read Matthew 22:37–40 out loud, together.

**Jesus replied: "'Love the Lord your God with all your heart and with all your soul and with all your mind.' This is the first and greatest commandment. And the second is like it: 'Love your neighbor as yourself.' All the Law and the Prophets hang on these two commandments."**
**—Matthew 22:37–40**

Would you circle "love the Lord" and then circle "love your neighbor."

### The Great Commission

Read this with me also:

**Therefore go and make disciples of all nations, baptizing them in the name of the Father and of the Son and of the Holy Spirit, and teaching them to obey everything I have commanded you. And surely I am with you always, to the very end of the age.**
**—Matthew 28:19–20**

In this verse, circle the phrases "go and make disciples," "baptizing them," and "teaching them to obey." In those five phrases that you just circled in the Great Commandment and the Great Commission we see the five purposes of the church.

### Five instructions for the church

1. **"Love God with all your heart": <u>WORSHIP</u>**

2. **"Love your neighbor as yourself": <u>MINISTRY</u>**

3. **"Go . . . make disciples": <u>EVANGELISM</u>**

4. **"Baptizing them": <u>FELLOWSHIP</u>**

5. **"Teaching them to do": <u>DISCIPLESHIP</u>**

### *The church exists to:*

1. **Celebrate God's <u>PRESENCE</u> (worship)**

   **"Exalt our Master."**

   **O magnify the LORD with me, and let us exalt his name together!**
   **—Psalm 34:3 (RSV)**

   **I was glad when they said to me, "Let us go to the LORD's house."**
   **—Psalm 122:1 (GNT)**

If we don't celebrate our relationship with God and his presence with us, we're ignoring the reason God made us!

Look at Psalm 34:3, and circle the word "together." We are to worship God as individuals, in private times with him. But if we do not worship him together with fellow believers we are cheating ourselves of the hope and joy that we so desperately need in this world. Look at Psalm 122:1—"I was *glad* . . ."

Have you ever had one of those days when you woke up and didn't feel at all like going to church? But, for whatever reason, you decided to go anyway. I've found on those days when I least feel like worshiping God with others I need it the most. Those are the days when I sense the greatest change in my heart and leave church saying, "I'm glad I went today!"

2. **Communicate God's <u>WORD</u> (evangelism)**

**"Evangelize our mission field."**

**The most important thing is that I complete my mission, the work that the Lord Jesus gave me—to tell people the Good News about God's grace.**

**—Acts 20:24** (NCV)

**You will be my witnesses . . .**

**—Acts 1:8**

We're often better at worship and fellowship than we are at spreading the Good News. It's easy for the church or a person to become so "worship of God focused" and "fellowship with us" focused that we forget that God put us in this world to be his witnesses.

This is so important in God's priority list that he has shown himself to be more than willing to give us a push to get us out into the world. The first church in Jerusalem likely had the greatest fellowship and the purest worship of any church that has ever existed. They met with each other every day, they sold what they had to meet the needs of others, they saw God working great miracles as a common occurrence. Yet God allowed a great persecution to come upon this church, a persecution that scattered those believers throughout the world. He was obviously more interested in their sharing their faith around the world than in preserving a perfect fellowship in Jerusalem.

3. **Incorporate God's <u>FAMILY</u> (fellowship)**

**"Encourage our members."**

**You are members of God's very own family . . . and you belong in God's household with every other Christian.**

**—Ephesians 2:19** (LB)

The *koinonia* we talked about earlier is one of the purposes of God's church in the world. Jesus told his disciples that others would see that we are Christians because of the love that we have for one another (John 13:35).

We relate to one another as a spiritual family. Let me ask you a question. Is your physical family perfect? Of course not. You say the wrong thing from time to time, aren't always as aware as you should be of one another's needs, and have to put up with the idiosyncrasies of each person in the family. But if you're a healthy family, you've learned how to work through your difficulties and put up with your differences.

God does not expect us to be a perfect fellowship as a church. How could we be? We are all imperfect people. But he does call us to be a healthy spiritual family: to go to one another if there is a problem, to forgive one another when we have been hurt, to love one another in spite of our differences. As we do this, the world has a chance to see Jesus working in the real lives of real people.

**4. Educate God's <u>PEOPLE</u> (discipleship)**

**"Educate for maturity."**

**Building up the church, the body of Christ, to a position of strength and maturity; until . . . all become full-grown in the Lord.**
—Ephesians 4:12–13 (LB)

The church is in this world so that you and I can grow to become more like Christ. We need others in the body of Christ if we're to grow to be all that God wants us to be.

Sometimes we can get the idea that growing in spiritual maturity is something you do alone. You have a devotional time with the Lord or read a book or even attend a Bible study pretty much on your own. These habits need to be a part of our lives—but don't miss the fact that the majority of our growth is going to happen through our relationships with other believers. It is as you see how others are growing that you see God's direction and challenge to mature in your own life. We grow together in the body of Christ!

**5. Demonstrate God's <u>LOVE</u> (ministry)**

**"Equip for ministry."**

**To equip the saints for the work of ministry.**
—Ephesians 4:12 (NRSV)

In the church, every member is a minister. We're not all involved as full-time pastors, but we are all called to minister in the name of Christ in this world. Don't let the word "minister" throw you—it simply means to serve. When you serve anyone because of your love for Christ, you are living out one of God's purposes for your life. It could be someone at home, someone with a need at your work, another believer at church, or a person you have just met.

Discussion question 3 can be used here.

Let me say something important about the importance of all five of these purposes. God does not want a church to focus on just one or two of these purposes. He wants us, both as a church and as individuals, to effectively accomplish all five of these purposes in our lives.

You might remember the modern parable of the lighthouse. It gives us a picture of how easily we can begin to leave a gap in our mission by slowly beginning to ignore one or more of the purposes. This is true for us as a church. It's also true for each of us as individuals in the body of Christ.

On a dangerous sea coast where shipwrecks often occur there was once a crude little life-saving station. The building was just a hut, and there was only one boat but the few devoted members kept a constant watch over the sea, and with no thought for themselves went out day and night tirelessly searching for the lost. Some of those who were saved and various others in the surrounding area wanted to become associated with the station and give of their time and money and effort for the support of its work. New boats were bought and new crews trained. The little life-saving station grew.

Some of the members of the life-saving station were unhappy that the building was so crude and poorly equipped. They felt that a more comfortable place should be provided as the first refuge of those saved from the sea. They replaced the emergency cots with beds and put better furniture in the enlarged building. Now the life-saving station became a popular gathering place for its members, and they decorated it beautifully and furnished it exquisitely, because they used it as a sort of club. Fewer members were now interested in going to sea on life-saving missions, so they hired life-boat crews to do this work. The life-saving motif still prevailed in this club's decoration, and there was a liturgical life-boat in the room where the club initiations were held. About this time a large ship was wrecked off the coast, and the hired crews brought in boat loads of cold, wet and half-drowned people. They were dirty and sick and they messed up the beautiful new clubhouse. The property committee soon met and had a shower house built outside the club where victims of shipwreck could be cleaned up before coming inside.

At the next meeting, there was a split in the club membership. Most of the members wanted to stop the club's life-saving activities as being unpleasant and a hindrance to the normal social life of the club. Some members insisted upon life-saving as their primary purpose and pointed out that they were still called a life-saving station. But they were finally voted down and told that if they wanted to save the lives of all the various kinds of people who were shipwrecked in those waters, they could begin their own life-saving station down the coast. They did.

As the years went by, the new station experienced the same changes that had occurred in the old. It evolved into a club, and yet another life-saving station was founded. History continued to repeat itself, and if you visit that sea coast today, you will find a number of exclusive clubs along that shore. Shipwrecks are frequent in those waters, but most of the people drown![5]

What's the point? A church can become a clubhouse. Any church can. We *must* protect ourselves from becoming so concerned about us that we forget the world. If you know anything about human nature, you know how easy that is to do. God's goal for the church is that we be a light to the world!

As important as our witness is, even that cannot become the sole purpose of the church or our lives. We need all five purposes to be healthy as a church, and healthy as individual believers.

Without the purpose of worship, we become heartless.

Without the purpose of ministry, we become selfish.

Without the purpose of evangelism, we become aimless.

Without the purpose of fellowship, we become joyless.

Without the purpose of discipleship, we become useless.

It takes all five! In any church there obviously are some who are better at one or more of these purposes. Some of us are more natural witnesses for Christ, while others find it easier to turn our hearts to God in worship. That's the value of a church: we can be strong together and learn from one another in all five of these purposes. But that doesn't mean that you should focus on only one purpose and I should focus solely on another. Just as we need all five purposes in the church, we need all five in our lives to be the growing believers that God wants us to be. The church is a place where I can learn to balance and strengthen all five of these biblical purposes in my life.

Remember this: *you* are the church.

So the question is, What are *you* going to do about God's purposes for the church? Do you need to make the commitment to join a church—to get off the sidelines as a Christian? How are you taking advantage of the opportunities to grow in the church? How are you following God's call to ministry? Who do you need to bring to Jesus?

Those five purposes are summed up in a purpose statement that I would like us to read together. Let's say this aloud together with the spirit of renewing our commitment to these purposes. Our commitment is:

### Purpose Statement for the Church

To bring people to Jesus and to membership in his family, to develop them to Christlike maturity, and to equip them for their ministry in the church and their life mission in the world in order to magnify God's name.

Let's pray together:

*Jesus, thank you for making the church. We are grateful that through the body of Christ you meet our need to belong to a spiritual family, to be a part of something significant. Jesus, thank you that you are building your church. We make a fresh commitment to be involved in what you are doing in the world through your church. We make ourselves available to you as the head of this church and ask that you would work through us as the body of Christ.*

*We commit ourselves in a fresh new way to your purposes in our own lives. As your ekklesia—called together to live for your purposes—it is our desire to love you with all of our hearts and to love our neighbor as ourselves. Use us as your hands and feet, Jesus, to go into all of the world and make disciples, baptizing them in your name and teaching them to do what you have taught us.*

*In Jesus' name, amen.*

### Teaching Tip

If it is appropriate in the setting where you are teaching this study, end this session by taking the Lord's Supper together as a church.

**Begin working on memory card 10, "The Truth about the Church."**

## Discussion Questions

1. How does the idea of the unity of the church really work in your life? Here are some points of struggle that it would be helpful to discuss honestly.

   • How do you handle it when you disagree strongly on some issue (political, for instance) with a Christian brother or sister?

   • How do you survive the temptation to compare: to think "I wish I had their gift" or "I have better gifts than they do. Why are they being noticed more than I am?"

   • Is our unity in Christ always stronger than the prejudices we grew up with? How can that unity break down those prejudices?

2. Look back at the seven characteristics of *koinonia* fellowship. Which of these is the most important to you personally?

3. Suppose you came home to find five phone messages for you from different people:

   • From someone asking you for your opinion about a new mission project.

   • From a friend asking about how to help two fellow Christians with a disagreement they've been having.

   • From someone asking a question about understanding a Bible verse or Bible truth.

   • From another with an idea for starting a new ministry.

   • From a friend who has some questions about how to truly worship God.

All things being equal, which of these calls would you return first?

*Small Group Leaders:* While knowing that all of the purposes of the church are vital, we each seem to have a passion for one of the purposes. This question helps to see which of the purposes you and those in your group are the most passionate about.

# The Church
## Part 2

**Life Change Objectives**

- To gain a new appreciation for what the church can be in your life and in the world.

- To let go of false pictures of a perfect church and commit to the true picture of a powerful church (filled with weak people!).

**Summary Teaching Outline**

The Metaphors for the Church

    The body of Christ

    The flock of God

    The family (household) of God

    The building of God

    The bride of Christ

A Final Word

A quick review of the last session:

- The church was envisioned by God.
- The church was established by Jesus.
- The church is energized by the Spirit.

The church was made possible by Jesus' death and resurrection.

Our mandate from God is to live out the Great Commission and the Great Commandment through the five purposes of evangelism, fellowship, discipleship, ministry, and worship.

**The New Testament lists sixty-seven names and metaphors for the church, each one giving another dimension and aspect of the nature and mission of the church. Today we'll be looking at five of the most significant metaphors for the church.**

I asked you in the last session what picture came to mind as I said the word *church*. What picture comes to mind now? Is it still the picture of a building that we meet in or has that first impression begun to change a bit? Do you also now see the unity, or the mission, or the fellowship of the church?

There is no doubt that God wants to do a great work in each of our hearts. He wants us more and more to picture what *he* pictures when we think of the church. That is why he has filled his Word with his pictures of the church. These pictures tell us what the church truly is. If you picture the church as weak, God's pictures show you how powerful it truly is. If you think it is a perfect place, God's pictures reveal the church to be a real place. If you think of the church in terms of location and buildings, God's photo album shows the church to be about God's people and God's purposes.

### Teaching Tip

Consider bringing an actual photo album with you to show at this time. If you're really creative you might put pictures in it that represent the body, the flock, etc.—but most of us are not that creative! A photo album with blank pages will do almost as well. Show it to those you're teaching at this point, and then turn the pages as you come to each of the five pictures we'll be looking at in this study.

## The Metaphors for the Church

### *The body of Christ*

**The church is Jesus' body and Jesus is the head of the body.**

**And God placed all things under his feet and appointed him to be head over everything for the church, which is his body, the fullness of him who fills everything in every way.**

**—Ephesians 1:22–23**

Your head tells your body what to do, and your body does it! Anything other than that is unhealthy.

Have you seen those plywood cutouts that you stick your head through as someone takes your photo—maybe at an amusement park? There is a hole where the head should be, and you put your head in the hole and have your picture taken. The picture then looks like your head is on the cartoon character or animal. The hilarious thing about these pictures is that the head and the body don't match! It's funny with a wooden cutout, but this can be a tragedy for the church. Jesus is the head of the church—the head determines what the body looks like and how it acts. It is tragic when the church does not reflect our head, Jesus Christ.

In fact, if he's not the head, then it's not a church.

**Two words are crucial as we study the body of Christ, the church:**

1. **<u>UNITY</u>**

2. **<u>DIVERSITY</u>**

It takes both! Your body has both. Your hand is different from your foot—aren't you glad. God has built your body with amazing diversity, but that diversity must work together in unity.

It's important to understand the foundation for our unity as believers. It's not based on something so fragile as whether I like you today or you complimented me yesterday. It is a historical and theological unity that is built on the character and actions of God.

You and I need to understand that this unity and diversity in the body of Christ are not simply good organizational principles or psychological practices. They are deeply theological priorities for the church.

## Our unity is built upon:

- **Christ breaking down the wall of <u>SEPARATION</u>.**

 **For Christ himself is our way of peace. He has made peace between us Jews and you Gentiles by making us all one family, breaking down the wall of contempt that used to separate us.**
 —Ephesians 2:14 (LB)

- **Our <u>ONENESS</u> in Christ's body.**

 **By his death he ended the angry resentment between us, caused by the Jewish laws which favored the Jews and excluded the Gentiles, for he died to annul that whole system of Jewish laws. Then he took the two groups that had been opposed to each other and made them parts of himself; thus he fused us together to become one new person, and at last there was peace.**
 —Ephesians 2:15 (LB)

- **Our <u>EQUAL</u> <u>STANDING</u> at the cross.**

 **As parts of the same body, our anger against each other has disappeared, for both of us have been reconciled to God. And so the feud ended at last at the cross.**
 —Ephesians 2:16 (LB)

- **Our common <u>CITIZENSHIP</u>, common <u>FAMILY</u>, and common <u>FUTURE</u> destination.**

**Now you are no longer strangers to God and foreigners to heaven, but you are members of God's very own family, citizens of God's country, and you belong in God's household with every other Christian.**
— Ephesians 2:19 (LB)

Jesus broke down the wall, that's a fact. He made us one in him, that's a fact. He gave us equal standing before him and a common future with him, fact and fact.

Think with me for just a moment about that wall that Jesus broke down. If he broke down the wall, then where does the disunity among us come from? It's our choice! A choice that treats as meaningless what Jesus did for us on the cross and what he is planning for us in eternity. When you think, "I can't have unity with that believer because of their culture or the color of their skin or the language that they speak," you are choosing to ignore the facts of what Jesus has done. When you say, "I won't ever talk to that person in my church again because of what they did to me or said about me," you're attempting to rebuild a wall that Jesus tore down a long time ago.

There is one side of us that says, "That's just the way it is. Christians are only human, after all. We struggle with jealousy and with prejudice and with fear of getting close to others just like everyone else. It's always been that way and it always will be." But these truths will not let us stay there. Once they take hold of your life, you cannot help but begin to think in a different way. "Jesus died for that person, how could I hate him?" "We're going to spend eternity together celebrating God's goodness to us. Why not start now?" "Jesus broke down the wall. Who am I to try to build it up again?"

While history tells us that believers have always struggled with unity, it also clearly reveals that any time we have decided to embrace the unity that Christ provides, the results are immediate and powerful. There is incredible power in our unity as believers. That's why Satan fights it so!

> We are olive-skinned, curly-haired, blue-eyed and black.
> We come from boarding schools and ghettos, mansions and shacks.
> We wear turbans, we wear robes. We like tamales. We eat rice.
> We have convictions and opinions, and to agree would be nice,
> But we don't, still we try and this much we know:
> 'Tis better inside with each other than outside living alone.[1]

Let's take a moment to bring this down to a day-to-day reality.

### Key Personal Perspective

*How Do I Handle a Disagreement with a Fellow Believer?*

### The wrong way: <u>GOSSIP</u>

**Gossip separates the best of friends.**

—**Proverbs 16:28** (NLT)

There is no sin that can tear a church apart quite so quickly as gossip. Gossip is simply talking to others about a problem that you have with someone rather than talking to the someone with whom you have a problem. We never call it gossip: we might call it talking about the problem or relating a spiritual concern or even sharing a prayer request. The truth is, if you're talking with someone who is not part of the problem or part of the solution, it's gossip. What's so destructive about gossip? It magnifies the problem rather than dealing with the problem. You've involved a lot more people now—the problem is bigger. You've intensified your feelings by talking with others about the problem without getting to the root of the problem—the problem is bigger.

### The right way: <u>CONFRONT</u> <u>IT</u>

**If another believer sins against you, go privately and point out the fault. If the other person listens and confesses it, you have won that person back. But if you are unsuccessful, take one or two others with you and go back again, so that everything you say may be confirmed by two or three witnesses. If that person still refuses to listen, take your case to the church. If the church decides you are right, but the other person won't accept it, treat that person as a pagan or a corrupt tax collector.**

—**Matthew 18:15–17** (NLT)

**Therefore, if you are offering your gift at the altar and there remember that your brother has something against you, leave your gift there in front of the altar. First go and be reconciled to your brother; then come and offer your gift.**

—**Matthew 5:23–24**

Look at Matthew 18. *You* go to the person with whom you have a problem—talk it out face to face. The majority of the time, the problem is solved right then and there. If you realize that someone has a problem with you, are you supposed to sit back and wait for them to come to you? Look at Matthew 5:23–24. *You* go to the person who you know has a problem with you. In every case, God makes you personally responsible for confronting the problem.

## Our diversity

**Now the body is not made up of one part but of many. If the foot should say, "Because I am not a hand, I do not belong to the body," it would not for that reason cease to be part of the body. And if the ear should say, "Because I am not an eye, I do not belong to the body," it would not for that reason cease to be part of the body. If the whole body were an eye, where would the sense of hearing be? If the whole body were an ear, where would the sense of smell be?**

**—1 Corinthians 12:14–17**

Sometimes we miss God's humor in the Bible. We read verses with a solemn look frozen on our face, when God is looking for a smile or an outright laugh. One of the places in the Bible where the laugh is warranted is Paul's words about the need for diversity in the human body in 1 Corinthians 12.

> Suppose the whole body were an eye—then how would you hear? Or if your whole body were just one big ear, how could you smell anything?
>
> —1 Corinthians 12:17 (NLT)

Picture yourself as one big eyeball or as one big ear trying to flop to work in the morning, and you'll get the point. It's ridiculous to think that unity means we need to all be the same. It's in the diversity that the real beauty and the real power of the body of Christ shine forth.

Diversity means that instead of expecting me to be exactly like every other Christian, God's real joy is when I express the unique gifts that he has given me. One of my favorite stories about this is the parable of "A rabbit on the swim team."

> Once upon a time, the animals decided they should do something meaningful to meet the problems of the new world. So they organized a school. They adopted a curriculum of running, climbing, swimming, and flying. To make it easier to administer the curriculum, all the animals took all the subjects.
>
> The duck was excellent in swimming; in fact, better than his instructor. He made only passing grades in flying, however, and was very poor in running. Since he was slow in running, he had to drop swimming and stay after school to practice running. This caused his webbed feet to be badly worn, so that he was only average in swimming. But average was quite acceptable, so nobody worried about that—except the duck.
>
> The rabbit started at the top of his class in running, but developed a nervous twitch in his leg muscles because of so much make-up work in swimming. The squirrel was excellent in climbing, but he encountered constant frustration in flying class because his teacher made him start from the ground up instead of from the treetop down. He developed "charlie horses" from overexertion and only got a C in climbing and a D in running.

The eagle was a problem child and was severely disciplined for being a non-conformist. In climbing classes, he beat all the others to the top of the tree but insisted on using his own way to get there.[2]

It's unity *with* diversity that makes the church a body. Look at Romans 12:4 and 5.

**Just as each of us has one body with many members, and these members do not all have the same function, so in Christ we who are many form one body, and each member belongs to all the others.**

**—Romans 12:4–5**

Unity with diversity makes a symphony orchestra. Without the diversity all the instruments would sound alike. Who would go to hear an all-tuba symphony!? And without the unity, all you would hear is a jumble of noise. It takes both!

Unity with diversity creates a beautiful quilt. Without the diversity you'd have a bedspread of only one color. Without the unity of the pieces of material being sewn together, all you have is a bunch of scraps. It takes both!

Unity with diversity results in a winning baseball team. Without the diversity you'd have nine guys trying to pitch or play first base. Without the unity every player would be in it for themselves. "You want me to sacrifice myself to move the runner to second? I don't think so!" It takes both unity and diversity.

> Discussion question 1 can be used here.

The church as the body of Christ is one of the most common pictures of the church in the New Testament, so we spent the most time on this. There are, however, some other pictures that help us to fill in all that God means for the church to be in the world; and all that he means for you and me to be in the church.

## The flock of God

**I have other sheep that are not of this sheep pen. I must bring them also. They too will listen to my voice, and there shall be one flock and one shepherd.**

**—John 10:16**

1. **We are the sheep.**

**This image emphasizes that members of the church, as the sheep of Christ, <u>BELONG TO HIM</u>.**

But you do not believe because you are not my sheep. My sheep listen to my voice; I know them, and they follow me. I give them eternal life, and they shall never perish; no one can snatch them out of my hand. My Father, who has given them to me, is greater than all; no one can snatch them out of my Father's hand.

—John 10:26–29

I've always thought it fascinating that God compares us to sheep, considering what helpless animals sheep can be. Some sheep become so top heavy when their wool grows out that if they fall onto their backs, they cannot right themselves. They have to lie in the grass, their four little legs kicking in the air, until the shepherd comes to set them on their feet again. Sometimes we're not even as smart as the sheep. We find ourselves on our back, kicking and bleating, but when the shepherd comes by, *we refuse his help!* "If only I kick a little harder or a little longer," we tell ourselves, "I know I can get myself righted on my own."

Say this together with me, "I . . . am . . . a . . . sheep." We are spiritually helpless. We'd save ourselves a lot of pain if only we'd recognize that sooner. We'd be a more powerful force for change in this world if only we'd see that more clearly.

2. **Jesus is the shepherd.**

   **The metaphor of Jesus as our shepherd shows his love and care for us.**

   I am the good shepherd. The good shepherd lays down his life for the sheep. I am the good shepherd; I know my sheep and my sheep know me—just as the Father knows me and I know the Father—and I lay down my life for the sheep. I have other sheep that are not of this sheep pen. I must bring them also. They too will listen to my voice, and there shall be one flock and one shepherd.

   —John 10:11, 14–16

We are the body, Jesus is the head. We are the sheep, Jesus is the shepherd. Do you see a pattern here?

Let me take a moment to picture for you what it means for Jesus to be our shepherd, through Max Lucado's comparison of a shepherd and a cowboy.

> Behold a hero of the west: the cowboy.
> He rears his horse to a stop on the rim of the canyon. He shifts his weight in his saddle, weary from the cattle trail. One finger pushes his hat up on his head. One jerk of the kerchief reveals a sun-leathered face. . . .
> He needs no one. He is a cowboy. The American hero.
> Behold a hero in the Bible: the shepherd.

On the surface he appears similar to the cowboy. He, too, is rugged. He sleeps where the jackals howl and works where the wolves prowl. Never off duty. Always alert. Like the cowboy, he makes his roof the stars and the pasture his home.

But that is where the similarities end.

The shepherd loves his sheep. It's not that the cowboy doesn't appreciate the cow; it's just that he doesn't know the animal. He doesn't even want to. Have you ever seen a picture of a cowboy caressing a cow? Have you ever seen a shepherd caring for a sheep? Why the difference?

Simple. The cowboy leads the cow to slaughter. The shepherd leads the sheep to be shorn. The cowboy wants the meat of the cow. The shepherd wants the wool of the sheep. And so they treat the animals differently.

The cowboy drives the cattle. The shepherd leads the sheep.

A herd has a dozen cowboys. A flock has one shepherd.

The cowboy wrestles, brands, herds, and ropes.

The shepherd leads, guides, feeds, and anoints.

The cowboy knows the names of the trail hands.

The shepherd knows the names of the sheep.[3]

> Discussion question 2 can be used here.

> **Split Session Plan:** If you're teaching this study over two sessions, end the first session here.

## *The family (household) of God*

17

As we're looking through God's "photo album" of the church, we've seen that he pictures us as a body and that he sees us as a flock. Turn the page and the next picture that you see is of a family.

We've all been at school events or children's performances where we see the row of parents with cameras in the back of the room. A child is recognized—flash goes the camera. Someone onstage smiles—flash. He or she gets their graduation certificate—flash!

If God were at the back of some imaginary room looking at his church, when would his camera flash? What is it that brings him great joy as he looks at his church? It is every time we live out one of these pictures that he is showing us. Every time we act like his family.

We trust him as our Father and share our faith in spite of the risk. Flash!

We make the effort to love one another in spite of our differences. Flash!

We notice one of the world's "unnoticed" people, and love them in Jesus' name.

We invest our lives in eternity rather than the here and now.

We honestly confess our sin and weakness to another believer.

Flash, flash, flash. God is rejoicing in his family.

What does it mean that the church is the family of God?

1. **God adopts us into his family.**

   **In the physical world, individuals automatically become part of a family unit when they are born. God wisely made the same provision for his spiritual children as well. At salvation, we are placed by the Holy Spirit into God's family, and God is now our Father.**

   God adopts us into his family through his Spirit. Look at 1 Corinthians 12:13.

   **For we were all baptized by one Spirit into one body—whether Jews or Greeks, slave or free—and we were all given the one Spirit to drink.**
   **—1 Corinthians 12:13**

   And we are not adopted as God's *only* child. We are a part of the church, this huge family of God; all adopted by him because of his love. Romans 8:15 tells us that as we see this truth it changes our relationship with God.

   **And so we should not be like cringing, fearful slaves, but we should behave like God's very own children, adopted into the bosom of his family, and calling to him, "Father, Father."**
   **—Romans 8:15 (LB)**

   God is not an overbearing and unwilling parent—he is a loving Father. That is a truth that you and I grow to recognize throughout our lives on this earth. And as each one of us grows it helps all of us to grow. Just as the attitude that any child in a family has toward his or her parents deeply affects everyone in that family, the attitude each of us has toward God rubs off on everyone around us.

   Every time you call God "Father," it strengthens not only your own heart but God's own family—the church. Every time you choose to relate to God out of faith and not fear, it strengthens you and it also strengthens God's church.

   At what point in your life do you need to begin to trust God as your Father?

## 2. We're to treat one another as family.

**Do not rebuke an older man harshly, but exhort him as if he were your father. Treat younger men as brothers, older women as mothers, and younger women as sisters, with absolute purity.**

—1 Timothy 5:1–2

First Timothy 5:1–2 tells us that our relationships in the church are family relationships. In the last session we talked about the fact that God does not expect us to be a perfect family. But he does expect us to be a healthy family. These verses take the idea of family even deeper. We should be family in the way that we relate to one another on a day-to-day basis.

Give an older man the kind of respect that you would, or should, give to your own father. Treat an older woman as if she were your mother. (The only problem with applying this part of the verse is finding a woman who will admit she's an "older woman"!) Treat younger men as brothers and women as sisters. Don't you love the honesty of the Bible? Paul recognizes that our close relationships as believers could be used by Satan to create a temptation—and so warns Timothy to treat younger women as sisters, with absolute purity.

The church is a family! Look at the person next to you and say, "Hi, brother" or "Hi, sister." If they are a *lot* older than you, you can take the risk and say, "Hi, Mom" or "Hi, Dad." It feels a little bit strange, doesn't it? But it is what God means for his church to be.

Who do you need to begin to treat as part of the family?

> Discussion question 3 can be used here.

## *The building of God*

There is a famous story from the days when Sir Christopher Wren was building St. Paul's cathedral in London. Wren was making a tour one day and asked a man working on the building, "What are you doing?"

The workman replied, "I am cutting this stone to the right size."

He asked a second man working elsewhere, "What are you doing?"

"I am earning money," he retorted.

When Wren asked a third man, the man paused from his work and excitedly replied, "I am helping Sir Christopher Wren to build St. Paul's cathedral!"

As Christians, we must hold before us the loftiest ideal of our presence in the church—we are here, in the Spirit's energy, working to help the Lord Jesus build His church.[4]

When I say "church building," what do you picture? A cathedral? A little brown church in the vale? One man filling out some medical forms wrote in the blank next to the question "Church Preference" the words "Red Brick." Is that what you think of when you think of a church building?

When God writes the word "building" next to "church" he is thinking of you!

**You are also God's building (1 Cor. 3:9 TEV).**

**In contrast to the Old Testament period in which Israel <u>HAD</u> a temple (Ex. 25:8), the church <u>IS</u> a temple: a living, vital temple.**

> **Consequently, you are no longer foreigners and aliens, but fellow citizens with God's people and members of God's household, built on the foundation of the apostles and prophets, with Christ Jesus himself as the chief cornerstone. In him the whole building is joined together and rises to become a holy temple in the Lord. And in him you too are being built together to become a dwelling in which God lives by his Spirit.**
> **—Ephesians 2:19–22**

Circle "the whole building." That not only means believers in this particular church but believers of all churches around the world who follow Jesus Christ. That not only means Christians in this particular time but believers from every century. We are all being built together to show the awesome greatness of God.

**In this metaphor, Jesus is pictured as the <u>CHIEF</u> <u>CORNERSTONE</u>.**

**The cornerstone was placed at the juncture of two walls to tie them together. In arches, a stone was placed between the supporting sides. The weight of the arch was on that stone, and if the stone was removed, the arch could collapse.**

He is the head; we are the body. He is the shepherd; we are the sheep. He is the cornerstone; we are the building. Do you get the feeling that this is a picture that God does not want us to miss?

The cornerstone in ancient buildings was not a decorative commemoration. It was the stone on which all of the weight of the building rested.

All of the weight rests on Jesus! He does not expect you to be a cornerstone—that's his job. If you feel that all the weight of the church or the Christian life is on your shoulders, you are trying to do Jesus' job. It's not your job to hold the universe together. It's not your job to make everything work. But God does have a job for you:

Individual believers are pictured as <u>LIVING</u> <u>STONES</u>.

In the construction of the church as a temple, each stone is a living stone because it shares the divine nature, and the building as a whole becomes a dwelling place for God through his Spirit.

> As you come to him, the living Stone—rejected by men but chosen by God and precious to him—you also, like living stones, are being built into a spiritual house to be a holy priesthood, offering spiritual sacrifices acceptable to God through Jesus Christ.
>
> —1 Peter 2:4–5

What a clear picture this is of the importance of individual responsibility combined with the complete interdependence we have in the church. Two things about dwellings built of stone:

First, if you've ever looked at a rock or brick wall, you know that every stone is important. Take out even one, and the hole that it leaves will be glaring. The first thing that you see when you look at that wall will be the missing stone. Each one of us has more importance than we realize. You may think that what you do goes unnoticed, but God sees how it fits perfectly into the temple that he is building.

Second, you know that a single brick, no matter how wonderful a brick it may be, cannot make a building. Take the greatest, most beautiful, most perfect brick that has ever been made, and by itself it is only a brick. It takes a lot of bricks to make a building. It takes all of us together to make the church. This is not a matter of it being a good idea that we work together. We *must* work together to be the church.

---

### Key Personal Perspective

**How readily do you accept believers from other denominations and churches as being "real" Christians? Have you been trying to carry all the weight of the Christian life on your shoulders? Do you need to see the importance of your place in God's building? Do you need to recognize your need to depend on others in the body of Christ?**

---

Discussion question 4 can be used here.

### *The bride of Christ*

**This is the one metaphor that is used of the church in a prophetic sense.**

There is a moment in every wedding that is unforgettable. The doors at the back of the church swing open, and the bride enters the room. Every eye turns to her, and they miss seeing the groom's reaction. Grooms have a great variety of reactions as their bride starts her walk down the aisle. Some smile, others sweat. Some look like they're about to jump out of their skin, others get a look of quiet strength in their eyes. More than a few have been known to faint. These are all different reactions to the same emotion: experiencing a supremely important moment of life.

We look forward to the day when Jesus will bring his bride to heaven. Jesus is the groom; his bride is the church. If you were able to look into his eyes as he watches his bride—the church—preparing to come down the aisle of eternity, what would you see? Joy! Unadulterated, unending, unmatched joy!

This picture of the bride is a picture that God took a long time to develop. From the Old Testament through the New, this is an image that slowly comes into focus.

- **Israel was often portrayed in the Old Testament as being the <u>WIFE</u> or <u>BRIDE</u> of God.**

   **And I will make you my promised bride forever. I will be good and fair; I will show you my love and mercy. I will be true to you as my promised bride, and you will know the LORD.**
   —**Hosea 2:19–20** (NCV)

- **However, Israel was repeatedly <u>UNFAITHFUL</u> to her vows of love to God.**

   **This message from the Lord came to me during the reign of King Josiah: Have you seen what Israel does? Like a wanton wife who gives herself to other men at every chance, so Israel has worshiped other gods on every hill, beneath every shady tree. I thought that someday she would return to me and once again be mine; but she didn't come back. And her faithless sister Judah saw the continued rebellion of Israel.**
   —**Jeremiah 3:6–7** (LB)

As you read these verses you can see how *personally* God takes his relationship to his people. He compares the unfaithfulness of Israel to a "wanton wife who gives herself to other men at every chance." Even in these words of judgment, you can hear the deep love relationship that God desires to have with us as his people.

- Unlike faithless Israel, the church is portrayed in Scripture as being a <u>VIRGIN BRIDE</u> awaiting the coming of her bridegroom.

> I am jealous for you with a godly jealousy. I promised you to one husband, to Christ, so that I might present you as a pure virgin to him.
>
> —2 Corinthians 11:2

True Love Waits is a concept that has swept the country. Some of you may have teenagers who have made a True Love Waits commitment to sexual purity until marriage. As a part of this commitment, many girls put on a ring given to them by their parents. It's a symbol of their commitment to God and of their decision to remain pure.

God has placed a symbol of purity into our hearts today in the person of the Holy Spirit. As the bride of Christ, the church awaits the day when we will celebrate the joy of our commitment to him throughout eternity. As the bridegroom, Jesus awaits the day when he will bring the church to himself in perfect purity and glorious beauty. That purity and beauty are never in question because they were bought with Jesus' sacrifice on the cross.

**In Ephesians 5:22–33, the analogy is drawn comparing the husband and wife relationship in marriage to Christ and his bride, the church. The illustration is powerful because it reveals the magnitude of Christ's love for his church. He loved her enough to die for her. It also reveals the obedient response the church is to have to the bridegroom, Jesus Christ.**

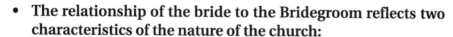

> Husbands, love your wives, just as Christ loved the church and gave himself up for her to make her holy, cleansing her by the washing with water through the word.
>
> —Ephesians 5:25–26

- **The relationship of the bride to the Bridegroom reflects two characteristics of the nature of the church:**

As we launch into this look at what we can learn from Jesus' words in Matthew 25, it is important to understand how a wedding happened in Jesus' day. Far different than what most of us experience, the Jewish wedding in first-century Israel was a detailed and drawn-out process.

First, there was an engagement period. During this period of a year or so the couple was not married, but they were committed to one another. So committed, in fact, that they would have had to get a divorce in order to separate during this engagement.

At the end of this engagement period came the fetching of the bride. The groom would go to the bride's home to take her to the ceremony. While she knew at about what time he would arrive, she did not know the exact hour.

Then there was the wedding ceremony.

After this came the wedding feast. And this was no little feast! It was a weeklong celebration of the new bride and groom in their new home. They would be called prince and princess throughout this week—for many it was the happiest week of their lives.

What does God want us to learn about the church from this picture?

1. **The church lives with a sense of urgency to always be <u>PRE-PARED</u> for the Bridegroom.**

> At that time the kingdom of heaven will be like ten virgins who took their lamps and went out to meet the bridegroom. Five of them were foolish and five were wise. The foolish ones took their lamps but did not take any oil with them. The wise, however, took oil in jars along with their lamps. The bridegroom was a long time in coming, and they all became drowsy and fell asleep. At midnight the cry rang out: "Here's the bridegroom! Come out to meet him!" Then all the virgins woke up and trimmed their lamps. The foolish ones said to the wise, "Give us some of your oil; our lamps are going out." "No," they replied, "there may not be enough for both us and you. Instead, go to those who sell oil and buy some for yourselves." But while they were on their way to buy the oil, the bridegroom arrived. The virgins who were ready went in with him to the wedding banquet. And the door was shut. Later the others also came. "Sir! Sir!" they said. "Open the door for us!" But he replied, "I tell you the truth, I don't know you." Therefore keep watch, because you do not know the day or the hour.
> —Matthew 25:1–13

Dr. J. Alexander Findlay tells of what he experienced in Israel.

> When we were approaching the gates of a Galilean town, I caught a sight of ten maidens gaily clad and playing some kind of musical instrument, as they danced along the road in front of our car; when I asked what they were doing, the driver told me that they were going to keep the bride company till her bridegroom arrived. I asked him if there was any chance of seeing the wedding, but he shook his head, saying in effect: "It might be tonight, or tomorrow night, or in a fortnight's time; nobody knows for certain." Then he went on to explain that one of the great things to do, if you could, at a middle-class wedding in Israel was to catch the bridal party napping. So the bridegroom comes unexpectedly, and sometimes in the middle of the night; it is true that he is required by public opinion to send a man along the street to shout: "Behold! The bridegroom is coming!" but that may happen at any time; so the bridal party have to be ready to go out into the street at any time to meet him, whenever he chooses to come.[5]

These next two sessions, as we study the Second Coming of Jesus, we'll be looking at how we can live with an attitude of anticipation and hope as we wait for Jesus' return.

## 2. The church is to <u>INVITE</u> <u>OTHERS</u> into the new relationship with the Bridegroom.

At the coming of Jesus there will be a great banquet celebrating the love of Jesus for his church. God wants as many at that feast as possible. Look at these verses.

> **Then he said to his servants, "The wedding banquet is ready, but those I invited did not deserve to come. Go to the street corners and invite to the banquet anyone you find."**
>
> —Matthew 22:8–9

> **Blessed are those who are invited to the wedding supper of the Lamb!**
>
> —Revelation 19:9

> **The Spirit and the bride say, "Come!" And let him who hears say, "Come!" Whoever is thirsty, let him come; and whoever wishes, let him take the free gift of the water of life.**
>
> —Revelation 22:17

As a church, God has given us the incredible privilege of handing out as many invitations as we can, letting others know that they are as welcome at this banquet as we are. We should not just lean back and think, "I'm glad I have my invitation to the banquet." As the bride of Christ, we are to invite everyone to this wedding feast.

This is an invitation that is filled with the anticipation of joy. We are in the "engagement" period now—committed to Jesus—and yet our relationship is not yet all that it will be in heaven. We still do not have all that is promised us in this eternal "marriage" to Jesus. We still have not yet had the feast—the great wedding supper of the Lamb that the book of Revelation talks about.

### Key Personal Perspective

**Being the bride of Christ is a spiritual love affair. Is this a reality in your life? Or does the idea seem too sentimental? Is there submission in your heart to Jesus as your Bridegroom? Are you ready to meet him? Are there some priorities you need to rearrange so that you can concentrate more on loving him?**

Discussion question 5 can be used here.

# A Final Word

**Is the church a useless, worn-out institution? It doesn't have to be. God has made all the provisions necessary for local churches to be vibrant, transformational groups of believers who live inter-dependent, authentic lives of ministry and mission, building bridges so that lost people can find hope in God. The Devil can't stop us; the pervasive culture around us can't stop us. We are the only ones who can cause the church to lose its place of importance by not acting like the body of Christ, the flock of God, the family of God, the building of God, and the bride of Christ.**

Cyprian, the bishop of Carthage, wrote this to a friend in the third century:

> It is a bad world—an incredibly bad world. But in the midst of it, I have found a quiet and a holy people who have learned a great secret. They are the despised and the persecuted, but they care not. They have overcome the world. These people are called Christians, and I am one of them.
>
> —Cyprian, bishop of Carthage

God's church is *God's* church, and so can never be defeated! We are imperfect, but we are also God's holy people. Listen to these words:

> God has always had a people.
>
> Many a foolish conqueror has made the mistake of thinking that because he had forced the Church of Jesus Christ out of sight, He had stilled its voice and snuffed out its life.
>
> But God has always had a people!
>
> The powerful current of a rushing river is not diminished because it is forced to flow underground. The purest water is the stream that bursts crystal clear into the sunlight after it has forced its way through solid rock.
>
> There have been charlatans, like Simon the magician, who sought to barter on the open market that power which cannot be bought or sold. But, God has always had a people, men who could not be bought, and women who were beyond purchase. God has always had a people!
>
> There have been times of affluence and prosperity when the Church's message has been diluted into oblivion by those who sought to make it socially attractive, neatly organized, and financially profitable.
>
> It has been gold-plated, draped in purple, and encrusted with jewels. It has been misrepresented, ridiculed, lauded, and scorned.
>
> These followers of Jesus Christ have been, according to the whim of the times, elevated as sacred leaders, and martyred as heretics. Yet, through it all there marches on that powerful army of the meek—God's chosen people who cannot be bought, flattered, murdered, or stilled! On through the ages they march! God's Church triumphant, alive and well![6]

These people are called Christians, and you are one of them!

You are a part of his body. Live in unity and rejoice in our diversity. You are his flock; follow your shepherd. You are his family; love one another. You are his building and you are his bride, showing others what God is like and inviting others to the great wedding supper of Jesus.

Read with me the words of Jesus as we close.

**I will build my church, and the gates of Hades will not overcome it!**
—Matthew 16:18

**Finish memorizing memory card 10, "The Truth about the Church," before the next session. We're sure there will be a quiz on these cards when you get to heaven!**

 ## Discussion Questions

In our group discussion, we're going to look back at the questions we've asked about how the pictures of the church challenge us in a *personal* way.

1. *The church is the body of Christ:* every part of the body is important. (What part would *you* want to give up?) Do you feel like you're an important part of the body of Christ?

2. *The church is the flock of God:* what are the things that we can do that make sure that Jesus is the shepherd leading us, that we aren't trying to lead ourselves?

3. *The church is the family of God:* how does this help you to picture your responsibilities toward other believers?

4. *The church is the building of God:* how readily do you accept believers from other denominations and churches as being "real" Christians? Have you been trying to carry all of the weight of the Christian life on your shoulders? Do you need to see the importance of your place in God's building? Do you need to recognize your need to depend on others in the body of Christ?

5. *The church is the bride of Christ:* being the bride of Christ is a spiritual love affair. Is this a reality in your life? Or does the idea seem too sentimental? Is there submission in your heart to Jesus as your Bridegroom? Is your life ready to meet him? Are there some priorities you need to rearrange so that you can concentrate more on loving him?

## For Further Study

Getz, Gene. *Sharpening the Focus of the Church.* Chicago: Moody Press, 1974.

MacArthur, John, Jr. *Body Dynamics.* Wheaton, Ill.: Victor, 1983.

Moore, John, and Ken Neff. *A New Testament Blueprint for the Church.* Chicago: Moody Press, 1985.

Radmacher, Earl D. *The Nature of the Church.* Portland, Ore.: Western Baptist Press, 1972.

Warren, Rick. *The Purpose-Driven Church.* Grand Rapids, Mich.: Zondervan, 1995.

# The Second Coming
## Part 1

### Life Change Objective

**That you will see the Second Coming not as a source of confusion or fear but as a source of hope.**

### Summary Teaching Outline

Any study of the Second Coming has to come with some "warning labels" attached.

Signs of Jesus' Coming
    Signs pointing to the end
    Signs preceding the end
    Signs accompanying the end

The Time of the Second Coming
    Descriptions by Jesus
    Facts about the timing

People of the End Times
    The Man of Lawlessness/The Beast/The Antichrist
    A second beast/the False Prophet
    The two witnesses
    The 144,000
    Jesus Christ

I once knew a woman whose stated goal was to outlive three husbands so that she could marry four different men. She even knew exactly what jobs she wanted these men to have and in what order she wanted to marry them, feeling that this would best prepare her for what she needed most in life.

First, a banker, then a movie star, then a pastor, and finally a funeral director:

Or, to say it another way,

One for the money, two for the show, three to get ready, and four to go!

When it comes to the Second Coming, you'd better do a better job of getting ready than that!

Let me ask you as we begin,

**What do you feel about the truth of Jesus' Second Coming?**

**Apathy? Anticipation? Anxiety?**

Some people live in anxious fear of the Second Coming. It all sounds so strange and scary. The majority of believers today are fairly apathetic—indifferent—about Jesus' Second Coming. We know that it's something that will happen, but don't see much meaning for today.

As we study the Second Coming of Christ in these next few sessions, my goal is simple: to help those of you who are indifferent to become inspired, to lead those of you who live in fear of the Second Coming to begin to live in anticipation. *Hope* is the message of the Second Coming of Jesus. If you don't feel hope as we study these truths, we've missed the main point.

Do you watch a basketball game any differently if you've taped it and already know the score? If your team won (and why would you watch a game on tape that you knew your team had lost!) you don't have any anxiety about the outcome. You just enjoy watching how the victory was won. As believers in Christ I can tell you for certain, our team wins! We're just watching God's victory play itself out. That is a truth that has the power to inspire the way you live every day of your life!

Attitude is all important as you look toward the Second Coming. The Bible, particularly the book of Revelation, is very clear about the attitude needed to fully understand what God is saying to us about the end. The attitude is not worry but worship. Worship—keep your eyes on Christ—and you'll find yourself being filled with hope as we study these truths.

**Any study of the Second Coming has to come with some "warning labels" attached.**

An electric hair dryer will have a warning label saying, "Don't use near water!" You could be in for a real shock if you ignore the warning. The truth of the Second Coming is a *powerful* truth—and can become a dangerous truth unless you observe a few simple guidelines.

### Teaching Tip

You may want to actually write out some large warning labels that have the three statements below written on them ("Don't lose responsibility in the midst of curiosity," "Don't lose delight in the details," and "Watch out for polarization"). Hold these warning labels up for everyone to see as you begin each of these points. Again, it's amazing how you can help to focus people's attention and sharpen their retention through an object that you hold in your hand.

**_Warning:_ Don't lose personal <u>RESPONSIBILITY</u> in the midst of historical and theological <u>CURIOSITY</u>.**

We have missed the whole purpose of the study of prophecy if it does not cause us to become more like the Lord Jesus Christ in our daily living.

You apply to your life the truths of the Second Coming the same way that you apply any other Scripture. This "application bridge" illustration is a guide for faithfully interpreting and living the truths of the Bible.[1]

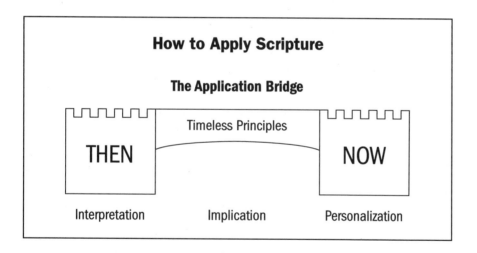

The application bridge moves from the then to the now—with the bridge between the two being the timeless principle from God's Word. In order to "walk across" this bridge, you must ask three questions concerning a Bible passage. Look with me at these three questions as you would ask them of any Bible passage, and then at how we would answer them when looking at the book of Revelation.

1. **What did the Bible passage mean to the original hearers?**

   **Much of the prophecy about the Second Coming is apocalyptic literature (from the Greek word *apocalypse*, "to unveil, to reveal"), a type of writing designed to make the truth clear to some while hiding it from others.**

   You'll soon understand why God chose to hide the meaning from some.

   All of the things that you read about beasts and horns and seas that we have a difficult time understanding were understood perfectly by those who first read Revelation.

   Look at this political cartoon as an example of what I mean.

   **Teaching Tip**

   Add a picture of a current political cartoon to the PowerPoint presentation at this point, or just remind participants of some symbols in a political cartoon by asking, "When you see a donkey it means . . . When you see an elephant it symbolizes . . ."

   What does the elephant mean? How about the donkey? We know that today. But would people 2,000 years from now understand our meaning? The best example we have today of what apocalyptic writing was like is the political cartoon.

   The reason, by the way, that this kind of writing was used was because the Christians were under the control of foreign oppressors, such as the Romans. Through this kind of writing the Christians could get away with veiled references to these powers.

   These pictures of beasts and angels around the throne of heaven are unfamiliar to many of us—but we need to realize that they are meant to help us understand. Merrill Tenney wrote

   > However difficult of interpretation [Revelation] may be for its modern readers, it was not designed to mystify, but rather to explain the truth of God more clearly. For this reason one should approach it with the expectation of learning, and not with the expectation of being confused.[2]

2. **What is the underlying timeless principle?**

   **In a word, <u>HOPE</u>.**

The Scriptures concerning Jesus' Second Coming not only talk about hope for the believers living at that time but about hope for us. It's obvious as you read that we're looking at many prophecies that have yet to be fulfilled.

3. Where or how could I practice this principle?

As much as we talk about the time and events of the Second Coming, the Bible emphasizes the application of this truth in our lives. *It is a sin* to study the Second Coming looking only for timetables. The message of hope must make an impact on the way we live.

Remember:

It is a message to obey, not just to listen to (James 1:22).

Knowing what is right to do and then not doing it is sin (James 4:17).

Far too many believers have a fascination with the future without any application for today.

*Warning:* Don't lose the <u>DELIGHT</u> in the <u>DETAILS</u>.

Listen to what Billy Graham had to say about losing delight in the details.

> Once in the Louvre Museum in Paris, I stood inches away from a large impressionistic painting by Renoir. "What in the world is that?" I wondered aloud. My wife answered, "Stand back, Bill, and you will see it." I had stepped too close to the masterpiece and each individual detail, each oil splotch, each brush stroke kept me from seeing the whole. I was bogged down by the details. But when I stood back, the mysterious puzzle disappeared and the beautiful vision of the artist formed in my brain.
>
> For too long, too many of us have stood too close to the Apocalypse of John. We have turned that great masterpiece into a series of blotches and brush marks. We have tried to outguess each other at the modern meaning of every star, every dragon, and every number, and we have lost the grand design of the prophet's vision and have missed the urgency of his warnings.[3]
>
> —Billy Graham

My prayer is that during these next two sessions we'll be able to step back together to take in the beauty of God's plan. I want to deepen your delight in what God is preparing to do.

*Warning:* Watch out for "polarization" in teaching about the Second Coming.

When it comes to teaching about the Second Coming, it's good to spend some time at the "equator" before being drawn away by the magnetic attraction of the "polar regions." In other words, look at the whole truth before being drawn aside by one or another slant on the truth.

Anytime there are two sides to an issue, people's tendency is to polarize—to draw apart to extremes. All of a sudden they are arguing and debating rather than communicating. Most books on the Second Coming spend more than half of their pages telling you why Christians who have a different view of how the details of the Second Coming will occur are wrong.

So, with these warning labels in clear view . . .

In the next two sessions we'll be looking together at:
- The signs of the return of Jesus
- The time of the Second Coming
- The "cast of characters" involved in Jesus' return
- The events surrounding the return of Jesus
- The meaning for my everyday life

---

 **A Closer Look**

Is the Second Coming of Christ an important perspective that God wants us to have?

Just remember . . .

One out of every 30 verses in the Bible mentions the subject of the end of time, or of Christ's return.

There are 216 chapters in the New Testament. There are well over 300 references to the return of Christ in the New Testament.

Only four of the 27 New Testament books fail to mention Christ's return.[4]

—Chuck Swindoll

---

Discussion question 1 can be used here.

# Signs of Jesus' Coming

When you drive down a freeway you see all kinds of signs giving you directions and distances. The Bible tells us that God has set up clear signposts in our world to tell us that Jesus is coming again. Some of these signs can be seen today, and others are coming later. In fact, there are three types of signs we need to be aware of.

**Three types of signs:**
1. Signs pointing to the end (the beginning of birth pains)
2. Signs immediately preceding the end time events
3. Signs accompanying the end time events

## *Signs pointing to the end*

There are a number of things that Jesus said would happen before his Second Coming. He called these the "beginning of birth pains." These are signs, but not signs that we will see only at the very end. They are signs that have shown believers for 2,000 years that this world is not God's final plan. These are signs that we can see now. They are the signs of the deterioration and inadequacy of this world. For thousands of years we've been able to look at these and say, "This world is not as stable as it sometimes seems. Jesus could be coming at any moment!"

> Jesus said to them: "Watch out that no one deceives you. Many will come in my name, claiming 'I am he,' and will deceive many. When you hear of wars and rumors of wars, do not be alarmed. Such things must happen, but the end is still to come. Nation will rise against nation, and kingdom against kingdom. There will be earthquakes in various places, and famines. These are the beginning of birth pains."
>
> —Mark 13:5–8

Since Jesus' first coming, here are some of the signs that we have always had with us.

- **<u>FALSE</u> <u>CHRISTS</u> (with false signs and miracles)**

These false christs are those who claim "I am he." It is amazing how in every generation there are those who claim to be Jesus, and in every generation there are those who are deceived by their lies.

- **Wars**

Where are there wars right now? Where are there rumors of wars?

- **Earthquakes**

Why are we so fascinated with earthquakes? In California, a relatively small earthquake can become a big story, and the scientists who measure quakes are familiar faces on the news. Earthquakes fascinate us partly because they remind us of how fragile this world is. They are a sign that this world will not last.

- **Famine**

   We should do all we can to feed the hungry. But that does not change the fact that even in our modern age, famine is still widespread.

**These signs that point to the end will all be summed up at the end. There will be wars, leading to a great final war. There will be false christs with false signs, leading to a great final Antichrist with great false signs that fool many (2 Thess. 2:9; Rev. 19:20). There will be famine in various places, leading to a great worldwide famine in the end (Rev. 6:5–6).**

   Let me tell you something that husbands don't like. They don't like it when their wives point out noises the car is making. "Did you hear that? What was that squeaky, clunking, grinding noise?" Know why they don't like it? Because they'd rather ignore the noise and hope that it goes away. The noise is a "sign" that there is something wrong with the engine. If you admit the noise is there, it means you need to do something about it. But if you ignore the noise, the damage (and the bill) is almost always worse in the end.

   The noise from your car can be compared to the beginnings of birth pangs leading to the Second Coming.

**There are indications for the wise to see throughout history. And there are signs that no one could miss at the end of time. It's the difference between hearing a grinding noise under the hood of your car and seeing the engine fall out!**

**Jesus' warning about these signs: <u>DON'T</u> <u>BE</u> <u>DECEIVED</u>!**

   It is *very* easy for people to make predictions about the future. Don't be deceived. False teachers appeal to our pride by telling us we can know something that no one else knows. Don't be deceived. The future is a scary place for many of us. We'd love to have someone tell us they have it figured out exactly. Don't be deceived.

   Maybe you don't think you're susceptible to this type of prediction. Let me ask you, have you ever cast even a glance at those predictions of the future in the *National Enquirer* at the checkout stand? "Earth will be invaded by Martians who look like televangelists." Even though we know it's a lie, it tends to draw us in!

## Signs preceding the end

These signs preceding the end are the signs that tell true believers that the end is right around the corner. These signs don't tell us exactly when Jesus will return, but that the time is close. I'd compare it to when you go to a movie theater. When the lights dim, you know the movie is just about to begin. There may be a few previews and ads first, but you know the time is close.

- **<u>APOSTASY</u>**

  *Apostasy* is a word you need to know. It refers to those who seemed to have faith, yet turned away in total denial.

  Notice a couple different kinds of apostasy in these verses in Matthew and Second Timothy.

  **At that time many will turn away from the faith and will betray and hate each other.**

  —Matthew 24:10

  **For the time will come when men will not put up with sound doctrine. Instead, to suit their own desires, they will gather around them a great number of teachers to say what their itching ears want to hear.**

  —2 Timothy 4:3

  In Matthew 24:10, people turn away from the faith entirely. They are the fair-weather Christians, trying to get a blessing from God but without making any real commitment. Second Timothy 4:3 tells about a different kind of apostasy—those who want to stay in the church but change its teaching to suit their wants rather than God's Word.

- **<u>INCREASE</u> of personal evil**

  **But mark this: There will be terrible times in the last days. People will be lovers of themselves, lovers of money, boastful, proud, abusive, disobedient to their parents, ungrateful, unholy, without love, unforgiving, slanderous, without self-control, brutal, not lovers of the good, treacherous, rash, conceited, lovers of pleasure rather than lovers of God—having a form of godliness but denying its power. Have nothing to do with them.**

  —2 Timothy 3:1–5

  **Brother will betray brother to death, and a father his child. Children will rebel against their parents and have them put to death.**

  —Mark 13:12

- **<u>SCOFFERS</u> will come**

  **First of all, you must understand that in the last days scoffers will come, scoffing and following their own evil desires.**

  —2 Peter 3:3

- **Many false prophets**

   **And many false prophets will appear and deceive many people.**
   —Matthew 24:11

   Again, what has been here throughout history will increase at the end.

   People will turn away from the faith. Evil will increase. People will make fun of the faith. False teachers will be very popular. Could any of this affect you or me in a personal way? Of course it will! We need to be ready for that. Determine now that these experiences will not make you think that God has abandoned you, but that he is just bringing this world to a close. Doesn't it make sense that at the end there will be a strong and clear "for or against" when it comes to faith? I can't imagine Jesus returning with even one person sitting on the fence as to their salvation. It's clear that people will separate into two camps.

## *Signs accompanying the end*

   The end is the "engine falling out." By this time everyone will know that the end is here. These are very dramatic signs.

- **Signs in the sun, moon, and stars**

   **There will be signs in the sun, moon and stars.**
   —Luke 21:25

   **Immediately after the distress of those days "the sun will be darkened, and the moon will not give its light; the stars will fall from the sky, and the heavenly bodies will be shaken."**
   —Matthew 24:29

   When the stars fall out of the sky, it's a pretty good indication that something is wrong!

- **Roaring of the sea, heavenly bodies shaken**

   **On the earth, nations will be in anguish and perplexity at the roaring and tossing of the sea.**
   —Luke 21:25

   **Men will faint from terror, apprehensive of what is coming on the world, for the heavenly bodies will be shaken. At that time they will see the Son of Man coming in a cloud with power and great glory.**
   —Luke 21:26–27

- **Great distress (unparalleled)**

   **For then there will be great distress, unequaled from the beginning of the world until now—and never to be equaled again.**
   —Matthew 24:21

### A Closer Look

**The most detailed descriptions of the end time events are found in the book of Revelation.**

| The seven seals (Final Conflict) | The seven trumpets (Final Destruction) | The seven bowls (God's Wrath Is Finished) |
|---|---|---|
| 1. White horse: Conquest | 1. Earth | 1. Sores |
| 2. Red horse: War | 2. Sea | 2. Sea to blood |
| 3. Black Horse: Famine | 3. Rivers | 3. Rivers to blood |
| 4. Pale Horse: Death | 4. Lights (3 woes) | 4. Fire from sun |
| 5. Martyrs | 5. Demons (Locusts) into darkness | 5. Beast's kingdom |
| 6. Earthquakes | 6. Angels and earthquakes (1/3 of men) | 6. Euphrates River dried up (Armageddon) |
| 7. The 7th seal is the 7 trumpets | 7. The 7th trumpet is the 7 bowls | 7. Earthquake (It is done!) |

Notice that this is like one of those stacking toys—seven bowls inside of seven trumpets inside of seven seals. One leads to the other leads to the other. We'll see in the next session that the time that these things take place is called the time of Tribulation.

White horses, seas turned to blood—these are pictures that are confusing to many of us. Listen to what Billy Graham said concerning this:

**Don't think of John's vivid language as a barrier to understanding; see it instead as the way he painted the picture of God's plan for the future in incredibly vivid colors.**[5]

—Billy Graham

God wants us to see something both terribly and wonderfully real: *This world will not last!* There is an amazing thing you'll discover as you read the book of Revelation—many who have their hearts turned against God will not look to him even in the chaos of our world coming to an end. They'll do the opposite! As it becomes clearer and clearer that this world will not last, those who have all of their hope set on this world will become more and more angry with God. And those who have their hope set on God will become more and more confident of his return.

In an earlier study we looked at what happens to people after they die. The Bible also very clearly explains to us exactly how this world will end. And it is heading to an inevitable end.

> The heavens will disappear with a roar; the elements will be destroyed by fire, and the earth and everything in it will be laid bare. . . . That day will bring about the destruction of the heavens by fire, and the elements will melt in the heat.
>
> —2 Peter 3:10, 12

**That's not the end of the story!**

> Then I saw a new heaven and a new earth, for the first heaven and the first earth had passed away.
>
> —Revelation 21:1

> Discussion questions 2 and 3 can be used here.

Suppose I'm holding two pieces of stock, one in each hand. One is guaranteed to fall—in fact the company will go bankrupt soon. The other will increase thirty-, sixty-, one-hundred-fold year after year and eventually will become the only important company in the world. Which would you take?

Put simply, that's the choice we make when we decide where we're going to invest our lives. This world will not last; heaven will last forever.

> **Split Session Plan:** If you're teaching this study over two sessions, end the first session here.

# The Time of the Second Coming

17

I wonder if there is any subject more packed with spiritual TNT than that of the time of the Second Coming? It is a doctrine that is accompanied by both great confusion and great inspiration. Jesus himself told us he did not know the time of his return, but that does not keep us from guessing. As if we could guess and get it right when even Jesus does not know.

Although the Bible does not tell us the exact time when Jesus will come again, it does give us real insight into the nature of God's timing.

Jesus wants us to understand the timing because it has a great impact on our hearts and readiness for his return. A picture of timing is the arrival of a season: like winter or spring. There is a day marked on the calendar that is the first day of winter, but that often has little to do with the actual arrival of that season's weather. There is a morning when you realize that the air is a little colder and crisper than it was the day before, and you sense that the season of winter is about to arrive.

There are sophisticated weather satellites and tracking stations that should be able to tell us exactly when a storm will arrive or the weather will clear. But the intricacy of this technology is no match for the special sensitivity of many older farmers. They can't tell you how they know the weather is about to change, but because of their years of experience they know. That's the kind of heart that God desires for you and me concerning the Second Coming of Christ. We don't need intricate calculations. We don't know the exact day of his coming. But, like the old farmer, we know it is getting closer. Because of our years of experience with our Savior, there are days when we can just feel it in our bones.

Look at how Jesus described the timing of his coming.

## Descriptions by Jesus

- **Like a <u>BRIDEGROOM</u>** (Matt. 25:1–13)

Remember our look at the weddings of Jesus' day in our study of the church? For the bride, the arrival of the bridegroom was an anticipated but also surprising joy. She knew he was about to arrive, but she didn't know exactly when.

An experience we have that is somewhat like this is that of waiting for a baby to be born. The signs tell us that the birth of that baby is getting closer and closer, yet we are not sure what day it will be. Like the bride waiting for her wedding or parents waiting for their child to be born, you and I should live with a sense of joyous anticipation as we await the return of Jesus.

- **Like the destruction of Sodom**

> **It was the same in the days of Lot. People were eating and drinking, buying and selling, planting and building. But the day Lot left Sodom, fire and sulfur rained down from heaven and destroyed them all. It will be just like this on the day the Son of Man is revealed.**
>
> **—Luke 17:28–30**

For the evil people in Sodom, the destruction that came was the last thing they expected. They may have said it came without warning, but the truth is they ignored the warnings.

- Like **NOAH'S** **FLOOD**

  **When the Son of Man comes again, it will be as it was when Noah lived. People were eating, drinking, marrying, and giving their children to be married until the day Noah entered the boat. Then the flood came and killed them all.**

  —Luke 17:26–27 (NCV)

- Like a **THIEF** in the **NIGHT**

  **Therefore keep watch, because you do not know on what day your Lord will come. But understand this: If the owner of the house had known at what time of night the thief was coming, he would have kept watch and would not have let his house be broken into. So you also must be ready, because the Son of Man will come at an hour when you do not expect him.**

  —Matthew 24:42–44

Each of these pictures is a picture of an unexpected arrival. Look with me at some of the truths that are seen in these pictures.

## *Facts about the timing*

- **The time of Jesus' return is SOON.**

  **Behold, I am coming soon! Blessed is he who keeps the words of the prophecy in this book.**

  —Revelation 22:7

Any prophetic teaching that takes the "soon" out of Jesus' coming ignores the words of Jesus.

"Wait a minute," you might be thinking, "how could Jesus be coming soon when these words were first written almost 2,000 years ago?"

Think of it this way: The word *soon* as used here does not mean so much this year or today or even in the next hour. It means "at any moment." For 2,000 years the world has lived in anticipation of Jesus returning at any moment. It's like looking up to see a huge boulder teetering on the edge of a cliff. It hasn't fallen yet, it may not fall today, but as you look at it you realize that it could fall at any moment.

This world for 2,000 years has been right on the verge of Jesus' return.

Soon is a word filled with immediacy. Not "sometime soon," but "*now* soon."

If I tell you you're going to move someday, what do you do? Nothing.

If I tell you you're moving soon, what do you do? *You start packing!*

- **The time of Jesus' return is known only by God.**

**No one knows about that day or hour, not even the angels in heaven, nor the Son, but only the Father.**
—Matthew 24:36

**So when they met together, they asked him, "Lord, are you at this time going to restore the kingdom to Israel?" He said to them: "It is not for you to know the times or dates the Father has set by his own authority."**
—Acts 1:6–7

It's amazing how someone who boldly proclaims the date of Jesus' return is able to draw people in—even to lead them to their death. I need say only two names: Jim Jones, David Koresh.

One of the many books written about the Second Coming is titled *99 Reasons Why No One Knows When Christ Will Return.*[6] Sometimes you can get most of what you need from a book in just the title! The number one reason, of course, is that Jesus said, "No one knows the day or the hour."

- **The time of Jesus' return is <u>UNEXPECTED</u>.**

**For you know very well that the day of the Lord will come like a thief in the night.**
—1 Thessalonians 5:2

**So you also must be ready, because the Son of Man will come at an hour when you do not expect him.**
—Matthew 24:44

Does the fact that his return is unexpected tell you anything? Although we may be able to see the signs, we won't know the exact time. It will be a wonderful surprise!

It's important for us to see that unexpected does not mean scary. Jesus is not coming to scare us, he is coming to save us! The only people who should be nervous about Jesus' coming are those who have not prepared themselves.

Discussion question 4 can be used here.

## People of the End Times

In any movie there is a cast of characters—names of actors you see scroll across the screen who provided the drama throughout the story. There are a number of people who are associated with the events of the end time—villains and heroes, the strong and the weak.

### 1. The Man of Lawlessness/The Beast/The Antichrist

> Don't let anyone deceive you in any way, for that day will not come until the rebellion occurs and the man of lawlessness is revealed, the man doomed to destruction.
>
> —2 Thessalonians 2:3

Hollywood is fascinated by this "ultimate villain." In their zeal they often miss the simple truths Paul tells us in 2 Thessalonians:

> He will oppose and will exalt himself over everything that is called God or is worshiped, so that he sets himself up in God's temple, proclaiming himself to be God. . . . The coming of the lawless one will be in accordance with the work of Satan displayed in all kinds of counterfeit miracles, signs and wonders, and in every sort of evil that deceives those who are perishing.
>
> —2 Thessalonians 2:4, 9–10

This beast will be the ultimate false christ. He will say that he is God and will show signs that deceive many into believing that he is God.

---

 **A Closer Look**

This will be one final Antichrist among many—the end of a long line that began after Jesus' first coming. The Beast is the final and worst Antichrist, not the *only* Antichrist.

> For many will come in my name, claiming, "I am the Christ," and will deceive many.
>
> —Matthew 24:5

> Dear children, this is the last hour; and as you have heard that the antichrist is coming, even now many antichrists have come. This is how we know it is the last hour. . . . Who is the liar? It is the man who denies that Jesus is the Christ. Such a man is the antichrist—he denies the Father and the Son.
>
> —1 John 2:18, 22

---

There are a number of biblical pictures attached to the Antichrist. These pictures are the subject of literally thousands of prophetic speculations!

Some pictures obviously point to Rome in John's day—for instance the seven hills point to Rome as the city built on seven hills. But these pictures also have clear meaning for the end times. These are symbols we can speculate about now, but will be abundantly clear when the Beast

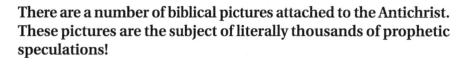

arrives. God doesn't give us signs to confuse us and bring us fear, but to direct us and give us hope! When this Beast arrives, then the signs are clear. Trying to use the signs to figure out where the Beast might come from—that's working backward.

- **The woman/Babylon—riding the Beast**
- **7 heads**
- **7 hills on which the woman sits**
- **7 kings—5 have fallen, one is, the other is yet to come**
- **In Revelation 17 the Beast is identified as "an eighth king"**
- **666—the number of the Beast**
- **The 10 horns = 10 kings who will serve along with the beast**

This number—666—has been the subject of more speculation and misinformation than anything else in all of prophecy. Rumors have circulated that every license plate in Israel begins with 666 (not true) or that every JC Penney credit card begins with 666 (again simply untrue). The speculations done with this number are incredible. People have added the numerical equivalents in the names of Hitler and Mussolini, for example, to prove that they were the Antichrist. When they died, these proofs were shown to be false.

Just to show you how silly this can become, let me prove to you that the Antichrist is Mickey Mouse:

|   |                          |     |
|---|--------------------------|-----|
|   | 10 Letters in WALT DISNEY | 10  |
| + | 10 Letters in DONALD DUCK | 20  |
| + | 101 Dalmatians           | 121 |
| - | 7 dwarfs                 | 114 |
| - | 3 ugly stepsisters       | 111 |
|   | (drum roll, please)      |     |
| x | 6 letters in M I C K E Y |     |
| = | 666                      |     |

I'm joking for a reason. You can prove just about anything with math magic. Don't get so caught up in playing with numbers that you lose the focus—*Jesus is coming again!* Revelation tells us that 666 is the number of a man. Whoever this is, it's just a man, playing at being God. He won't play for long.

### A Closer Look

Revelation is an example of the double application of prophecy, both to those to whom it was originally written and to saints of a later time.

> If you fail to see the hope that the book of Revelation gave to first-century Christians, you've missed the point of the book. If you fail to see the hope that the book of Revelation has given to Christians of every nation for the last 2,000 years, you've missed the point of the book. If you fail to see the hope that the book of Revelation gives to those who live during the end times, you've missed the point of the book.

Jesus' first coming had many examples of this double application of prophecy. Prophecies that were fulfilled in a partial way in Old Testament events found their ultimate and complete fulfillment in the life of Christ.

The book of Revelation obviously points to the Roman Empire and the emperor Domitian in its pictures of the Beast. But it is also just as obvious that there is a greater fulfillment to be seen here—one that can come only at the end of time.

Is it wrong to speculate about what these pictures might mean? No, as long as you never confuse speculation about God's Word with the perfect truth of God's Word. During World War II many believers were absolutely certain that Hitler was the Antichrist. They turned out to be wrong. We must have the humility to recognize that we could be just as wrong about many of our speculations today.

2. A second beast/the <u>FALSE</u> <u>PROPHET</u>

   In order to promote his program more efficiently, the Antichrist will have an important lieutenant. He is the "second beast" (Rev. 13:11–18), and his sole duty is to promote the purposes and expedite the worship of the first Beast, the Man of Sin.

3. The two <u>WITNESSES</u>

   Revelation 11 talks about two witnesses who will prophesy and picture the judgment of God, much like the great Old Testament prophets. They will be killed by the Beast in Jerusalem and will be resurrected by God into heaven as their enemies look on.

You can't help but be struck with their similarity to prophets such as Elijah and Jeremiah. They proclaimed God's truth to people who did not want to hear the truth. They brought the message of God's judgment. At the end, God will send messengers to make his plans clear. But just as Jeremiah was rejected, these witnesses will be rejected. And just as God took care of his prophets in the Old Testament, he'll take care of these prophets.

4. **The 144,000**

**12,000 sealed saints from each of the tribes of Israel (Rev. 7:4–8)**

**Pure believers in the midst of the tribulations of the last days (Rev. 14:1, 5)**

Some think these are two different groups of 144,000. Others think they are the same. The important thing is the number. The number 12 is important in the Bible as a picture of God's plan. He had 12 tribes in Israel as a witness to the world and Jesus chose 12 apostles to carry his message to the world; 12,000 from each of 12 tribes represent the overwhelming fulfillment of God's plan.

**(These are all individuals or specific groups of individuals. In the next session we'll look in a more comprehensive way at what will happen to believers, to the Jewish people, and to unbelievers.)**

**Don't forget. All of these characters play only bit parts when compared to the leading character in this drama. Never fail to give top billing to Jesus Christ.**

If this were a movie, you probably wouldn't remember one of these other characters after you left the theater. They aren't even supporting actors; they are just a backdrop to the great return of Jesus Christ. I've counseled with a number of Christians who are frightened by thoughts of the Second Coming. Their minds are filled with images of a beast and a time of judgment. Those are very powerful and vivid pictures. But they pale in comparison to the glory of Jesus Christ. The Bible tells us very clearly where our focus should be—on the soon and coming King. He is at the center of and controls the action in every part of this great drama.

• **Jesus will <u>DESTROY</u> the Beast and his lieutenant.**

**The lawless one will be revealed, whom the Lord Jesus will overthrow with the breath of his mouth and destroy by the splendor of his coming.**
**—2 Thessalonians 2:8**

• **Jesus will redeem the two witnesses.**

Then they heard a loud voice from heaven saying to them, "Come up here." And they went up to heaven in a cloud, while their enemies looked on.

—Revelation 11:12

- Jesus will lead the 144,000 to <u>VICTORY</u>.

  They follow the Lamb wherever he goes. They were purchased from among men and offered as firstfruits to God and the Lamb.

  —Revelation 14:4

- Jesus will return in absolute <u>GLORY</u>.

  For the Lord himself will come down from heaven with a mighty shout and with the soul-stirring cry of the archangel and the great trumpet-call of God.

  —1 Thessalonians 4:16 (LB)

  Look, the Lord is coming with many thousands of his holy angels to judge every person.

  —Jude 1:14–15 (NCV)

  Look, he is coming with the clouds, and every eye will see him.

  —Revelation 1:7

  We wait for the blessed hope—the glorious appearing of our great God and Savior, Jesus Christ.

  —Titus 2:13

Circle these words: "mighty shout," "cry of the archangel and the great trumpet-call of God" in 1 Thessalonians 4:16; "thousands of his holy angels" in Jude 1:14; "every eye will see him" in Revelation 1:7. Look at Titus 2:13 and circle the words "the blessed hope" and "the glorious appearing."

*Get the picture!* It is a picture of victory. It is a picture of hope. It is a picture of eternity. And, more than anything, it is a picture of Jesus!

Pray with me:

> *Jesus, we anticipate your return. You've told us clearly that you're coming back because you want us to be with you. In the midst of our busy lives or our boring lives or our anxious lives, we take a moment right now to picture your return. You will come in absolute glory and will lead us to total victory. We choose in a fresh new way to not put our hope in this world, but to see that our security and our everlasting joy is in you alone. Amen.*

**Begin working on memory card 11, "The Truth about the Second Coming." If you haven't done them all, don't let that keep you from memorizing this one. If you've memorized each card up until now, you will be completing a life-changing commitment.**

## Discussion Questions

1. How would the fact that Jesus is coming at any moment have changed the way you faced one situation today, or how could it change the way you face one situation tomorrow?

2. Does knowing that this world will not last cause a change in your attitude toward any specific material thing, human government or institution, problem or struggle you are facing?

3. Is there anything good about knowing that things will get worse before they get better?

4. To give us hope, God has told us some of the truths of the Second Coming of Jesus and the end of the world. Many Christians, however, feel fear when they study the Second Coming. Why do you think we feel fear? How can we move from fear to hope? Why do you think Christians who are facing persecution have always found incredible hope in the truth of Jesus' Second Coming?

# The Second Coming
## Part 2

 **Life Change Objective**

To decide to live in anticipation of Jesus' Second Coming in one significant way this next week.

**Summary Teaching Outline**

Events of the End Times

    Jesus Christ is coming to this earth again

    The Tribulation

    The Rapture

    The visible return of Christ

    The Millennium

At the end of time what will happen to . . .

    Believers

    The Jewish people

    Unbelievers

What Should Our Attitude Be?

    Be alert and watchful.

    Be alert and self-controlled.

    Live holy lives.

    Be patient and eagerly wait.

    Long for his return.

In January 1961, a few days before John F. Kennedy was inaugurated as president of the United States, the president-elect invited Billy Graham to spend a day with him in Key Biscayne, Florida. The invitation surprised the evangelist because of Kennedy's well-known dislike for Graham and lack of interest in spiritual matters. After a round of golf, Kennedy and Graham were returning to their hotel when Kennedy stopped the white Lincoln convertible he was driving by the side of the road.

"Billy, do you believe that Jesus Christ is coming back to earth one day?"

"Yes, Mr. President, I certainly do."

"Then why do I hear so little about it?"[1]

Good question! One of the reasons is the fact that so few of us talk about the Second Coming of Jesus. A few talk a lot about it, but most of us ignore this great subject almost entirely. I've found that I tend to shy away from discussing things I don't understand. Do you ever feel that way? It is hard to understand the variety of occurrences and opinions surrounding Jesus' return. But there is no doubt that God wants us to understand these things. That's why he put them in his Word. It's my prayer that the time we're spending looking at this will give you confidence to talk more about one of the greatest news stories this world will ever hear.

To quickly review:

**In the last session we focused on the signs of Jesus' coming, the descriptions of his coming, and some of the persons involved in the end times.**

**Three types of signs:**

1. **Signs pointing to the end (the beginning of birth pains)**
2. **Signs immediately preceding the end time events**
3. **Signs accompanying the end time events**

**Jesus' descriptions of the time of the Second Coming:**

- **Like a bridegroom**
- **Like the destruction of Sodom**
- **Like Noah's flood**
- **Like a thief in the night**

**People of the end times:**

- **The man of lawlessness/the Beast/the Antichrist**
- **A second beast/the False Prophet**
- **The two witnesses**
- **The 144,000**

**Never fail to give top billing to Jesus Christ.**

How did our study of Jesus' Second Coming affect your life this last week? Did it cause you to see any circumstances in a different light? Did it make you act toward others in a different way? Did it give you hope where you needed it? Remember: the truth that Jesus is coming again should make you think and act in a different way. Jesus' return is not just an interesting fact; it is a life-changing truth!

If I were to lecture today on economics, I could present hundreds of interesting facts concerning such things as supply and demand, interest rates and inflation. And I have no doubt that most of you would be asleep in about ten minutes! However, if I were to say to you the single sentence, "I am presenting to you a surprise check in the amount of $10,000," you would feel a charge of electricity through your body that would last for days. You would tell everyone you met about it. "They handed out $10,000 checks in my Bible study today. I told you, you should have come!"

As we study together the details of Jesus' coming again, let's do so with the spiritual electricity of a single sentence: "Jesus is coming again!"

**We're now going to focus on the events of the end times and what our daily attitude toward Jesus' Second Coming should be.**

# Events of the End Times

**It would be great to cover these events in order. Unfortunately no one agrees on the order! Before we look at some of the things that believers see from different perspectives, let's look at one thing we all clearly agree on.**

### *Jesus Christ is coming to this earth again*

**Just like he came the first time—in a visible, physical, bodily form—Jesus is coming to this earth again! Although Christians disagree about the order of events surrounding his return, of his actual return there can be no doubt. His Second Coming is spoken of even more clearly than his first coming.**

Pretend with me for a moment that you are standing with Jesus' disciples in Acts chapter 1 as Jesus leaves them to go to heaven. He has been with them as the resurrected Lord for over a month, but has told them all along that he did not intend to stay. He gives them a final command to be his witnesses, and then the most amazing thing happens.

Jesus' resurrected body physically ascends to heaven! They stand there and watch him go into the clouds and disappear from their sight. I don't know how long they stood frozen in shocked amazement, but gradually questions must have begun to intrude on this moment of awe. "How did he do that? Where did he go? When is he coming back?"

Because of the uniqueness of this moment in our spiritual history, some angels were there to give the answer. Look at Acts 1:9–11:

**After he [Jesus] said this, he was taken up before their very eyes, and a cloud hid him from their sight. They were looking intently up into the sky as he was going, when suddenly two men dressed in white stood beside them. "Men of Galilee," they said, "why do you stand here looking into the sky? This same Jesus, who has been taken from you into heaven, will come back in the same way you have seen him go into heaven."**

—Acts 1:9–11

Did you notice that the word *same* is used a lot in that last sentence? God sent a message that we could not mistake. "This same Jesus"— not a different Messiah, but Jesus himself will return. "In the same way." He won't come invisibly or spiritually, but physically. They saw him go up into the clouds, and he will return through the clouds. The fact that Jesus would return was no surprise to the disciples. Jesus had already promised that he would return.

**They will see the Son of Man coming on the clouds of the sky, with power and great glory.**

—Matthew 24:30

Listen to his tender words to his followers as he saw the tension in their faces the night before he was to go to the cross.

**There are many rooms in my Father's house; I would not tell you this if it were not true. I am going there to prepare a place for you. After I go and prepare a place for you, I will come back and take you to be with me so that you may be where I am.**

—John 14:2–3 (NCV)

I want you to notice two things about this verse. Jesus is preparing a place—for you! Heaven is not tract housing; it is custom built for you by the person who knows you best!

Then notice the phrase "with me so that you may be where I am." That's obviously what thrills Jesus about heaven; he's looking forward to our being with him! The truth of the return of Jesus is the truth that he who loves you most is coming back for you, because he wants to be with you.

Have you seen the movie or stage play *Beauty and the Beast*? You probably wonder what in the world that could have to do with Jesus' Second Coming. Near the end of the movie there is a moment that fits what we are talking about. The beast has released his hoped-for love, Belle, to return to her father. He thinks he will never see her again. He is in despair, seemingly not caring even when he is struck down in a battle. But then Belle arrives at his side, and he looks at her with wide-eyed amazement and says, "Belle? You came back! You came back!"

Why do I give you that picture? Jesus is coming back for you, and I don't want you to miss that at its core this is a story of a holy romance—a love story. Jesus loves the church as his bride, and he is coming back for her. Jesus loves you as his spiritual brother, sister, friend—and he is coming back for you.

**We're going to look at some different opinions about how this coming will take place. But don't let this study deter you from the fact that the world needs to hear: Jesus Christ is coming again!**

Discussion question 1 can be used here.

**There are four end time events that every believer needs to understand: the Tribulation, the Rapture, the visible return of Christ, and the Millennium.**

## *The Tribulation*

**Revelation 4–18 describes the Tribulation in detail. The signs that accompany Jesus' Second Coming that we studied in the last session were a description of many of the occurrences in this period of tribulation. The time of Tribulation includes the Battle of Armageddon, the great final battle (Rev. 16:16).**

**Two characteristics will distinguish the Tribulation from other difficult times in history:**

- **First, it will be <u>WORLDWIDE</u>, not localized.**

Now there are certain areas of the world that are at peace while others are at war. Christians suffer persecution in some parts of the world, but not all. Famine is experienced in some countries, but not in every country. In the Tribulation, these will be worldwide occurrences. A newspaper will not have the room to print all of the top stories of what will be going on in the world in that day.

- Second, the Tribulation will be unique because <u>ALL</u> will realize and act like the end is at hand.

The Scriptures divide the seven years of the Tribulation into two equal parts. In Revelation, the two halves of the Tribulation are designated either by "time, times and half a time" (Rev. 12:14), or "forty-two months" (11:2; 13:5), or "1,260 days" (11:3; 12:6), each of which works out to three and one-half years.

> There is an important historical perspective behind the truth of the Tribulation. The Tribulation means that as this world draws to an end, things will get worse before they get better. We'd all like to think that everything in this world would approach near perfection as we get ready for Jesus' return, but that's not the picture the Bible gives us.
>
> Why would God do this? One reason is certainly that he wants to draw a clear dividing line as this world draws to a close. It's as if God were putting up a sign as the end approaches that says, "No fence riding allowed." You'll have to make your decision, clearly and immediately. No more room for equivocation. No more time for procrastination. World events will make clear to everyone that the time for commitment is now.

Question: Will Christians go through this time of Tribulation?

In order to answer that we must first look at the event called the Rapture.

### *The Rapture*

The title "Rapture" comes from the Latin word used in 1 Thessalonians 4:17. The original Greek word is translated "caught up" in English.

The Rapture is when Jesus gathers all believers to be with him, giving each a resurrected, glorified body. This is to be distinguished from the visible return of Jesus in which all will see him and he will judge the nations and establish his kingdom. Many see the Rapture as an event hidden to all but believers and occurring years before Jesus' visible return. Others see the Rapture and Jesus' visible return as happening simultaneously.

Although there is some question about the exact time of the Rapture (see the box at the end of this section), the questions we have about exactly when it will happen shouldn't detract from the assurance that it will happen.

First Thessalonians 4:13–18 gives the most detail about what will happen when the Lord raptures the church.

The believers in Thessalonica were worried. They felt that somehow those in their church who had already died were not going to be able to be in heaven with the Lord, or that they might have gotten cheated out of having a resurrected body in heaven. Paul writes to calm their concerned hearts—by explaining to them the order of how God will do things.

**For the Lord himself will come down from heaven, with a loud command, with the voice of the archangel and with the trumpet call of God, and the dead in Christ will rise first. After that, we who are still alive and are left will be caught up together with them in the clouds to meet the Lord in the air. And so we will be with the Lord forever. Therefore encourage each other with these words.**

**—1 Thessalonians 4:16–18**

- **First: The Lord <u>DESCENDS</u>.**

**"For the Lord himself will come down from heaven . . ."**

**In the clouds (Acts 1:11). On God's conditions (Matt. 24:14). Unexpectedly (Matt. 24:37).**

Clouds. Although the word just means sky, I have to admit that I'm partial to those great billowy thunderclouds with the sunlight streaming through them as the kind Jesus will burst through.

- **Second: The dead in Christ <u>RISE</u>.**

**"And the dead in Christ will rise first . . ."**

First Corinthians 15 talks about this resurrection of our bodies.

**So will it be with the resurrection of the dead. The body that is sown is perishable, it is raised imperishable; it is sown in dishonor, it is raised in glory; it is sown in weakness, it is raised in power.**

**—1 Corinthians 15:42–43**

Remember our study of what happens after we die? A believer's body rises out of the ground to become a resurrected body that then meets its spirit coming with Jesus in the air. Every believer is involved in the Rapture. If you die before his return, your spirit immediately goes to be in the presence of the Lord. When Jesus returns; your spirit will come with him in the air, your body will rise out of the ground, and BAM! the spirit and the body will reunite in midair.

Now that's what I'd call a thrill ride!

- **Third: We who are alive shall be <u>CAUGHT</u> <u>UP</u> with them.**

**First Thessalonians 4 says, "We who are still alive and are left will be caught up together with them."**

This is our most familiar picture of the Rapture. Those believers who are walking the earth at that time will somehow immediately have their earthly bodies transformed into resurrected bodies and will rise to meet Jesus in the air.

- **Fourth: We <u>MEET</u> the Lord in the air and we will be with the Lord forever.**

  How many have been to your twentieth high school reunion? Have you noticed that sometimes reunions don't quite match their hype? You see people who had long hair who now have no hair. The guy who was wide receiver on the football team is now just ... wide. The brightest person in your class is the dullest person at the party.

  Imagine *this* reunion. People with broken bodies now have resurrected bodies. Family members see each other as they rise to meet Jesus. Seeing people from your past who you would never have dreamed would become believers. United with people from this church. People from all over this city, nation, world. And most important, Jesus Christ is at the very center of this reunion.

  Without even knowing you, I can tell you about the most exciting experience in your life. It hasn't happened yet! You're looking forward to your greatest experiences.

 **A Closer Look**

**What is the difference in timing between the Rapture of the church and the visible Second Coming of Jesus to judge the nations and set up his kingdom?**

**Some (amillennial and postmillennial views) regard these two as occurring one right after the other or at the same time.**

**Others (premillennial view) see an order. There are three general ideas as to what this order might be:**

1. **Pretribulation Rapture: the Rapture occurs right before the Tribulation begins.**
2. **Midtribulation Rapture: the Rapture occurs 3-1/2 years into the time of Tribulation.**
3. **Posttribulation Rapture: the Rapture occurs at the end of the seven-year Tribulation.**

**What should these different views say to you on a personal basis? Rejoice if God takes you out of the Tribulation of those last days. But don't be surprised, and don't lose faith if God chooses to leave us as witnesses during those last days.**

Discussion questions 2 and 3 can be used here.

Here is my very untheological way of looking at this, because I want it to happen as soon as possible. I'm looking forward to a pretribulation Rapture. But if we're still around when the tribulations begin, I'll immediately move to believing in a midtribulation Rapture. And if we're still here 3-1/2 years into the Rapture, I'll quickly move to the posttribulation view!

I want you to understand some of these details about Jesus' Second Coming. However, my one warning is that you don't become so involved in the details that you miss the big picture. Tell an older Christian that Jesus is coming again and they ask, "Is that pre-, post-, or midtribulation?" Tell a new believer that Jesus is coming and they just look up! Never lose that spirit.

## The visible return of Christ

**The visible return of Jesus is different from the Rapture. At his return, all the earth will see Jesus returning, and he will establish his reign and rule on the earth.**

> At that time the sign of the Son of Man will appear in the sky, and all the nations of the earth will mourn. They will see the Son of Man coming on the clouds of the sky, with power and great glory.
>
> —Matthew 24:30

> Look, he is coming with the clouds, and every eye will see him, even those who pierced him; and all the peoples of the earth will mourn because of him. So shall it be! Amen.
>
> —Revelation 1:7

In Matthew 24:30 and Revelation 1:7 we read about all the nations mourning when they see Jesus. They will mourn because it will become immediately apparent that they've built their lives on the wrong foundation.

Our goal as believers is simply this: to have more people rejoice and fewer people mourn at the return of Jesus. Help someone to put their faith in Christ and you assure that his return will be a moment of inexpressible joy rather than one of excruciating grief.

## The Millennium

**The Millennium is the term used to point to the thousand-year reign of Christ spoken of in Revelation 20:1–6.**

> And I saw an angel coming down out of heaven, having the key to the Abyss and holding in his hand a great chain. He seized the dragon, that ancient serpent, who is the devil, or Satan, and bound him for a

thousand years. He threw him into the Abyss, and locked and sealed it over him, to keep him from deceiving the nations anymore until the thousand years were ended. After that, he must be set free for a short time.

I saw thrones on which were seated those who had been given authority to judge. And I saw the souls of those who had been beheaded because of their testimony for Jesus and because of the word of God. They had not worshiped the beast or his image and had not received his mark on their foreheads or their hands. They came to life and reigned with Christ a thousand years. (The rest of the dead did not come to life until the thousand years were ended.) This is the first resurrection. Blessed and holy are those who have part in the first resurrection. The second death has no power over them, but they will be priests of God and of Christ and will reign with him for a thousand years.

—Revelation 20:1–6

Over the years there have arisen three major ways of looking at this thousand-year reign of Christ:

1. Postmillennial (Jesus comes again after the Millennium)

   This view holds that the kingdom of God is now being extended in the world through the preaching of the Gospel and the saving work of the Holy Spirit in the hearts of individuals. The world will eventually be Christianized, and the return of Christ will occur at the close of a long period of righteousness and peace commonly called the "Millennium." This will not be a literal 1,000 years, but actually an extended period of time.

   *Strength:* Optimistic view of the power of the Gospel to change the world, hope for the fulfillment of the Great Commission.

   *Weakness:* Practically, this view is hard to reconcile with what's happening in the world. Biblically, it is hard to reconcile with the strong teaching of the final period of tribulation.

2. Amillennial (Jesus comes again without an earthly Millennium)

   Until the end, there will be parallel development of both good and evil, God's kingdom and Satan's. After the Second Coming of Christ at the end of the world, there will be a general resurrection and general judgment of all people. The thousand-year reign of Christ is not literal; it is symbolic of Jesus' work on earth from his resurrection until his Second Coming.

   *Strength:* Answers questions about such things as resurrected saints living in an unregenerate world for a thousand years until the final judgment.

*Weakness:* **Must see a great deal of the Second Coming prophecies as spiritual symbols rather than actual events.**

The truth of the Millennium is a puzzling truth. Questions abound. Are we going to be interacting with an imperfect world in our resurrected bodies for a thousand years? What about those who become believers during this time? The Bible doesn't give us answers to these questions. The amillennial view deals with these many difficult questions by seeing the Millennium as symbolic. But there is a weakness to that: there is a very literal (not just symbolic) feel to much of what you read as the Bible speaks of Jesus' Second Coming.

3. **Premillennial (Jesus comes again before the Millennium)**

**Premillennialism is the view that holds that the Second Coming of Christ will occur prior to the Millennium and will establish Christ's kingdom on this earth for a literal 1,000 years. The duration of Christ's kingdom will be 1,000 years. Its location will be on this earth. Its government will be the personal presence of Christ reigning as King. And it will fulfill all the yet unfulfilled promises about Christ's earthly kingdom.**

*Strength:* **Attempts to seek understanding of all Scriptures relating to the Second Coming rather than ignoring those that are difficult to understand. A more literal view of Scripture.**

*Weakness:* **Is often marked by overcomplicated charts and with wrong guesses and differing opinions about the meaning of the symbols.**

I know that a look at these events of the Second Coming brings up some questions and I hope it gets you thinking. Part of the reason for *Foundations* is to get you thinking! Thinking theologically! It's important to see how people come to the conclusions they do about the timing of the Second Coming. It's not simply a matter of "This one feels good to me." There are deep and expansive biblical foundations behind our views of the Second Coming of Jesus.

You've just had a quick course in the Tribulation, the Rapture, the visible return, and the Millennium. If you feel a little overwhelmed, you're not alone! Christians have struggled with getting a grip on these events of the Second Coming for a couple of thousand years now.

As with all God tells us about the Second Coming, he does not teach us this just to excite our curiosity. God is encouraging us. God is giving us hope.

**Key Personal
Perspective**

*Four Encouragements in These Four Events*

1. The truth of the Tribulation encourages me. Just because things get worse does not mean God will not soon make them better.

2. The truth of the Rapture encourages me. God will take his children home.

3. The truth of Jesus' visible return encourages me. Jesus will ultimately be Lord of all.

4. The truth of the Millennium encourages me. God has a plan that extends into eternity.

What can be seen lasts only for a time, but what cannot be seen lasts forever.

—2 Corinthians 4:18 (GNT)

**Teaching Tip**

Remember the principle of transformation. The Bible was not written just to inform our minds or even to excite our interest. God is in the process of transforming lives. A truth such as the Millennium is not meant to simply inform us of God's plan. God wants to transform us, to give us hearts of hope.

**Split Session Plan:** If you're teaching this study over two sessions, end the first session here.

Some of you are optimists in how you look at this world, and some of you are pessimists. You pessimists look at a rainy day and think, "It's going to flood." You optimists think, "God is sending his gentle rain" even if it is flooding! I want you to know that the *hope* we are talking about has nothing to do with whether your personality is optimistic or pessimistic. The optimist sees the glass as half full. The pessimist sees the glass as half empty. The person of hope sees the glass as firmly held in the hand of God.

The truth is, we are in for some tough times in this world. And this world is in for some tough times before Jesus' final return. But that makes the real hope that we look forward to that much sweeter. Don't settle for anything less than the genuine hope that the Bible offers us. There is a false kind of hope out there—the hope that says that somehow everything is going to turn out okay for everyone. Thinking about that idea for just a few moments tells you that simply can't be true. You cannot take opposite paths and end up in the same place.

These Second Coming truths are a powerful reminder of the fact that the way things are is not the way things will remain. This world is facing massive change. I'd like to be able to say that it will be a positive change for all of us, but that depends on where you are putting your faith. If your faith is in things that are not going to last, this change will be terrifying when all those things are lost. But if your faith is in that which will last forever, the closer you get to forever, the greater your joy!

The Bible tells us very specifically what happens at the end of time.

# At the end of time what will happen to . . .

## *Believers*

**In a word, <u>REWARD</u>!**

> **So Christ was sacrificed once to take away the sins of many people; and he will appear a second time, not to bear sin, but to bring salvation to those who are waiting for him.**
>
> —Hebrews 9:28

> **And when the head Shepherd comes, your reward will be a never-ending share in his glory and honor.**
>
> —1 Peter 5:4 (NLT)

> **Dear friends, now we are children of God, and we have not yet been shown what we will be in the future. But we know that when Christ comes again, we will be like him, because we will see him as he really is.**
>
> —1 John 3:2 (NCV)

Jesus brings salvation to us. That's a reward. We worship him in a perfect eternity. That's a reward. He gives us crowns of glory. And that's a reward.

You don't deserve this! I don't deserve this! The rewards come to us solely based on God's grace. Any share that you and I get in his glory and honor only serves to give him more glory and honor throughout eternity.

Look at 1 Peter 5:4. We look forward to the reward of "a never-ending share in his glory and honor." When we read "share in his glory," the first thought is that we'll somehow get a portion of Jesus' eternal riches.

But the deeper meaning here is not that we will get some of what Jesus has but that we will become more fully who Jesus is. First John 3:2 tells us, "When Christ comes again, we will be like him, because we will see him as he really is."

## The Jewish people

In a word, <u>RESTORATION</u>.

Paul's clear statements in Romans 11 cannot be ignored.

> Again I ask: Did they stumble so as to fall beyond recovery? Not at all! Rather, because of their transgression, salvation has come to the Gentiles to make Israel envious. But if their transgression means riches for the world, and their loss means riches for the Gentiles, how much greater riches will their fullness bring! . . . I do not want you to be ignorant of this mystery, brothers, so that you may not be conceited: Israel has experienced a hardening in part until the full number of the Gentiles has come in. And so all Israel will be saved, as it is written: "The deliverer will come from Zion; he will turn godlessness away from Jacob."
>
> —Romans 11:11–12, 25–26

Some say this means that the literal nation must be restored under the rule of King David. That's what you think if you believe the covenant promises in the Old Testament will be fulfilled in the Millennium. Others believe these verses simply say that there will be a great revival among the Jewish people. Whichever way you see these verses, they clearly tell us that before the end, many Jewish people will be brought to faith in Christ.

## Unbelievers

In a word, <u>JUDGMENT</u>.

> Then I saw a great white throne and him who was seated on it. Earth and sky fled from his presence, and there was no place for them. And I saw the dead, great and small, standing before the throne, and books were opened. Another book was opened, which is the book of life. The dead were judged according to what they had done as recorded in the books. . . . If anyone's name was not found written in the book of life, he was thrown into the lake of fire.
>
> —Revelation 20:11–12, 15

Look at Revelation 20. Underline the statement "the dead were judged according to what they had done." The dead refers here to unbelievers. If we do not trust Christ in this life, all that we have to stand on when we come before God is what we have done—and it's not enough. It's a terrifying thing to think of standing before a perfect God depending only on what I have done to get me into a perfect heaven.

Make sure your name is written in the book of life! How do you get your name in that book? Trust Jesus Christ with your life! It is Jesus' book. Revelation 13:8 and 21:27 call it the Lamb's book of life. And Jesus said, "I am the resurrection and the life" (John 11:25). "I am the way and the truth and the life" (John 14:6).

Hope means that you are a realist. A realist about sin and its effect on the world. A realist about judgment and the fact that it will come. A realist about salvation and our need to trust Jesus.

## What Should Our Attitude Be?

19

We need to understand the truths concerning the Second Coming. Why? So that we can be better informed? So that we can be better able to argue with those who have an opinion different from ours? No! The Bible tells us very clearly how our study should impact our attitude.

- **Be alert and <u>WATCHFUL</u>.**

20

21

**Be on guard! Be alert! You do not know when that time will come.**

—Mark 13:33

**If he comes suddenly, do not let him find you sleeping.**

—Mark 13:36

The word *alert* is often used to point to our attitude toward the Second Coming. Ever been driving along in your car and fall asleep for a few seconds, awakened by oncoming lights in the other lane? Wakes you up, doesn't it? You become very alert!

The truth of the approaching light of his coming should "wake us up" to the real life and crying needs that are all around us. Because of the hope that we have, we should stand out as ones who are full of life in a sleep-walking world.

It's easy to become a bit dull in your spiritual life. Let's just admit it. It's all too easy to slip into complacency about your relationship with God and begin to focus on the things in this world. One of the reasons why Jesus so clearly taught us that he will come again was to help us to stay spiritually alert! The truth of the Second Coming is a spiritual alarm clock.

- **Be alert and <u>SELF-CONTROLLED</u>.**

22

**So then, let us not be like others, who are asleep, but let us be alert and self-controlled.**

—1 Thessalonians 5:6

Look at 1 Thessalonians 5:6. "Let us not be like others, who are asleep." This is telling us that if you do not know Christ, you're asleep at the wheel. Those who know Christ are alive to things that the rest of this world is asleep to.

Look at 1 Peter 1:13 and 4:7.

**Therefore, prepare your minds for action; be self-controlled; set your hope fully on the grace to be given you when Jesus Christ is revealed.**

—1 Peter 1:13

**The end of all things is near. Therefore be clear minded and self-controlled so that you can pray.**

—1 Peter 4:7

How does the truth of his coming make us more self-controlled? How does it make us more clear minded? By helping us to keep the truth in perspective, to see things as they really are.

One of the greatest ways that you exercise self-control is through the simple two-letter word "no." Obviously, you show self-control when you say no to temptations. Did you know that you also exhibit self-control when you say no to the weight of trying to do too much or have too much in this world? Listen to one woman's testimony about being released from the burden of too many good things.

> Three years ago our family moved 14,000 pounds of stuff into a new home. That move convinced me to begin the tedious process of evaluating what we really need to keep and what needs to go. Sorting and discarding so many things has helped me realize again how easily our hearts can be entangled by the stuff of this life. I want to free myself from any unnecessary, binding weights that might keep me from important things in life: my relationships with Christ, my family, and others. I don't want anything to distract me from the priorities that really matter as I wait expectantly for His return.[2]

Remember, we're just traveling through this world. There is a lot to be said for traveling as light as you possibly can.

- **Live holy lives.**

When you see where this world is headed, does that cause you to lessen your grip on the worldly? The truth of the Second Coming shows us that this world is a shaky place. But if the instability of this world is all you see, you've missed the point! We need to also see that heaven is a solid place—unshakable.

Read with me 2 Peter 3:11–12. There are three words at the end of this verse that will be a real surprise to some of you.

**Since everything will be destroyed in this way, what kind of people ought you to be? You ought to live holy and godly lives as you look forward to the day of God and speed its coming.**

—2 Peter 3:11–12

"Speed its coming"! What do you think that means? Is the Bible saying that I can do something that moves the time of his coming closer? It certainly is! The way that the church witnesses for Christ in some way speeds the coming of Christ. If you think that no one cares about your character, that it goes unnoticed, you are wrong. "Live holy lives." Your character in some way impacts God's timetable.

Let's look at these next two attitudes together.

- **Be <u>PATIENT</u> and <u>EAGERLY</u> wait.**

  **You too, be patient and stand firm, because the Lord's coming is near.**
  —James 5:8

  **Therefore you do not lack any spiritual gift as you eagerly wait for our Lord Jesus Christ to be revealed.**
  —1 Corinthians 1:7

Now wait a minute. Does he want me to be patient or does he want me to be eager? He wants both. You can be patient and eager at the same time. The single word for that attitude is *anticipation*.

It's crazy. We act as if we can't enjoy Jesus' return until it actually happens. But if I can enjoy the anticipation of something as small as a vacation or even a new flavor of ice cream waiting in my freezer ("I'll eat it after the kids go to bed"), why wait until he comes again to begin enjoying it? You can enjoy his coming now by longing for it in your heart. Try praying this way every once in a while, "Lord, I can hardly wait until the day when we will be able to . . ."

> Discussion question 4 can be used here.

As you anticipate his return, then you'll begin to do the final thing in this list:

- **Long for <u>HIS</u> <u>RETURN</u>.**

  **Now there is in store for me the crown of righteousness, which the Lord, the righteous Judge, will award to me on that day—and not only to me, but also to all who have longed for his appearing.**
  —2 Timothy 4:8

  **For the grace of God that brings salvation has appeared to all men. It teaches us to say "No" to ungodliness and worldly passions, and to live self-controlled, upright and godly lives in this present age, while we wait for the blessed hope—the glorious appearing of our great God and Savior, Jesus Christ.**
  —Titus 2:11–13

The blessed hope. I want to end this study with a few honest moments of making sure that this hope does not elude us.

Listen to this straightforward statement concerning our struggle with hope in the all-too-real world.

> If there was a police lineup of all that had ever robbed anyone of hope, certainly the most fingered culprit would be that foul menace called Circumstance. *Circumstantia* means "stand around." The word points to those events and people that crowd in around us, loitering in the halls of our lives and blocking the view out the window to the broader reality beyond. . . .
>
> When positive circumstances crowd around us, we are tempted to deposit our hope in them, not the Lord. The stock market climbs, and our portfolio grows. We tiptoe our way through some tough circumstances and come out unscathed. . . . How tempting it is to believe that circumstances like these are solid enough to stand on, to bear the weight of our confidence, our identity, or our future. . . .
>
> Negative circumstances are equally adept at crowding out our view of deeper realities. When illness strikes, we cannot look beyond the pain. Grief blocks the view when a loved one dies, embarrassment clouds our vision when we are fired from a job, weariness and resentment get in our way when we care for an aging parent, and loneliness crowds the window when an engagement falls through.
>
> The hulking obviousness of our present circumstances, combined with the frustrating remoteness of our future redemption . . . make it tough to hold fast to hope.[3]

Would you agree with me that this great truth of the Second Coming usually takes a back seat to the struggles we have with everyday life? The circumstances that are so in our face keep us from looking for the hope that is so in our future. If this truth of the Second Coming does not make it easier for us to hold on to hope, then we have missed the point. It is meant to drench us in hope.

You struggle with the pain of physical suffering in this world—Jesus is coming again! You grieve over the injustice that is rampant in this world—Jesus is coming again. Your heart breaks with loneliness—Jesus is coming again. This world does not offer you the excitement and adventure that you know you were born for—Jesus is coming again.

How do we hang on to that hope? How does the Second Coming become more than simply a study that you now put in the back of a drawer? How can the truth of Jesus' Second Coming make a real difference in your life this next week, and the week after that, and the week following that? I want to encourage you to act with the attitude that the apostle John was drawn toward as God revealed to him the hope of eternity.

**Key Personal Perspective**

For the believer the knowledge of prophecy draws our hearts out in worship toward God. From the beginning to the end of the book of Revelation, the apostle John had a habit of responding to God's prophetic future with an attitude of worship.

> When I saw him, I fell at his feet as though dead. Then he placed his right hand on me and said: "Do not be afraid. I am the First and the Last."
> —Revelation 1:17

> I, John, am the one who heard and saw these things. And when I had heard and seen them, I fell down to worship at the feet of the angel who had been showing them to me. But he said to me, "Do not do it! I am a fellow servant with you and with your brothers the prophets and of all who keep the words of this book. Worship God!"
> —Revelation 22:8–9

There is no better summation of our study of the end times than those two powerful words of invitation, "Worship God!"

Hope is realizing that God will have the last word.

So worship God with me right now.

*Our Father, we turn to you whom we will spend eternity honoring with our worship. We admit to you what you already know. Our problems seem so immediate, and our hope sometimes seems so distant—and so we focus on our problems and not our hope. We pray that this truth of Jesus' coming again will bring a new immediacy of hope into our lives. We pray that that hope will enable us to see just one circumstance or problem differently this next week, with eyes of faith. We pray that this hope will enable us to have minds that are alert, lives that are self-controlled, and hearts that long for that day when you will return.*

*And, Jesus, thank you for loving us. Thank you for telling us that you are looking forward also to that day when we will be with you where you are.*

*In your name, amen.*

> **Finish memorizing memory card 11, "The Truth about the Second Coming."**

## Appendix
### Views Concerning Last Things

| Categories | Amillennialism | Postmillennialism | Historic Premillennialism | Dispensational Premillennialism |
|---|---|---|---|---|
| Second Coming of Christ | Single event; no distinction between Rapture and Second Coming. Introduces eternal state. | Single event; no distinction between Rapture and Second Coming; Christ returns after Millennium. | Rapture and Second Coming simultaneous; Christ returns to reign on earth. | Second Coming in two phases: Rapture for church; Second Coming to earth seven years later. |
| Resurrection | General resurrection of believers and unbelievers at Second Coming of Christ. | General resurrection of believers and unbelievers at Second Coming of Christ. | Resurrection of believers at beginning of Millennium. Resurrection of unbelievers at end of Millennium. | Distinction in resurrections: 1. Church at Rapture 2. Old Testament/Tribulation saints at Second Coming 3. Unbelievers at end of Millennium |
| Judgments | General Judgment of all people | General Judgment of all people | Judgment at Second Coming Judgment at end of Tribulation | Distinction in Judgment: 1. Believers' works at Rapture 2. Jews/Gentiles at end of Tribulation 3. Unbelievers at end of Millennium |
| Tribulation | Tribulation is experienced in this present age. | Tribulation is experienced in this present age. | Posttribulation view: church goes through the future Tribulation. | Pretribulation view: church is raptured prior to Tribulation. |
| Millennium | No literal Millennium on earth after Second Coming. Kingdom present in church age. | Present age blend into Millennium because of progress of Gospel. | Millennium is both present and future. Christ is reigning in heaven, Millennium not necessarily 1,000 years. | At Second Coming Christ inaugurates literal 1,000-year Millennium on earth. |
| Israel and the Church | Church is the new Israel. No distinction between Israel and the church. | Some distinction between Israel and the church. Future for Israel but church is spiritual Israel. | Some distinction between Israel and the church. Future for Israel but church is spiritual Israel. | Complete distinction between Israel and church. Distinct program for each. |
| Adherents | L. Beckhof; O. T. Allis; G. C. Berkhouwer | Charles Hodge; B. B. Warfield; W. G. T. Shedd; A. H. Strong | G. E. Ladd; A. Reese; M. J. Erickson | L. S. Chafer; J. D. Pentecost; C. C. Ryrie; J. F Walvoord; C. Swindoll |

*Source:* Taken from Paul Enns, *The Moody Handbook of Theology* (Chicago: Moody Press, 1989). Used by permission.

## Discussion Questions

1. What does the fact that Jesus is preparing a place for you communicate to you about his love for you? How would you like to grow in understanding the depth of Jesus' love for you?

2. Can you even imagine what the Rapture of God's church will be like? (Sort of like skydiving in reverse!) Who do you know whose resurrected body will come out of the grave to meet their spirit coming with Jesus in the air? Who would you like to clasp hands with on the way up to meet Jesus? What would you like your first thought to be when you realize what is happening?

3. What does the fact that there are so many differing opinions on subjects like the Millennium say to you?

4. Talk together about how the attitudes God teaches us to have toward the visible return of Jesus fit into our everyday lives.

   *Be alert and watchful.* What helps you to think about the fact that Jesus *is* going to come again?

   *Be alert and self-controlled.* How does the truth of the visible return of Jesus help you to say no to temptation and yes to spiritual disciplines such as prayer and serving others?

   *Live holy lives.* Do you live a holy life more out of fear that he will catch you doing something wrong when he returns or out of a desire to use the short time you have to live to please the Lord? What helps you to live less with fear and more with a desire to please him?

   *Be patient and eargerly wait.* We all struggle with patience. What lessons have you learned (or seen in others) that help you to remember to not try to hurry God?

   *Long for his return!* What are you looking forward to when Jesus comes again?

## For Further Study

Clouse, Robert G. *The Meaning of the Millennium.* Downers Grove, Ill.: InterVarsity Press, 1977.

Elwell, Walter, ed. *Topical Analysis of the Bible.* Grand Rapids, Mich.: Baker, 1991.

Graham, Billy. *Storm Warning.* Dallas: Word, 1992.

Lightner, Robert. *The Last Days Handbook.* Nashville: Nelson, 1990.

Little, Paul. *Know What You Believe.* Wheaton, Ill.: Victor, 1987.

Rhodes, Ron. *The Heart of Christianity.* Eugene, Ore.: Harvest House, 1996.

# Wrap-Up Study

### Life Change Objective

**To map out eleven personal ways you want to live the truths that we've learned together from God's Word.**

---

### Summary Teaching Outline

What Is Christian Doctrine?

What Is the Value of the Doctrine You Have Learned?

1. You know God better.
2. You have fed your soul.
3. You will be able to share with others.
4. You are protected against error.
5. You have changed the way you think.
6. You have built an essential foundation.

The Foundation of My Life Is Determined By:

1. Where I set my heart
2. Where I set my mind
3. Where I fix my eyes

---

You might remember that as we started this study together some months ago we looked together at this encouragement from Jude 1:20.

**But you, dear friends, must continue to build your lives on the foundation of your holy faith.**

—Jude 1:20 (NLT)

That is my continuing encouragement to you. My prayer for you is the prayer Paul prayed in Philippians 1:9–10.

**And this is my prayer: that your love may abound more and more in knowledge and depth of insight, so that you may be able to discern what is best.**

—Philippians 1:9–10

That, in knowledge and depth of insight, you have seen and will continue to see your love for the Lord and others grow, and that your knowledge of the things of God will enable you day by day to make great choices in your life.

This study is going to be different from any other study in *Foundations*. *You* are going to be the primary teachers as we look at the ways that God works in our lives through his truth. I'm going to give you a chance to talk to each other in your groups, and we'll have an opportunity to hear a few of those stories that you tell in your groups in our larger group.

## Teaching Tip

Even if you have not been sitting in groups or using discussion questions for the majority of this study, we'd encourage you to use groups in this final study. As people hear from others, the truth will be further cemented in their lives.

You can encourage discussion in these groups by giving people an opportunity to think about the questions in advance. Give them a card the week before this study (or even as they come in) with the following statement and questions:

In our final study we will be looking at how God's truth has made an impact on our lives. As part of this study you'll have an opportunity to discuss the following questions:

1. What truth that we learned together has helped you to deepen your relationship with God?

2. What truth or truths did you find giving you strength throughout the day?

3. Can you recall an opportunity when you had to share a truth that you learned in *Foundations* with someone: your family, a friend, your small group, someone at work?

4. Did a truth in this study protect you from making a wrong decision or heading in a wrong direction or falling to a temptation?

5. What do you see differently than you did before this study?

6. How has this study increased the sense of security that you have in your relationship with God?

## What Is Christian Doctrine?

Christian doctrine is an <u>ORGANIZED</u> <u>SUMMARY</u> of what the <u>BIBLE</u> <u>TEACHES</u>.

A working definition of theology is <u>FAITH</u> <u>SEEKING</u> <u>UNDER-STANDING</u>.

Would you say the word *doctrine* with me. Doctrine.

I hope you have a greater appreciation for that word as a result of our time together these last weeks and months. You understand what the Bible teaches. Your faith has sought understanding. And this makes an impact on your life.

## What Is the Value of the Doctrine You Have Learned?

1. You <u>KNOW</u> <u>GOD</u> <u>BETTER</u>.

   **We are cruel to ourselves if we try to live in this world without knowing the God whose world it is and who runs it. The world becomes a strange, mad, painful place . . . for those who don't know about God.**[1]
   —J. I. Packer

   **Let not the wise man boast of his wisdom or the strong man boast of his strength or the rich man boast of his riches, but let him who boasts boast about this: that he understands and knows me, that I am the LORD.**
   —Jeremiah 9:23–24

   I'm going to let you be the teachers tonight. You've heard a lot from me over the time of this study. Tonight let's hear from each other. Take a moment in your groups to answer this question:

   What truth that we learned together has helped you to deepen your relationship with God?

### Teaching Tip

After they've had time to share in their groups, ask for a few people to share with the entire group. If you have group leaders, ask them to raise their hand to let you know if there is something that was said in their group that everyone should hear. Otherwise, just ask for a couple volunteers.

### 2. You have <u>FED</u> <u>YOUR</u> <u>SOUL</u>.

**In pointing out these things to the brethren, you will be a good servant of Christ Jesus, constantly nourished on the words of the faith and of the sound doctrine which you have been following.**

—1 Timothy 4:6 (NASB)

Once our church, as a part of this doctrinal study, decided to have a "doctrinal potluck." Each person was encouraged to bring a food that fit some doctrinal theme. Besides the inevitable angel food cake, the group also feasted on heavenly ambrosia, triple layer cake (for the Trinity, I suppose), bread of life, and hellfire and brimstone chili.

That's funny, but may be taking the truth that doctrine feeds our soul just a little too literally! Food helps our physical bodies to grow; the truth of God grows our soul. Our soul is the source of our feelings, our decisions, and the way that we relate to God and others. As our soul is nourished we are better able to feel God's presence in our lives, and we find ourselves making more godly decisions. We discover a new depth to our relationships. Don't miss the obvious point here. We need food every day and throughout the day in order to thrive physically. The truths that feed our souls are the truths that we have allowed to become a part of our everyday lives.

Take a moment in your groups to answer this question:

What truth or truths did you find giving you strength throughout the day?

### 3. You will be able to <u>SHARE</u> <u>WITH</u> <u>OTHERS</u>.

**He must hold firmly to the trustworthy message as it has been taught, so that he can encourage others by sound doctrine and refute those who oppose it.**

—Titus 1:9

Take a moment in your groups to answer this question:

Can you recall an opportunity you had to share a truth that you learned in *Foundations* with someone: your family, a friend, your small group, someone at work?

### 4. You are protected against <u>ERROR</u>.

**But solid food is for the mature, who by constant use have trained themselves to distinguish good from evil.**

—Hebrews 5:14

Take a moment in your groups to answer this question: Did a truth in this study protect you from making a wrong decision or heading in a wrong direction or falling to a temptation?

5. **You have changed the way you THINK.**

**For as he thinks within himself, so he is.**

—Proverbs 23:7 (NASB)

### How a person thinks determines how they act.

Suppose for a moment that I had handed each of you a can with a lid on it when you walked into the room tonight. You were given instructions not to open the lid until I told you to. Throughout the study you would have been trying to figure out what was in the can, right? What if by shaking the can and hearing a rattle you were convinced that it contained a live snake? Would that affect how you opened the can? Of course it would. You'd bring it to me and say, "*You* open it." Suppose that instead you were convinced that it was filled with chocolate chip cookies? You would take the lid off with a very different attitude!

There are a lot of things in this world that are like the can with a lid on it to us human beings. We can't see heaven. The lid hasn't been taken off yet. We don't physically see Jesus or God's Holy Spirit. We must trust what God tells us about himself. We can't always see how the tough times we go through are working for God's good in our lives. That too is a matter of faith.

Take a moment in your groups to answer this question: What do you see differently than you did before this study? How has your perspective on life changed?

6. **You have built an ESSENTIAL FOUNDATION.**

**Therefore leaving the elementary teaching about the Christ, let us press on to maturity, not laying again a foundation of repentance from dead works and of faith toward God, of instruction [doctrine] about washings [baptism], and laying on of hands, and the resurrection of the dead, and eternal judgment.**

—Hebrews 6:1–2 (NASB)

Take a moment in your groups to answer this question: How has this study increased the sense of security that you have in your relationship with God?

As we close, let me remind you of three simple truths.

# The Foundation of My Life Is Determined By:

 17

### 1. Where I set my heart

**Since, then, you have been raised with Christ, set your hearts on things above, where Christ is seated at the right hand of God.**
—Colossians 3:1

When you read a verse such as Colossians 3:1, one of the natural questions is, "How do I do that?" What are some of the practical decisions I must make and actions I must take in order to set my heart on things above?

Take a look at the chart at the end of this study labeled "Building a Foundation That Lasts." You'll see at the top of this chart a simple truth about how our heart is changed for the better. First we must learn the truth. Then we begin to love the truth. And out of that love for the truth we naturally begin to live that truth.

What is the next step that God is asking you to take in response to his truth? In the last column in that chart, with the heading "Live It," you'll see some questions designed to help you to think about what that next step might be. Go back to this chart from time to time and check on how you are doing.

### 2. Where I set my mind

Look at Colossians 3:2 and Psalm 1:2.

**Set your minds on things above, not on earthly things.**
—Colossians 3:2

**They love the Lord's teachings, and they think about those teachings day and night.**
—Psalm 1:2 (NCV)

What you set your mind on is what you think about during the day. What if I were to tell you that we had been able to videotape the things that your mind focused on today, and that we'd now be showing that tape on a giant screen to the entire group. I'd guess that not one of us in this room would be thrilled with that announcement, myself included!

Want to change your life? Change what you think about during the day! God's truth gives us God's power to turn our thoughts in a different direction. Read with me Philippians 4:8.

Brothers and sisters, think about the things that are good and worthy of praise. Think about the things that are true and honorable and right and pure and beautiful and respected.

—Philippians 4:8 (NCV)

### 3. Where I fix my eyes

Let us fix our eyes on Jesus, the author and perfecter of our faith, who for the joy set before him endured the cross, scorning its shame, and sat down at the right hand of the throne of God.

—Hebrews 12:2

So we fix our eyes not on what is seen, but on what is unseen. For what is seen is temporary, but what is unseen is eternal.

—2 Corinthians 4:18

Anne Ortlund writes in the introduction to her book *Fix Your Eyes on Jesus:*

> I was chatting last Sunday with my in-laws; they're dear people. We covered this and that, and got to discussing a particular pastor. Oh, so subtly, so delicately, I managed to allude to his struggles, perils, possible problems. . . . I rattled on. . . .
> Suddenly I saw my self—fangs, claws, and all.
> I was making sure they understood that Ray and I had never had such struggles, perils, possible problems—that we must obviously be superior. . . . I was too well-bred to say it; I only inferred it. My relatives are savvy people; they'd understand.
> The Spirit stopped me cold.
> My eyes weren't on Jesus, they were on my family—to make sure Ray and I looked good in their sight. That gave freedom to my "old nature" (my familiar, ugly, life-long enemy) to take control of my tongue, and there in front of all of them was my exposed heart, with all its lurking pride and jealousy.
> Embarrassing! Discouraging!
> I apologized, and my sweet family made light of it and of course forgave me.
> But I'm always just one step from disaster, aren't you? And there's no help, no winning, unless we follow Hebrews 12:2—fix our eyes on Jesus, one moment at a time.[2]

I love the honest hope expressed in that quote. Honest: it is so easy for us to get our eyes selfishly fixed on ourselves. We do it seemingly hundreds of times each day. But also hope: Jesus has the power to change us one moment at a time.

The question isn't who or what you had your eyes fixed on yesterday, or even who you hope to have your eyes fixed on tomorrow. Who will have the fixed focus of your attention throughout the day today? If you've tried to fix your eyes on Jesus and his plan for your life for even part of one day, you already know that this is not easy. Our gaze tends to wander—sometimes in mere seconds—from our resolution to "really think about

Jesus today." But the next moment always is before each of us, filled with the promise of how different my life will be as my eyes are fixed on him!

I'd like to pray for you as we come to the end of this study.

*Father,*

*Thank you for showing us the truth in your Word, through your Son and by your Spirit. Our heartfelt request is that the truths we have learned will be lived out in our daily lives. We make this request in confidence, knowing you want us to be doers of your Word. But we also ask this humbly. Lord, we can't live your truth on our own strength: although that hasn't kept us from falling flat on our faces trying! We need, desperately need, your presence and power in our lives. Through that power we pray that you will enable us to build our lives on the foundation of your truth.*

*In Jesus' name, amen.*

# Building a Foundation That Lasts

## Three Levels of Truth

Here's a brief look at what we've studied together these past few months. This chart helps you to see the different levels of learning that go along with grasping a truth. Being able to quote a truth does not mean I've fully grasped that truth.

| To grasp a doctrine I must . . . | Learn It (understand the truth) | Love It (change my perspective) | Live It (apply it to life) |
|---|---|---|---|
| **The Bible** | The Bible is God's perfect guidebook for living. | I can make the right decision. | I will consult the Bible for guidance in my decision about _____. |
| **God** | God is bigger and better and closer than I can imagine. | The most important thing about me is what I believe about God. | When I see how great God is, it makes _____ look small. |
| **Jesus** | Jesus is God showing himself to us. | God wants me to know him better. | I will get to know Jesus through a daily quiet time. |
| **The Holy Spirit** | God lives in me and through me now. | I am a temple of God's Holy Spirit. | I will treat my body like the temple it is by _____. |
| **Creation** | Nothing "just happened." God created it all. | I have a purpose in this world. | The reason I exist is to _____. |
| **Salvation** | Grace is the only way to have a relationship with God. | I am an object of God's grace. | I'll stop seeing _____ as a way to earn my salvation. I'll begin doing it simply in appreciation for God's grace. |
| **Sanctification** | Faith is the only way to grow as a believer. | I grow when I see myself in a new way. | I'll spend more time listening to what God's Word says about me and less time listening to what the world says about me. |
| **Good and Evil** | God has allowed evil to provide us with a choice. God can bring good even out of evil events. God promises victory over evil to those who choose him. | All things work together for good. | I am battling evil as I face _____. I will overcome evil with good by _____. |
| **The Afterlife** | Heaven and hell are real places. Death is a beginning, not the end. | I can face death with confidence. | I will have a more hopeful attitude toward _____. |
| **The Church** | The only true "world superpower" is the church. | The best place to invest my life is in God's church. | I need to make a deeper commitment to the church by _____. |
| **The Second Coming** | Jesus is coming again to judge this world and to gather God's children. | I want to be living alertly for him when he comes. | Someone I can encourage with the hope of the Second Coming is _____. |

# Notes

## Session 11. Salvation: Part 1

1. Charles R. Swindoll, *Grace Awakening* (Dallas: Word, 1990), 10.

2. Anne Ortlund, *Fix Your Eyes on Jesus* (Dallas: Word, 1994), 150.

3. Warren Wiersbe, *Key Words of the Christian Life* (Grand Rapids, Mich.: Baker, 2002), 16.

4. D. James Kennedy, *Evangelism Explosion*, 3d ed. (Wheaton, Ill.: Tyndale, 1983), 101.

5. Walter Maier, *Twenty Centuries of Great Preaching* (Waco, Tex.: Word, 1971), 2:52.

## Session 12. Salvation: Part 2

1. Max Lucado, *In the Grip of Grace* (Dallas: Word, 1996), 1–7.

2. The three bulleted points were adapted from Charles C. Ryrie, *So Great Salvation* (Wheaton, Ill.: Victor, 1989), 142–43.

3. J. F. Strombeck, *Shall Never Perish* (Grand Rapids, Mich.: Kregel, 1991), 15–16.

4. Charles Stanley, *Eternal Security: Can You Be Sure?* (Nashville: Nelson, 1990), 4–5.

5. Appendix adapted and abridged from Charles Stanley, *Eternal Security: Can You Be Sure?* (Nashville: Nelson, 1990), 135–83.

## Session 13. Sanctification: Part 1

1. Chris Rice, "Clumsy," *Deep Enough to Dream,* Rocketown Records, 1997.

## Session 14. Sanctification: Part 2

1. Chuck Smith, *Why Grace Changes Everything* (Eugene, Ore.: Harvest House, 1994), 95.

2. Bob Dylan, *Gotta Serve Somebody.* Copyright © 1979 by Special Rider Music. All rights reserved. International copyright secured. Reprinted by permission.

3. Richard Foster, *Celebration of Discipline: The Path to Spiritual Growth* (New York: Harper & Row, 1978), 6–7.

4. Max Lucado, *A Gentle Thunder* (Dallas: Word, 1995), 79–80.

## Session 15. Good and Evil: Part 1

1. Lee Strobel, *The Case for Faith* (Grand Rapids, Mich.: Zondervan, 2000), 29.

2. Taken from a tape of the teaching of this study at Saddleback Church, 21 February 2000.

3. Whittaker Chamber, "The Devil," *Life* (2 February 1948): 84–85, quoted in Thomas E. Trask and Wayde I. Goodall, *The Battle* (Grand Rapids, Mich.: Zondervan, 1997), 40.

4. Aleksandr I. Solzhenitsyn, *The Gulag Archipelago, 1918–1956*, trans. Thomas P. Whitney (New York: Harper & Row, 1985), 615.

## Session 16. Good and Evil: Part 2

1. From a personal testimony given at Saddleback Church, 7–8 March 1999.

2. ww.hillsdale.edu/academics/history/Documents/War/America/Indian/1876-BigHorn-Times.htm

3. J. I. Packer, *God's Words: Studies of Key Bible Themes* (Downers Grove, Ill.: InterVarsity Press, 1981), 85–86.

4. C. S. Lewis, *The Problem of Pain* (New York: Macmillan, 1962), 93.

5. Bruce H. Wilkerson, *Personal Holiness in Times of Temptation* (Eugene, Ore.: Harvest House, 1998), 148.

6. Quoted in Wilkerson, *Personal Holiness,* 127.

7. Thomas E. Trask and Wayde I. Goodall, *The Battle* (Grand Rapids, Mich.: Zondervan, 1997), 101–2.

## Session 17. The Afterlife: Part 1

1. David van Biema, reported by Richard N. Ostling, Elisabeth Kauffman, and Victoria Rainert, "Religion: Does Heaven Exist?" *Time* (24 March 1997): 70ff.

2. Jeffery L. Sheler, "Hell Hath No Fury," *U.S. News & World Report* (31 January 2000): 44.

3. Melanie Menagh, "Beyond Death and Dying," *Omni* 17 (22 September 1995): 62.

4. Billy Graham, *Facing Death and the Life After* (Waco, Tex.: Word, 1987), 220.

5. Lieghton Ford, *Good News Is for Sharing* (Elgin, Ill.: David C. Cook, 1977), 34.

6. C. S. Lewis, *The Great Divorce* (New York: MacMillan, 1946), 72–73.

7. Jill Briscoe, *Heaven and Hell: A Study of the Promise and the Peril of Eternity* (Wheaton, Ill.: Victor, 1990), 55.

## Session 18. The Afterlife: Part 2

1. Ray Stedman, *Jesus Teaches on Prayer* (Waco, Tex.: Word, 1975), 30–31.

2. Vance Havner, quoted in Billy Graham, *Facing Death and the Life After* (Waco, Tex.: Word, 1987), 232.

3. Graham, *Facing Death,* 215–16.

4. *Schindler's List,* dir. Stephen Spielberg, performers Liam Neeson and Ben Kingsley (Hollywood: Universal, 1993).

5. Jeff Jensen, "Whose Afterlife Is It, Anyway? Everything We Know about HEAVEN . . . We Learned from the Movies," *Entertainment Weekly* (4 December 1998): 54.

6. David van Biema, reported by Richard N. Ostling, Elisabeth Kauffman, and Victoria Rainert, "Religion: Does Heaven Exist?" *Time* (24 March 1997): 70.

7. Philip Yancey, "Heaven Can't Wait," *Christianity Today* (7 September 1984).

8. Quoted by Robert Mills in *I Believe: The Apostles' Creed for the Third Millennium* (Lenoir, N.C.: PLC, 1998), 143.

9. C. S. Lewis, *Mere Christianity* (Westwood, N.J.: Barbour, 1952), 113.

10. Source unknown.

11. William Barclay, *Matthew,* vol. 2 (Philadelphia: Westminster Press, 1958), 268.

## Session 19. The Church: Part 1

1. Findley B. Edge, *The Greening of the Church* (Waco, Tex.: Word, 1971), 36–37.

2. George W. Peters, *Theology of Church Growth* (Grand Rapids, Mich.: Zondervan, 1981), 55.

3. W. A. Criswell, *The Doctrine of the Church* (Nashville: Convention Press, 1980), 35–36.

4. Rick Warren, *The Purpose-Driven Church* (Grand Rapids, Mich.: Zondervan, 1995), 88–89.

5. Wayne Rice and Mike Yaconelli, *Right-On Ideas for Youth Groups* (Grand Rapids, Mich.: Zondervan, 1973).

## Session 20. The Church: Part 2

1. Max Lucado, *The Great House of God* (Dallas: Word, 1997), 136.

2. Chuck Swindoll, *Growing Strong in the Seasons of Life* (Portland, Ore.: Multnomah, 1983), 312.

3. Max Lucado, *A Gentle Thunder* (Dallas: Word, 1995), 73–74.

4. John MacArthur Jr., *Body Dynamics* (Wheaton, Ill.: Victor, 1983), 154–55.

5. William Barclay, *The Gospel of Matthew,* vol. 2 (Philadelphia: Westminster Press, 1975), 319–20.

6. Bill and Gloria Gaither and Don March, "God Has Always Had a People," *The Church Triumphant* (Alexandria, Ind.: Paragon/Gaither).

## Session 21. The Second Coming: Part 1

1. Application Bridge from Rick Warren's "Class 201: Discovering Spiritual Maturity," the second of four orientation classes at Saddleback Church. These materials are available at www.pastors.com.

2. Merrill C. Tenney, *Interpreting Revelation* (Grand Rapids, Mich.: Eerdmans, 1957), 28.

3. Billy Graham, *Approaching Hoofbeats: The Four Horsemen of the Apocalypse* (Waco, Tex.: Word, 1983), 19–20.

4. Charles R. Swindoll, *Growing Deep in the Christian Life* (Portland, Ore.: Multnomah Press, 1986), 268.

5. Graham, *Approaching Hoofbeats,* 23.

6. B. J. Oropeza, *99 Reasons Why No One Knows When Christ Will Return* (Downers Grove, Ill.: InterVarsity Press, 1994).

## Session 22. The Second Coming: Part 2

1. William Martin, *A Prophet with Honor* (New York: William Morrow, 1991), 281.

2. Rebecca Barlow Jordan, "Living in Joyful Anticipation of Christ's Return," *Discipleship Journal* 110 (March/April 1999).

3. David W. Henderson, "Hope: Anchoring Your Heart to a Sure and Certain Future," *Discipleship Journal,* 114 (November/December 1999).

## Wrap-Up Study

1. J. I. Packer, *Truth and Power* (Wheaton, Ill.: Shaw, 1996), 16.

2. Anne Ortlund, *Fix Your Eyes on Jesus* (Dallas: Word, 1994), 9.

# Resources Available

*Audiotapes of Foundations.* Audiotapes of each of the *Foundations* studies, taught by Tom Holladay and Kay Warren, are available at www.pastors.com.

*Purpose-Driven Church.* This award-winning book by Rick Warren shows how your church can help people live God's five purposes for our lives. Available in book and DVD in twenty languages. Millions of people have studied this book in churches and groups. (Zondervan)

*Purpose-Driven Life.* Rick Warren takes the groundbreaking message of the award-winning *Purpose-Driven Church* and goes deeper, applying it to the lifestyle of individual Christians. *The Purpose-Driven Life* is a manifesto for Christian living in the twenty-first century: a lifestyle based on eternal purposes, not cultural values. Written in a captivating devotional style, the book is divided into forty short chapters that can be read as a daily devotional, studied by small groups, and used by churches participating in a 40 Days of Purpose campaign. (Zondervan)

*40 Days of Purpose.* A forty-day campaign for churches that builds on *The Purpose-Driven Life* as a foundation, adding sermons, small group resources and video tapes, and training for leadership teams. This is a forty-day emphasis that promises to permanently change your church. (contact PurposeDriven.com)

*Purpose-Driven Youth Ministry.* The essentials of a healthy, Purpose-Driven youth ministry from Saddleback's youth pastor, Doug Fields. (Zondervan)

*Pastors.com and PurposeDriven.com* have additional resources for those in full-time ministry. Pastors.com specializes in messages and helps for the pastor as a communicator, including sermons and books. PurposeDriven.com specializes in tools and program materials to help churches focus on our God-given purposes.

# MEMORY CARDS

---

The Truth about the Bible

**1**

**The Bible is God's perfect guidebook for living.**

---

The Truth about God

**2**

**God is bigger and better and closer than I can imagine.**

---

The Truth about Jesus

**3**

**Jesus is God showing himself to us.**

---

The Truth about the Holy Spirit

**4**

**God lives in me and through me now.**

---

The Truth about Creation

**5**

**Nothing "just happened." God created it all.**

---

The Truth about Salvation

**6**

**Grace is the only way to have a relationship with God.**

---

The Truth about Sanctification

**7**

**Faith is the only way to grow as a believer.**

---

The Truth about Good and Evil

**8**

**God has allowed evil to provide us with a choice.**
**God can bring good even out of evil events.**
**God promises victory over evil to those who choose him.**

---

The Truth about the Afterlife

**9**

**Heaven and hell are real places.**
**Death is a beginning, not the end.**

---

The Truth about the Church

**10**

**The only true "world superpower" is the church.**

---

The Truth about the Second Coming

**11**

**Jesus is coming again to judge this world and to gather God's children.**

How great is the love the Father has lavished on us, that we should be called children of God!

—1 John 3:1

All Scripture is inspired by God and is useful to teach us what is true and to make us realize what is wrong in our lives. It straightens us out and teaches us to do what is right.

—2 Timothy 3:16 (NLT)

You alone are the LORD. You made the heavens, even the highest heavens, and all their starry host, the earth and all that is on it, the seas and all that is in them. You give life to everything, and the multitudes of heaven worship you.

—Nehemiah 9:6

Don't be drunk with wine, because that will ruin your life. Instead, let the Holy Spirit fill and control you.

—Ephesians 5:18 (NLT)

For in Christ all the fullness of the Deity lives in bodily form, and you have been given fullness in Christ, who is the head over every power and authority.

—Colossians 2:9–10

And we know that in all things God works for the good of those who love him, who have been called according to his purpose.

—Romans 8:28

I have been crucified with Christ and I no longer live, but Christ lives in me. The life I live in the body, I live by faith in the Son of God, who loved me and gave himself for me.

—Galatians 2:20

You have been saved by grace through believing. You did not save yourselves; it was a gift from God.

—Ephesians 2:8 (NCV)

Therefore, prepare your minds for action; be self-controlled; set your hope fully on the grace to be given you when Jesus Christ is revealed.

—1 Peter 1:13

You should not stay away from the church meetings, as some are doing, but you should meet together and encourage each other. Do this even more as you see the day coming.

—Hebrews 10:25 (NCV)

Set your minds on things above, not on earthly things.

—Colossians 3:2